W9-ASU-001

AFRICA TODAY

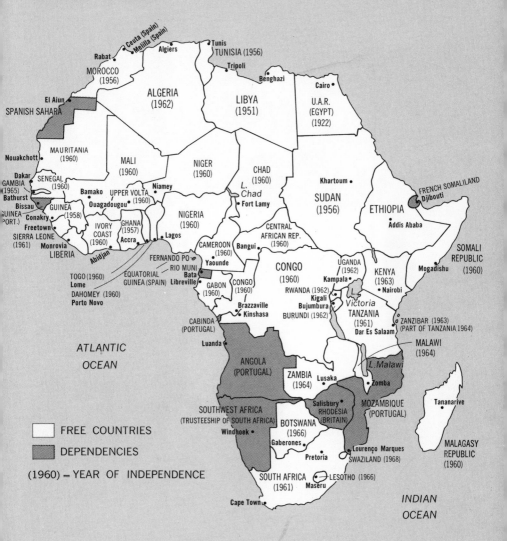

Ceuta (Spain)
Melilla (Spain)

Rabat • Algiers
Tunis
TUNISIA (1956)

MOROCCO
(1956)
Tripoli

Benghazi

Cairo •

El Aiun

SPANISH SAHARA

ALGERIA
(1962)

LIBYA
(1951)

U.A.R.
(EGYPT)
(1922)

Nouakchott •

MAURITANIA
(1960)

Dakar •
GAMBIA
(1965)
Bathurst

SENEGAL
(1960)

MALI
(1960)

NIGER
(1960)

CHAD
(1960)

Khartoum •

Bamako •
Niamey
UPPER VOLTA
(1960)

Bissau
GUINEA
(PORT.)

GUINEA
(1958)
Ouagadougou

L.
Chad
Fort Lamy

SUDAN
(1956)

ETHIOPIA

FRENCH SOMALILAND
Djibouti

Conakry •
Freetown

IVORY
COAST
(1960)

GHANA
(1957)

NIGERIA
(1960)

Addis Ababa •

SIERRA LEONE
(1961)
Monrovia •

Accra

Lagos

CENTRAL
AFRICAN REP.
(1960)

SOMALI
REPUBLIC
(1960)

LIBERIA

Abidjan

CAMEROON
Yaounde

Bangui •

Mogadishu •

TOGO (1960)
Lome
DAHOMEY (1960)
Porto Novo

FERNANDO PO
RIO MUNI
EQUATORIAL
GUINEA (SPAIN)

CONGO
(1960)

UGANDA
(1962)
Kampala •

KENYA
(1963)
Nairobi •

Bata
Libreville

GABON
(1960)

CONGO
(1960)

RWANDA (1962)
Kigali
Bujumbura

L.
Victoria

ATLANTIC

OCEAN

Brazzaville
Kinshasa

BURUNDI (1962)

TANZANIA
(1961)
Dar Es Salaam

ZANZIBAR (1963)
(PART OF TANZANIA 1964)

CABINDA
(PORTUGAL)

Luanda •

MALAWI
(1964)

ANGOLA
(PORTUGAL)

L. Malawi

ZAMBIA
(1964)
Lusaka

Zomba •

MOZAMBIQUE
(PORTUGAL)

Tananarive •

SOUTHWEST AFRICA
(TRUSTEESHIP OF SOUTH AFRICA)
Windhoek •

BOTSWANA
(1966)
Gaberones •

Salisbury •
RHODESIA
(BRITAIN)

MALAGASY
REPUBLIC
(1960)

☐ FREE COUNTRIES

■ DEPENDENCIES

(1960) = YEAR OF INDEPENDENCE

Pretoria •

SOUTH AFRICA
(1961)

Lourenço Marques
SWAZILAND (1968)

LESOTHO (1966)
Maseru •

INDIAN

Cape Town •

OCEAN

FROM THE
Library of

Linda Jennings

GROWING UP AFRICAN

Books by Jay David

THE KENNEDY READER

THE FLYING SAUCER READER

GROWING UP BLACK

GROWING UP JEWISH

TO BE A BLACK WOMAN (edited by Mel Watkins and Jay David)

LIVING BLACK IN WHITE AMERICA (edited by Jay David and
Elaine Crane)

GROWING UP AFRICAN (edited by Jay David and
Helise Harrington)

GROWING UP AFRICAN

Edited by JAY DAVID and HELISE HARRINGTON

WILLIAM MORROW AND COMPANY, INC.

New York 1971

Copyright © 1971 by William Morrow and Company, Inc.

Grateful acknowledgment is made for permission to reprint material as listed below: Farrar, Straus and Giroux, Inc., for *The Dark Child* by Camara Laye. G. Adali-Mortty for "Palm Leaves of Childhood" by G. Adali-Mortty. Harcourt Brace Jovanovich, Inc., for *I Was a Savage* by Prince Modupe, copyright © 1957 by Harcourt Brace Jovanovich, Inc. The Cambridge University Press on behalf of the Hakluyt Society for *The Travels of Ibn Battuta*, edited by H. A. R. Gibb, and *Awo: The Autobiography of Chief Obafemi Awolowo* by Chief Obafemi Awolowo, and *Kossoh Town Boy* by Robert Wellesley Cole. Northwestern University Press for "The Story of Rashid bin Hassani" from *Ten Africans*, edited by Margery Perham, copyright © 1963 by Northwestern University Press, Evanston, Illinois. Routledge and Kegan Paul Ltd. for "Song for the Dance of Young Girls" in *People of the Small Arrow* by J. H. Driberg, originally published by Payson and Clarke Ltd. in 1930. Frederick A. Praeger for *Baba of Karo* by Mary Smith. The Regents of the University of California for *Shinega's Village* by Sahle Selassie, copyright © 1964 by University of California Press. Editions Payot, Paris, for "Circumcision Songs" from *Les Rites Secrets des Primitifs de l'Oubangui* translated by A. M. Vergiat. Humanities Press, Inc., for "To a Farm in the White Highlands" by Solomon Kagwe from *Origin East Africa*, edited by D. Cook. Random House for *Tell Freedom* by Peter Abrahams. Curtis Brown Ltd. for *Down Second Avenue* by Ezekiel Mphahlele. Little, Brown and Company for *The African* by William Conton. Simon and Schuster for "Ibrahimo" from *The Lonely African* by Colin M. Turnbull. Atheneum Publications, Inc., for "On the Appeal from the Race of Sheba" from *Selected Poems* by Leopold Sedar Senghor. Translated and introduced by John Reed and Clive Wake, copyright © 1964 by Oxford University Press. Frederick A. Praeger, Inc., for *Equiano's Travels*, edited by Paul Edwards, copyright © 1966 by Frederick A. Praeger. Ibadan University Press for "Martyr" by David Diop. Oxford University Press for "Some Contexts of Blackness" by Sillaty K. Dabo and "Racialism at the Meeting Point" by Francis Deng from *Disappointed Guests* by H. Tajfel and J. L. Dawson, published by Oxford University Press for the Institute of Race Relations. African Affairs for "Song" published by the Journal of the Royal African Society. Panaf Books Ltd. for *Ghana: Autobiography of Kwame Nkrumah* by Kwame Nkrumah. The Ministry of Information, Accra, for "The Mosquito and the Young Ghanaian" by Kwesi Assah Nyako. The Macmillan Company for *Weep Not, Child* by James Ngugi, copyright © 1969 by The Macmillan Company. Faber and Faber Ltd. for *A Nigerian Villager in Two Worlds* by Dilim Okafor Omali. Walker and Company for *Ambiguous Adventure* by Cheikh Hamidou Kane, copyright © 1963 by Walker and Company, New York. *Africa Report* for "A Conversation with Eduardo Mondlane" by Helen Kitchen, published November, 1967. The Editors of *Ramparts* for "The Smuggled Account of a Guerrilla Fighter from Africa," copyright 1969 by *Ramparts* Magazine, Inc. *Africa Today* for "The Price of Nigerian Victory" by Charles Keil.

While we have made every possible effort to trace all persons having any rights or interests in material used in the anthology, and to clear reprint permissions, we have been unable, in some instances, to do so. We therefore apologize if any required acknowledgments have been unintentionally omitted, or rights overlooked.—THE EDITORS

All rights reserved. No part of this book may be reproduced or utilized in any form or by any means, electronic or mechanical, including photocopying, recording or by any information storage and retrieval system, without permission in writing from the Publisher. Inquiries should be addressed to William Morrow and Company, Inc., 105 Madison Ave., New York, N.Y. 10016. Printed in the United States of America by The Colonial Press, Inc., Clinton, Mass. Library of Congress Catalog Card Number 70-142415.

Maps by Dyno Lowenstein.

Foreword

by Edris Makward,

Associate Professor, Department of African Languages and Literature, University of Wisconsin

JAY DAVID AND HELISE HARRINGTON have put together a very interesting collection of texts written or told by Africans. Most of these texts are carefully chosen excerpts from African autobiographies written and published within the past two decades. There are also some excerpts from more ancient works by Africans—i.e., *The Travels of Ibn Battuta* (fourteenth century) and *Equiano's Travels* (eighteenth century)—as well as some very recent texts such as "The Smuggled Account of a Guerilla Fighter from Africa." Lastly the editors included a few poems by contemporary African writers and some traditional ritual songs.

In drawing from such varied sources, the editors have indeed been able to give a broad if not exhaustive picture of the major cultural and political problems of contemporary Africa. There is, however, one predominant theme that runs throughout almost all the selections collected here. And to use Léopold Sédar Senghor's own words, we should unmistakably read this collection as a book on "the kingdom of childhood [*le royaume d'enfance*]." It was indeed the Poet-President of Sénégal who took the defense of Camara Laye—the author of *The African Child* (originally *L'Enfant noir*)—whose novel was bitterly criticized by the young militant reviewers of *Présence Africaine* for indulging in a vain and lengthy account of his supposedly picturesque and exotic childhood memories, instead of denouncing aloud the abuses of colonialist France on African soil. Senghor's dismissal of these harsh criticisms was based on his firm belief that "to represent the Negro-African world in the colours of childhood was indeed the most suggestive way of condemning the capitalistic world of western Europe."

Thus unsurprisingly, two excerpts from *The African Child* are included here. Laye's autobiography, which was one of the first African books to draw the attention and praise of European critics and readers, remains indeed a masterpiece of the genre. Very few writers have portrayed their African childhood with equal authenticity and genuine emotion. The first excerpt describes the fascination with which the young narrator watches his blacksmith father in the performance of his craft—particularly when working with gold. The supernatural element which seems to accompany every single gesture of the blacksmith adds to the poetry of the scene. The second excerpt describes the initiation rites as they were undergone by the narrator himself, and members of his age-group. During the terrifying "ceremony of the Lions" he has to learn to overcome "his fear and his own baser nature," and show that he is now ready to be told "the real hidden secrets." We see here a vivid example of the way knowledge is upheld in traditional African society until the individual proves that he has reached the age to "know." This is indeed the stage when the African child begins to understand better the rules of his society; he then realizes that all that he thought was the work of "supernatural powers" during the initiation rites was in fact the work of older young men. There is, however, no condemnation of the purpose of all these practices, for the author, not unlike most African writers and intellectuals, appreciates the moral and psychological value of these endurance tests within the traditional African society.*

However, the narrator's "growing up" is on two levels. For in addition to his passage from childhood to manhood, there is the allusion that, for better or for worse, important changes are taking place in Africa and that the traditional culture is no longer going to be the same as it has always been for

---

* Birago Diop, *The Tales of Amadou Koumba.* London: Oxford University Press. (Translation by Dorothy Blair.)

centuries. And even though the author does not make any value judgments or accusations against the colonizing power, there still lingers a genuine feeling of nostalgia and regret over a disappearing world. This contributes in no small way to the poetry of the whole autobiography.

A similar feeling of discontinuity is also apparent in another African autobiography included in the third part of the present collection. The tone and atmosphere in Hamidou Kane's *Ambiguous Adventure* are more philosophical, however. Interestingly enough, though both authors are of Muslim backgrounds, there is very little Islamic flavor in Camara Laye's book, and much more of an animistic African flavor, whereas Kane's book is filled with a strong Islamic mysticism. Here the cultural discontinuity is symbolized by the hero's "night of the Koran." This is, of course, an old Muslim tradition, but Samba Diallo's "night" is evidently pregnant with more emotion than his father's, or his father's father's. For in addition to Samba's natural gift in communicating the beauty of the Holy Koran, there is the disturbing implication of Samba's awareness that his "night" represented the apotheosis, the end of the age-old tradition:

"For a long time, in the night, his voice was that of the voiceless phantoms of his ancestors, whom he had raised up. With them, he wept their death; but also, in long cadence, they sang his birth."

The hopeful note is quite apparent here, however, for Samba does also symbolize the coming of a new era.

With the excerpt from Baba of Karo's autobiography we see how education was received very informally within a traditional African society. This childhood was lived around the turn of the century in Northern Nigeria, that is, at a time when the impact of Western patterns—here British—on the African was almost nil. However, in these recollections of a Hausa girl, told in a very realistic and direct language, a less poetic note is sounded. Thus, we read that "some prostitutes were the daughters of *malams,* some were the daughters of noblemen, some were the daughters of commoners; if their parents had arranged marriages for them against their will, they ran away and became prostitutes. *Then and now, it's all the same; there have always been prostitutes."* (Italics mine.)

This narrative is quite legitimate and relevant, and would certainly meet the approval of the younger African writers who feel strongly that African literature should not consist of the representation of an over-idealized "innocent" Africa, a continent which was "great and pure . . . until the wicked white man came and started tampering with everything." *

In Part II there is a greater emphasis on the contact of Africa with Europe, and the various effects of this contact on the local African societies. The selection by Olaudah Equiano is a vivid and enlightening account of the life of a young eighteenth-century Nigerian boy, kidnapped from his peaceful village, sold as a slave and sent to the New World. There is no denying that this is one horrifying but true aspect of the early contact of Africa with the Western world.

A more contemporary representation is given by the autobiography of a well-known Nigerian political leader, Chief Obafemi Awolowo. And for a true understanding of the hopes as well as the frustrations of those Africans who are now sincerely and passionately concerned with true nation-building, it is quite appropriate to be reminded of the immediate consequences of the establishment of British rule in Yorubaland by the prestigious founder and leader of the Action Group†himself:

"The peace, tranquility and self-sufficiency of tribal African life contrasted with the fear of the new white lords, the fear of his 'carriers,' and 'messengers' of the local chieftains who were more or less *the agents of the British Government, and who as a result acquired new status, prestige and power."* (Italics mine.)

The excerpt from Sierra Leonian William Conton's autobiographical novel, *The African,* strikes a much more cultural note. Conton's commentary on the significance of the new

* Cf the works of the Senegalese novelist and movie-maker Ousmane Sembène, of the Ghanaian novelist Ayi Kwei Armah, and of the Malian novelist Yambo Ouoleguem.

† One of the major Nigerian political parties before the military coup d'état of January, 1966.

Western education for the young African is indeed a true picture of the post World War II era in colonial Africa. This was indeed the era when more and more West Africans were coming to the firm conclusion that Western education and the training of a modern "élite" in sufficient numbers were the surest way to end the humiliation of colonial rule in their respective native lands.

Still another authentic aspect of this contact of Africa with Europe is given by Solomon Kagwe's account of life in pre-independence Kenya. This vigorous description of the life of Africans living and working on a white-owned farm in the Kenya of the 1950's evokes at the same time a vision of what that "other" Kenya—a Kenya which would have been another "white man's country within Black Africa"—would have meant for the millions of Kenyans now living in Jomo Kenyatta's Kenya. For it has to be borne in mind that just over a decade ago there were still many "hopes" that the rich farmlands of Kenya would never be left in the hands of the "savage kaffirs" who were claiming them so forcefully. History obviously has not bowed to the whims of these "well-intentioned defenders of civilization against African savagery."

With the excerpts from the autobiographies of South Africans Peter Abrahams and Ezekiel Mphahlele, we are offered two equally vivid and enlightening accounts of childhood—a Black African's and a "coloured's"—in the land of *apartheid* where millions of Black Africans and other "non-whites" are dominated and inhumanly treated by a white minority. It is indeed natural that these accounts do not display the serenity that characterizes Camara Laye's recollections or Léopold Senghor's poetic evocations of his *"royaume d'enfance."*

Jay David and Helise Harrington have rightfully ended their collection with selections dealing with post-independence Africa. This is a very sound thing to do indeed; for ignoring, or even intentionally omitting, such burning questions as the Nigerian civil war would only be misleading. African intellectuals and writers themselves are now speaking up more and more on these questions, and are no longer prepared to leave them out in order not to hurt their own nationalist feel-

ings—or their fellow Africans'. The well-known eastern Nigerian novelist Chinua Achebe was indeed only emphasizing
this awareness of Africa's real problems when he quoted ap-
provingly David Diop's lines:

> "The White Man killed my father
> My father was proud.
> The White Man seduced my mother
> My mother was beautiful. . . ."

and then concluded that had David Diop lived to witness certain events in post-independence Africa, he would certainly
have known that "Black men could also kill, rape, torture
. . . other Black men, women and children." *

In putting together these selections the editors have indeed
provided us with a representation of Africa which illustrates
most eloquently its rich variety as well as its profound unity.
And having given the reader this very broad picture of Africa
past and present without leaving out the burning problems of
the post-independence era, as well as the humiliations and
horrors that plague the existence of millions of Africans living
in still white-dominated Africa, it was quite appropriate to
close the collection on the passionately hopeful lines of the
same David Diop mentioned above:

> In spite of the desolate villages of Africa
> Hope was preserved in us, as in a fortress,
> And from the mines of Swaziland to the factories of Europe
> Spring will be reborn under our bright steps.

* At a conference on "The Commitment of the African Writer" given at
the University of Wisconsin, Madison, in March, 1969.

Contents

FOREWORD by Edris Makward, Associate Professor,
Department of African Languages and Literature, University of Wisconsin   5

INTRODUCTION   15

I. TRIBAL CHILDHOOD: AFRICA BEFORE
THE EUROPEANS   19

  1. From *The African Child* (or *The Dark Child*)
     by Camara Laye, Guinea   21

  2. "Lullaby" (traditional), Ghana   29

  3. "Palm Leaves of Childhood" by G. Adali-
     Mortti, Ghana   31

  4. From *I Was a Savage* by Prince Modupe,
     Guinea   33

  5. From *The Travels of Ibn Battuta* by Ibn
     Battuta, Empire of Mali   42

  6. From "The Story of Rashid bin Hassani" by
     Rashid bin Hassani, Zambia, as told to
     W. F. Baldock   50

  7. "Song for the Dance of Young Girls"
     (traditional), Sudan   67

  8. From *Shinega's Village* by Sahle Selassie,
     Ethiopia   69

  9. From *Baba of Karo* by Baba of Karo as told to
     Mary Smith, Nigeria   72

10. "Circumcision Songs" (traditional Bangi),
     Central Africa   80

11. From *The African Child* (or *The Dark Child*)
     by Camara Laye, Guinea   83

II. COLONIAL CHILDHOOD: CONTACT
    WITH THE WEST   97

    1. From *The Interesting Narrative of the Life of
       Olaudah Equiano* by Olaudah Equiano,
       Nigeria   103
    2. "Martyr" by David Diop, Senegal   116
    3. From *Awo: the Autobiography of Chief
       Obafemi Awolowo* by Chief Obafemi
       Awolowo, Nigeria   118
    4. "Song" (traditional), Malawi   126
    5. From *The African* by William Conton, Sierra
       Leone   127
    6. From "Some Contexts of Blackness" by Sillaty
       K. Dabo, Sierra Leone   133
    7. From *Kossoh Town Boy* by Robert Wellesley
       Cole, Sierra Leone   136
    8. "To a Farm in the White Highlands" by
       Solomon Kagwe, Kenya   145
    9. From *Tell Freedom* by Peter Abrahams,
       South Africa   150
   10. From *Tell Freedom* by Peter Abrahams,
       South Africa   174
   11. From *Down Second Avenue* by Ezekiel
       Mphahlele, South Africa   177
   12. "Ibrahimo" by Colin Turnbull, Democratic
       Republic of the Congo   189

III. AFRICAN CHILDHOOD TODAY:
     NATIONALISM AND BEYOND   205

    1. From "On the Appeal from the Race of
       Sheba" by Leopold Senghor, Senegal   209
    2. From *Ghana: the Autobiography of Kwame
       Nkrumah* by Kwame Nkrumah, Ghana   213
    3. "The Mosquito and the Young Ghanaian" by
       Kwesi Assah Nyako, Ghana   219
    4. From *Weep Not, Child* by James Ngugi,
       Kenya   221

5. From "A Conversation with Eduardo
   Mondlane," Mozambique   240
6. "The Smuggled Account of a Guerrilla
   Fighter from Africa," Rhodesia   244
7. From "Racialism at the Meeting Point" by
   Francis Deng, Sudan   254
8. From "The Price of Nigerian Victory" by
   Charles Keil   257
9. From *A Nigerian Villager in Two Worlds* by
   Dilim Okafor Omali, Nigeria   259
10. From *Ambiguous Adventure* by Cheikh
    Hamidou Kane, Senegal   265
11. "Pardon Me" by Ismael Hurreh, Somalia   278
12. "The Vultures" by David Diop, Senegal   280

Some Highlights of Black African History   281
Starter Bibliography of Black Africa   284
Map of Africa in 1914   101
Map of Africa Today   207

Introduction

TO many, Africa remains the land of jungles and swamps, of lions and giraffes, of primitive tribes and army coups. This view of Africa reflects the distorted and oversimplified perception of the white Western world. African society, values, and history are as varied, complex, and sophisticated as that of the West. This book by Africans attempts to dispel distorted images and to portray the Africans' dreams and frustrations, and the vision of their destiny, of their own lives, of their own world. For too many people this view of Africa, the human Africa, is unknown.

Growing Up African consists of thirty-five selections by African adults who recount their childhood and by African children who reveal themselves through their songs. These selections were written in the eighteenth, nineteenth, and twentieth centuries, and portray the lives of Africans when their perception of the world is beginning to form. A child's impressions, born of innocence and curiosity, can be informative of the society in which he is raised and the men and women with whom he lives.

The childhoods of the contributors, like Africa itself, are diversified. Some of the writers grew up in a predominantly tribal setting and enjoyed the security of traditionally accepted norms. Others witnessed the arrival of Europeans and the confrontation of two different ways of life. Some grew up as sharecroppers on European farms and still others in the urban slums of South Africa. Some were burdened by an alien government whose agents they rarely saw, while others faced daily the brutality of racial prejudice and apartheid. A few of the younger contributors grew up at a time when the hope of Africa was at last being restored. African nationalism was in the ascendancy and European imperialism in decline. These children witnessed the birth of African nations, the assertion of African identity, and the attempts to solve the many economic and political problems which still plague Africa today.

The book includes only narratives from Africa south of the Sahara. Although North Africa maintained commercial ties with black Africa, culturally and historically it is closer to the Middle East than to the rest of Africa. More selections are included from West Africa than from the other areas partially because of its higher population density and partially due to the greater availability of West African materials.

Growing Up African is divided into three chronological sections. The first is tribal Africa before the European penetration of the late nineteenth century. Some of the selections are more contemporary than the nineteenth century, but all deal with a time and place scarcely influenced by European conquerors. The mood of the selections is serene, and the writers are nostalgic as they recount, at times, slightly romanticized memories of their secure African past.

The mood of the second section, which narrates the African confrontation with the West, is an antithesis of the first. The narrators are often confused, afraid, dismayed, and angry; for in the African encounter the West usually perpetrated physical or psychological violence. In the eighteenth century European slave dealers shipped Africans to American plantations; and in the nineteenth century colonialists, administrators, and missionaries challenged the Africans' national independence, their traditional technology, their spiritual capabilities, and their personal integrity. The African commentators, although often impressed by Western achievements, became—even as children—bitter and angry.

The final section is a collection of narratives from black-nationalist Africa. In the last forty years Africans have been reasserting their cultural traditions and have been demanding their countries' independence. With the important exceptions of South Africa, Rhodesia, Mozambique, Angola, Southwest Africa, and Portuguese Guinea, all the African colonies have become independent countries. This final section, in a sense, is a synthesis of the first two chapters. Africans in their nation building are not free from their past, either from their tribal heritage or from their colonial history. In fact one of the major problems facing African nationalism today is to resolve the innovations which contact with the West has inspired with the tribal customs of their forefathers. Children growing up in nationalist Africa are raised in a sea of conflicting emotions—loyalty to their own tribe but love for their nation, attachment to their own culture but attraction to the power of the West and the need to modernize. This problem of creating a modern Africa without loss of identity remains a dilemma for young Africans, and even in their childhood many recognize the complexity of their position.

In *Growing Up African* most of the childhood experiences are about moments of discovery, of children becoming aware of new dimensions to their own environments. In a larger context, we hope this collection will also provide for the reader moments of discovery, of historical and present-day Africa, of the Africa of children, of human Africa. For we believe that when all of us begin to appreciate the cultural heritage of others, then the possibility of international understanding will not seem so remote.

JAY DAVID and
HELISE HARRINGTON
New York City

TRIBAL CHILDHOOD:

AFRICA BEFORE THE EUROPEANS

AFRICA has never been isolated from the rest of the world. Until the nineteenth century its intercourse with the West was limited to an economic and coastal contact, but its relationship, particularly with North Africa and Arabia, is longstanding and intimate. In West Africa by the ninth century the Sudanic kingdom of Ghana established a prosperous trading alliance, particularly in gold, slaves and salt, with North African Berber tribes and Arab travelers. Its successors, Mali, Songhay, and Kanem-Bornu, enlarged this contact to include an adoption of the Islamic religion and cultural and intellectual exchanges. In East Africa Omani Arabs settled on the coast and intermarried with coastal Africans.

African peoples in the East African interior, in Central Africa, and in coastal West Africa had less direct contact with non-African peoples. Their societies were no less dynamic, however, nor their cultural traditions poorer. In fact, the complexity and wide diversity of African tribal traditions preclude any simple description of childhood in Africa. Some African tribes formed large states while others remained in small political units. Some African peoples became farmers while others became traders; and some groups developed belief systems which were highly divergent from those of their neighbors.

The childhood of an African also varied according to the time period in which he lived. Africa's history is complex, and the living conditions of any area changed from decade to decade. A child born in Timbuktu in the early 1500's, for instance, grew up in one of Africa's centers of trading and learning, but a youngster from the same city in the 1590's witnessed Timbuktu's fall to Moroccan invaders and the city's subsequent economic and intellectual decline.*

Still, childhood in any of Africa's eight hundred tribal units did have certain universal characteristics. Perhaps the most important was the psychological security fostered by the community in which the child lived. Political dynasties might rise or fall, disease might ravage a village, or religious convictions might change, but before the coming of the white man, the tribes' traditions were considered valid and were not challenged; the worth of the tribes' customs and the richness of their history were never doubted.

In this sense the African tribal child had a secure beginning. He was born into a nonindustrial society which, in comparison with contemporary society, was relaxed and personalized. He was a member of a close-knit group and had a definite place in a clearly defined universe. With childlike wonder, fear, and delight he entered the world of his forefathers, and grew to respect and revere their traditions and customs.

The traditional childhood is quickly disappearing in Africa, as the continent becomes more closely associated with modern industrial societies. While some of the following selections are contemporary, all point back to a time in Africa when children were taught the customs of their own peoples and were not as yet influenced by the West.

* For a brief chronology of some important events in African history, see Some Highlights of Black African History at the back of the book.

1

FROM

The African Child (or *The Dark Child*)

by Camara Laye

(1924–   )

Camara Laye, the son of a well-known metalsmith, was brought up in a small town in Guinea, West Africa. As a youngster, Camara Laye spent most of his time in his father's workshop where he learned the art of smithing just as his grandfather and great-grandfather had done before him.

In Laye's community smithing was not just a craft as it is in the West, but also an art and a way of life. His father when smelting gold purified his body and evoked the genies of fire and gold. In turn the griots—*the praise-singers—and the rest of the community held his father in great respect, for by smelting gold he proved himself to be in close communion with the spirit of creation.*

In the following passage Camara Laye as a young boy watches his father smelt gold. While he cannot understand or rationally explain his father's magic, he can accept the certainty of it and revere his father's dignity.

Despite his apprenticeship Laye did not follow in his father's footsteps. He attended the Technical College in Conakry, trained as an engineer in France, and has become one of West Africa's best-known novelists. His publications in-

clude The African Child, The Radiance of the King, *and* The Dream of Africa.

OF ALL the different kinds of work my father engaged in, none fascinated me so much as his skill with gold. No other occupation was so noble, no other needed such a delicate touch. And then, every time he worked in gold it was like a festival—indeed it *was* a festival—that broke the monotony of ordinary working days.

So, if a woman, accompanied by a go-between, crossed the threshold of the workshop, I followed her in at once. I knew what she wanted: She had brought some gold, and had come to ask my father to transform it into a trinket. She had collected it in the placers of Siguiri where, crouching over the river for months on end, she had patiently extracted grains of gold from the mud.

These women never came alone. They knew my father had other things to do than make trinkets. And even when he had the time, they knew they were not the first to ask a favor of him, and that, consequently, they would not be served before others.

Generally they required the trinket for a certain date, for the festival of Ramadan or the Tabaski [Islamic holidays] or some other family ceremony or dance.

Therefore, to enhance their chances of being served quickly and to more easily persuade my father to interrupt the work before him, they used to request the services of an official praise-singer, a go-between, arranging in advance the fee they were to pay him for his good offices.

The go-between installed himself in the workshop, tuned up his *cora,* which is our harp, and began to sing my father's praises. This was always a great event for me. I heard recalled the lofty deeds of my father's ancestors and their names from the earliest times. As the couplets were reeled off it was like watching the growth of a great genealogical tree that spread its branches far and wide and flourished its boughs and twigs before my mind's eye. The harp played an accompaniment to this vast utterance of names, expanding it with notes that were now soft, now shrill.

I could sense my father's vanity being inflamed, and I already knew that after having sipped this milk-and-honey he would lend a favorable ear to the woman's request. But I was not alone in my knowledge. The woman also had seen my father's eyes gleaming with contented pride. She held out her grains of gold as if the whole matter were settled. My father took up his scales and weighed the gold.

"What sort of trinket do you want?" he would ask.

"I want. . . ."

And then the woman would not know any longer exactly what she wanted because desire kept making her change her mind, and because she would have liked all the trinkets at once. But it would have taken a pile of gold much larger than she had brought to satisfy her whim, and from then on her chief purpose in life was to get hold of it as soon as she could.

"When do you want it?"

Always the answer was that the trinket was needed for an occasion in the near future.

"So! You are in that much of a hurry? Where do you think I shall find the time?"

"I am in a great hurry, I assure you."

"I have never seen a woman eager to deck herself out who wasn't in a great hurry! Good! I shall arrange my time to suit you. Are you satisfied?"

He would take the clay pot that was kept specially for smelting gold, and would pour the grains into it. He would then cover the gold with powdered charcoal, a charcoal he prepared by using plant juices of exceptional purity. Finally, he would place a large lump of the same kind of charcoal over the pot.

As soon as she saw that the work had been duly undertaken, the woman, now quite satisfied, would return to her household tasks, leaving her go-between to carry on with the praise-singing which had already proved so advantageous.

At a sign from my father the apprentices began working two sheepskin bellows. The skins were on the floor, on opposite sides of the forge, connected to it by earthen pipes. While the work was in progress the apprentices sat in front of the bellows with crossed legs. That is, the younger of the two sat, for the elder was sometimes allowed to assist. But the younger—this time it was Sidafa—was only permitted to work the bellows and watch while waiting his turn for promotion to less rudimentary tasks. First one and then the other worked hard at the bellows: the flame in the forge rose higher and became a living thing, a genie implacable and full of life.

Then my father lifted the clay pot with his long tongs and placed it on the flame.

Immediately all activity in the workshop almost came to a halt. During the whole time that the gold was being smelted, neither copper nor aluminum could be worked nearby, lest some particle of these base metals fall into the container which held the gold. Only steel could be worked on such occasions, but the men, whose task that was, hurried to finish what they were doing, or left it abruptly to join the apprentices gathered around the forge. There were so many, and they crowded so around my father, that I, the smallest person present, had to come near the forge in order not to lose track of what was going on.

If he felt he had inadequate working space, my father had the apprentices stand well away from him. He merely raised his hand in a simple gesture: at that particular moment he never uttered a word, and no one else would: no one was allowed to utter a word. Even the go-between's voice was no longer raised in song. The silence was broken only by the panting of the bellows and the faint hissing of the gold. But if my father never actually spoke, I know that he was forming words in his mind. I could tell from his lips, which kept moving, while, bending over the pot, he stirred the gold and charcoal with a bit of wood that kept bursting into flame and had constantly to be replaced by a fresh one.

What words did my father utter? I do not know. At least I am not certain what they were. No one ever told me. But could they have been anything but incantations? On these occasions was he not invoking the genies of fire and gold, of fire and wind, of wind blown by the blast-pipes of the forge, of fire born of wind, of gold married to fire? Was it not their assistance, their friendship, their espousal that he besought? Yes. Almost certainly he was invoking these genies, all of whom are equally indispensable for smelting gold.

The operation going on before my eyes was certainly the smelting of gold, yet something more than that: a magical operation that the guiding spirits could regard with favor or disfavor. That is why, all around my father, there was absolute silence and anxious expectancy. Though only a child, I knew there could be no craft greater than the goldsmith's. I expected a ceremony; I had come to be present at a ceremony; and it actually was one, though very protracted. I was still too young to understand why, but I had an inkling as I watched the almost religious concentration of those who followed the mixing process in the clay pot.

When finally the gold began to melt I could have shouted aloud—and perhaps we all would have if we had not been forbidden to make a sound. I trembled, and so did everyone else watching my father stir the mixture—it was still a heavy paste—in which the charcoal was gradually consumed. The next stage followed swiftly. The gold now had the fluidity of water. The genies had smiled on the operation!

"Bring me the brick!" my father would order, thus lifting the ban that until then had silenced us.

The brick, which an apprentice would place beside the fire, was hollowed out, generously greased with Galam butter. My father would take the pot off the fire and tilt it carefully, while I would watch the gold flow into the brick, flow like liquid fire. True, it was only a very sparse trickle of fire, but how vivid, how brilliant! As the gold flowed into the brick, the grease sputtered and flamed and emitted a thick smoke that caught in the throat and stung the eyes, leaving us all weeping and coughing.

But there were times when it seemed to me that my father ought to turn this task over to one of his assistants. They were experienced, had assisted him hundreds of times, and could certainly have performed the work well. But my father's lips moved and those inaudible, secret words, those incantations he addressed to one we could not see or hear, was the essential part. Calling on the genies of fire, of wind,

of gold and exorcising the evil spirits—this was a knowledge
he alone possessed.

By now the gold had been cooled in the hollow of the
brick, and my father began to hammer and stretch it. This
was the moment when his work as a goldsmith really began.
I noticed that before embarking on it he never failed to
stroke the little snake stealthily as it lay coiled up under the
sheepskin. I can only assume that this was his way of gathering strength for what remained to be done, the most trying
part of his task.

But was it not extraordinary and miraculous that on these
occasions the little black snake was always coiled under the
sheepskin? He was not always there. He did not visit my
father every day. But he was always present whenever there
was gold to be worked. His presence was no surprise to *me*.
After that evening when my father had spoken of the guiding
spirit of his race I was no longer astonished. The snake was
there intentionally. He knew what the future held. Did he
tell my father? I think that he most certainly did. Did he tell
him everything? I have another reason for believing firmly
that he did.

The craftsman who works in gold must first of all purify
himself. That is, he must wash himself all over and, of
course, abstain from all sexual commerce during the whole
time. Great respecter of ceremony as he was, it would have
been impossible for my father to ignore these rules. Now,
I never saw him make these preparations. I saw him address
himself to his work without any apparent preliminaries.
From that moment it was obvious that, forewarned in a
dream by his black guiding spirit of the task which awaited
him in the morning, my father must have prepared for it as
soon as he arose, entering his workshop in a state of purity,
his body smeared with the secret potions hidden in his
numerous pots of magical substances; or perhaps he always
came into his workshop in a state of ritual purity. I am not
trying to make him out a better man than he was—he was a
man and had his share of human frailties—but he was always
uncompromising in his respect for ritual observance.

The woman for whom the trinket was being made, and

who had come often to see how the work was progressing, would arrive for the final time, not wanting to miss a moment of this spectacle—as marvelous to her as to us—when the gold wire, which my father had succeeded in drawing out from the mass of molten gold and charcoal, was transformed into a trinket.

There she would be. Her eyes would devour the fragile gold wire, following it in its tranquil and regular spiral around the little slab of metal which supported it. My father would catch a glimpse of her and I would see him slowly beginning to smile. Her avid attention delighted him.

"Are you trembling?" he would ask.

"Am I trembling?"

And we would all burst out laughing at her. For she would be trembling! She would be trembling with covetousness for the spiral pyramid in which my father would be inserting, among the convolutions, tiny grains of gold. When he had finally finished by crowning the pyramid with a heavier grain, she would dance in delight.

No one—no one at all—would be more enchanted than she as my father slowly turned the trinket back and forth between his fingers to display its perfection. Not even the praise-singer whose business it was to register excitement would be more excited than she. Throughout this metamorphosis he did not stop speaking faster and ever faster, increasing his tempo, accelerating his praises and flatteries as the trinket took shape, shouting to the skies my father's skill.

For the praise-singer took a curious part—I should say rather that it was direct and effective—in the work. He was drunk with the joy of creation. He shouted aloud in joy. He plucked his *cora* [harp] like a man inspired. He sweated as if he were the trinket-maker, as if he were my father, as if the trinket were his creation. He was no longer a hired censer-bearer, a man whose services anyone could rent. He was a man who created his song out of some deep inner necessity. And when my father, after having soldered the large grain of gold that crowned the summit, held out his work to be admired, the praise-singer would no longer be able to contain himself. He would begin to intone the *douga*, the great chant which is sung only for celebrated men and which is danced for them alone.

But the *douga* is a formidable chant, a provocative chant, a chant which the praise-singer dared not sing, and which the man for whom it is sung dared not dance before certain precautions had been taken. My father had taken them as soon as he woke, since he had been warned in a dream. The praise-singer had taken them when he concluded his arrangements with the woman. Like my father he had smeared his body with magic substances and had made himself invulnerable to the evil genies whom the *douga* inevitably set free; these potions made him invulnerable also to rival praise-singers, perhaps jealous of him, who awaited only this song and the exaltation and loss of control which attended it, in order to begin casting their spells.

At the first notes of the *douga* my father would arise and emit a cry in which happiness and triumph were equally mingled; and brandishing in his right hand the hammer that was the symbol of his profession and in his left a ram's horn filled with magic substances, he would dance the glorious dance.

No sooner had he finished, than workmen and apprentices, friends and customers in their turn, not forgetting the woman for whom the trinket had been created, would flock around him, congratulating him, showering praises on him and complimenting the praise-singer at the same time. The latter found himself laden with gifts—almost his only means of support, for the praise-singer leads a wandering life after the fashion of the troubadours of old. Aglow with dancing and the praises he had received, my father would offer everyone cola nuts, that small change of Guinean courtesy.

Now all that remained to be done was to redden the trinket in a little water to which chlorine and sea salt had been added. I was at liberty to leave. The festival was over!

2

"Lullaby"

(traditional: Akan tribe of West Africa)

An African child may grow up with more than one mother to care for him. In many African societies a man can take several women in marriage, and the wives may cooperate with each other in caring for their offspring. Unlike Western society's nuclear family, the African traditional family is an extended family, and uncles, aunts, and distant cousins, as well as co-wives, maintain close ties and feel deeply responsible for one another's welfare.

Still, in Africa as elsewhere, the relationship between a mother and the child she bears is a special one. For the child it means warmth, tenderness, and security. The following verse is sung to a traditional Ghanaian tune which Akan mothers still sing to lull their children to sleep. The lullaby, like most traditional poetry, is part of Africa's oral tradition of passing literature and history from one generation to the next verbally. Neither the composer of the piece nor its age is known.

> Why do you cry?
> You are the child of a yam farmer,
> Why do you cry?
> You are the child of a cocoyam farmer,
> Why do you cry?
>
> Someone would like to have you for her child,
> But you are my own.

Someone wishes she had you to nurse on a good mat,
Someone wishes you were hers.
She would put you on a camel blanket,
But I have you to rear on a torn mat.
Someone wishes she had you,
But it is I who have you.

3

"Palm Leaves of Childhood"

by Gyormbeeyi Adali-Mortti

(1916–   )

A rural African child, often even as a youngster a tiller of the
soil, is intimately involved with the natural world about him.
Unlike the actions of Western urbanized man, who lives
apart from nature, the activities of a rural African youth are
closely identified with his environment. In the following
poem Gyormbeeyi Adali-Mortti comments that just as a
rural African boy feels he is part of his landscape, so his
landscape becomes part of him, becomes part of his "dream-
ing and becoming."

Adali-Mortti, a Ghanaian of West Africa, is an interpreter
of Ewe poetry, as well as a poet in his own right. Before at-
tending Cornell Graduate School, he was one of the founders
of the literary magazine Okyeame, *a publication of the*
Ghana Society of Writers. He is now a lecturer in business
management at the University of Ghana School of Adminis-
tration.

When I was very small indeed,
and Joe and Fred were six-year giants,
my father, they and I, with soil
did mix farm-yard manure.
In this we planted coconuts,
naming them by brothers' names.
The palms grew faster far than I;

and soon, ere I could grow a Man,
they, flowering, reached their goal!
Like the earrings that my sisters wore
came the tender golden flowers.
I watched them grow from gold to green;
then nuts as large as Tata's head.
I craved the milk I knew they bore.
I listened to the whispering leaves:
to the chattering, rattling, whispering leaves,
when night winds did wake.
They haunt me still in work and play:
those whispering leaves behind the slit
on the cabin wall of childhood's
dreaming and becoming.

4

FROM

I Was a Savage

by Prince Modupe

(1901–   )

Prince Modupe of the So-So tribe was born in 1901 in Guinea, West Africa. His mother experienced an extremely difficult delivery, and upon his birth she sighed, "Modupe Olurum— I thank God." From his mother's prayer, Modupe obtained his name. In naming her child his mother was following a custom of her people to name children for the first important object or the first significant words spoken after a birth.

Even from his moment of birth, Modupe's life, like the life of most other African children, was thus shaped by tribal custom. In the following selection Modupe as a young boy discovers the importance his tribe attaches to such traditions. He comes to realize that the punishment for transgressing tribal sanctions is severe, but at the same time discovers that the social and religious order they uphold is sacred and that the well-being of his tribe depends on his adherence to them.

Prince Modupe eventually left the security of his tribal world. In 1922 he traveled to America and attended the Hampton Institute in Hampton, Virginia. He has lectured widely on Africa and is currently living with his family in Los Angeles.

WHEN my father returned from his long overland trading trips, his clothing was always stained with the dust of the journey. There was in the cloth the smells of the cargo he carried—hides, ground nuts (peanuts), cola. I knew these things came from places which were only names to me—Bomako, Kauroussa, Kankan. They seemed as remote as the moon, and this made the odors seem exotic. The smell of leather was the smell of travel. I inhaled it as I walked one morning beside him, his country-cloth robe fluttering in the breeze, flapping against my face. He was taking me to call on my grandfather.

We were in the prayer room when a messenger arrived from the Bambara tribe [large tribal group of Guinea, West Africa]. I retreated with my father to a far corner of the room while my grandfather granted audience. Before my eyes, I saw the familiar, kindly old Grandfather become the stern majestic chief attending to important affairs.

Africans are a ceremonious people. There were long polite inquiries. The health of everybody? I could see that the messenger was fairly bristling with excitement under the calm surface of politeness. I hoped Grandfather would forget my presence in the room. I wanted to know what this was about!

They finally got around to the point and exciting enough it was! A *lappa* [wraparound skirt of African women] had been stolen from the house of a Bambara woman. A So-So warrior had been seen running from the village with something in his hand which resembled a *lappa*.

Theft was almost unknown among our people. It was punishable by death. If the Bambara were mistaken, if the accusation were false, tribal war would follow. If they were correct, if one of our people had stolen, the guilty So-So would have to be discovered and punished.

Grandfather's voice was terrible to hear. It was sort of a growl with a crack in it. Was the name of the So-So youth known to the Bambaras?

The witch doctor had called the name, a youth known as Santigi.

I felt my father stiffen. I no longer wanted to be in that room but I dared not move. Santigi!

Santigi was betrothed to my sister N'gadi. The marriage

had been arranged except for one detail—Santigi had not
accumulated all of the necessary dowry. The part he lacked
was a bright new *lappa,* the wraparound skirt which tribal
women wear.

Tribesmen do not "buy" their brides. The dowry is a sort
of marriage insurance. It means that the man appreciates the
value of the girl and he wants to make a token of this appre-
ciation to the girl's parents. It is the tangible way to show
his respect for the girl and her family.

Santigi was not rich, even by bush standards, but he was
strong and hard-working, and fearless, a well-liked fellow.
My sister N'gadi loved him and he was acceptable to our
family. N'gadi was studying to be a medicine woman and
already had her own house away from ours.

Grandfather dispatched a messenger to fetch Santigi to
the prayer room where we waited. The silence in the room
seemed jungle heavy. Neither my grandfather nor the Bambara spoke.

When Santigi came in, after what seemed a long time, he
stood straight and proud. He seemed to fill the doorway as
he came through it. The questioning began. Had Santigi
been to the Bambara town?

Santigi nodded, easily enough. He had gone to the Bambara market.

Why had he gone to a Bambara market? Was not every
needful thing to be had in our own market?

He had gone to look for a fine bright new *lappa!* He got
over the word *lappa* without a pause.

Had he brought a *lappa* back with him? He shook his
whole body with his head. No *lappa!*

There was nothing for it now but trial by ordeal. That was
the tribal way of establishing innocence. One's innocence
was one's protection. If after drinking the judgment poison,
a brew called *wobia,* Santigi was able to keep his feet under
him, war would follow. The Bambara's witch doctor's word
would have been challenged. The Bambara were a powerful
tribe.

There was a great commotion among our people when the

word got around. Some of the more excitable thought the warriors might as well get their weapons ready. It seemed unlikely that Santigi would steal, even more unlikely that he would be able to steal and then lie about it without a quiver of guilt showing in his face.

Excitement kept sleep away from me that night. I thought about N'gadi, the way she would feel if Santigi did not survive the judgment poison. N'gadi was thin as early-morning shadow and not robust in any part except her spirit which was staunch. She was probably sobbing alone in her medicine hut, forgotten in the turmoil by everyone except myself.

I thought about war, how exciting that would be, how disgusting that I was less than warrior age. How unspeakable to be left at home with women and children, probably hiding out in the forest in case our town should be taken.

I thought about Santigi. Would he be alive or dead after another sundown? If the poison caught him, and he were buried face down as criminals are, N'gadi would have to watch this disgrace. I wondered how it would feel to be dead, a dead criminal, unable to join the spirits of the reverenced dead, how lonely. How would a lonely dead feel when the feast was made to the spirits of deceased elders and he could not join the festival. I knew that a man who lives the laws of his tribe is never alone, living or dead. Surely Santigi had not risked becoming a lonely dead, not even for love of N'gadi!

Death was interesting to think about. I tried to imagine that the dark hut was a grave, that the *canda* mat beneath me was a burial mat. People would sing praise-songs over me, recounting deeds of great valor . . . N'gadi in mournful sing-song telling how I had saved her from a terror of a Bambara warrior . . .

N'gadi! Everything I thought about led my mind to my sister. I had given myself the shivers thinking about death. I wanted to feel the comfort of my sister's arms around me. I would run to N'gadi. Night is the roaming time of spirits and it would be terrifying to go out alone at night. I was so frightened by the thoughts I had been thinking that I had to leave them behind in this hut, so I would make a dash for it. In no time at all I would be with N'gadi and we could sob together.

No one stirred as I slipped out the door. Moonlight flooded the village but I stayed clear of it by moving between huts until my sister's house and the medicine man's behind it were the only ones to be seen in front of me.

I was gathering up my courage for the final spurt of distance when I saw a figure moving stealthily as a leopard toward the medicine man's hut. The figure was a woman and she carried a gourd carefully so as not to spill the contents. The figure was slim like N'gadi. In fact, it almost certainly was N'gadi! Was it her spirit walking? The figure disappeared behind the medicine hut for only as long as it takes an elephant to trumpet. When she reappeared there was still a gourd in her hands.

I slipped back to my *canda* as quickly as I could get there. I had seen something which no one should have looked upon because it should not have happened. I did not understand it but I knew it was evil. Curled up into a small ball of frightened humanity, I finally fell asleep.

The drums began talking early the next morning. As soon as the Bambara arrived, the people gathered for the trial. Santigi was at the center of a great circle, surrounded by elders and warriors and the witch doctor. My sister was there but I was afraid to meet her eyes. She had strange powers which I feared.

The witch doctor poured the *wobia* from a gourd into a larger pot over the fire. He talked to the steaming juice. The drums beat loud and fast, then ceased. All sound and motion ceased with the drums. In the silence, the witch doctor reached out a calabash full of the hot liquid to Santigi. I could not tell whether Santigi's hand shook or whether it only seemed to because of the heat waves above the poison pot. He planted his legs far apart as though to brace himself upright. He watched N'gadi as he drained the calabash. N'gadi looked at the ground. Everyone else seemed intent on Santigi. He seemed to sway once but quickly recovered himself. It was finally apparent to everyone that the poison was not going to topple him.

My grandfather stood up. The Bambara stood up. My grandfather spoke in a harsh voice. The warrior had proven his innocence. If war had to come, we were ready.

Santigi's friends swarmed around him, whooping their joy —all but N'gadi. She walked home with the rest of my family and was strangely quiet.

It was after the midday resting time when some exciting news went around the town. Matara, my mother, had dozed and dreamed that *uba,* the vulture, had perched in her house. There is no omen more terrible than this. Calamity of the worst sort is sure to follow. What had it to do with the strange thing I had seen in the moonlight? I must speak.

I found my father alone. His face became grim when I told him what I had to say. His first thought was to ask N'gadi whether she had substituted some innocent brew for the powerful *wobia.* Talking to himself rather than to me, he changed his mind. He would ask Santigi. He would tell Santigi of the ruin that was sure to fall on all of the people, even on N'gadi, if he had done an evil he would not confess.

We heard the message drums that evening: *Santigi guilty. . . . Santigi to die. . . . Santigi guilty. . . . Santigi to die. . . . We have lappa . . . Santigi to die.*

People gathered quickly in the central compound, Santigi in the center of the throng, his head bowed. The witch doctor held up a bright new *lappa* so that all could see it before Grandfather dispatched a runner to carry it to the Bambara town.

The witch doctor explained that the power of the *wobia* had been crossed. Santigi had confessed to this as well as to stealing and lying—all terrible crimes. N'gadi's lips were parted. I was afraid she was going to declare herself. I saw that Santigi was looking at N'gadi too. Ever so slightly, he shook his head at her. There was great pride in both of them as they stared at one another across the space which separated them.

Santigi was to die three sundowns hence. From the time grandfather announced the execution until it was carried out, the *taboole,* the sacred drums of sorrow, never ceased throbbing. They spoke slowly at first, gathering pace gradually as the death hour approached. Their voice seemed like great sobs, yet they were more sorrowful than anything that could come from a human throat. The vibrations shuddered the earth beneath our feet and I thought that the earth itself joined in the crushing lament.

By the third day no one found it possible to do any work. The call to sorrow and shame was too urgent. The adults went about with set, sad faces. For the first time in my childhood the days seemed long, endless. The death chant was taken up all through the town. A great many friends and relatives of Santigi's overflowed his home. As many as could find seating room on the floor wailed there and threw ashes over their heads. I looked for N'gadi but she was nowhere about. My mother stayed in her own house grieving over the sin of the youth who was to die because he loved her daughter above the laws of the tribe.

As the execution time neared, all women and children were shooed toward their homes. The women would continue their lament behind closed doors. What was to be done was not a thing for children to see.

I hid behind the trunk of a tree. In my overexcited imagination I had already witnessed the execution a hundred times over. I felt strangely a part of what was going on. If I had not told my father what I had seen in the moonlight, the warriors might at that moment have been going to war instead of to the sacrifice rock. I was horribly fascinated by this affair I had stumbled into and I wanted to stay with it to the end.

It was easy during the confusion to maneuver my way from tree to tree until I neared the great rock. The sacrifice altar was screened by trees. I scrambled up one of them and fastened myself tight against a horizontal limb.

The fire in the center of the clearing was burning brightly when I attained my lookout perch, but the death procession had not reached the place.

Boom . . . Boom, boom, boom . . . My tree trembled with the thuds. War drums joined in with the drums of sorrow.

Warriors of his own age group escorted Santigi to a spot

in front of the sacred rock. They were dressed in full regalia, hide shields, spears, plumed headgear. The dancing firelight glinted on the edges of the spears. The warriors formed a circle, leaving an opening for the entry of the older men, the tribal elders, the witch doctor, the executioner. These two came in last, wearing masks. The executioner carried a long, broad knife, curved on the end. It is called a sacrifice knife because this really was a sacrifice that was about to be made —the sacrifice of a life to the sacred principles of tribal law. The masks embodied the spirit of that law as it had come down to us from the ancient ones who had died, yet who live forever through the laws and the customs.

Santigi's expression was resigned as the warriors bound him. He must have thought that the best he could do was to die like a true tribesman, he who had not been able to live as one. Perhaps by this last bit of brave living he would be allowed to sit on the far edge of the conclave of tribal dead.

The warriors danced, spears in hand. At the edge of the circle was a large calabash filled with palm wine to which herbs of strange powers had been added. This was taken in great gulps by the dancers as the tempo of the drumming and dancing increased. The longer they danced, the higher they leaped, the faster they whirled. The light and heavy drums, combined with the thud of feet and the chorus of chant, shook the tree where I perched. I dug my hands into the bark of the branch. If I fell like a ripe fruit, the executioner might have double duty that night!

Sweat gleamed on the bodies of the frenzied dancers, their eyes rolled, some of them were overcome with paroxysmal spasms and fell at the edge of the circle with foam on their lips.

The executioner did not dance. He stood with folded arms looking down at Santigi. When the big drum stopped, every sound and movement stopped with it. The executioner grasped the end of the knife with both hands, raised it high and swung. After that single sweeping motion, Santigi's head rolled sideways. A gush of blood rose out of his neck. The sacred rock was red.

The drums came to life again. The booming was no longer

frenzied, but sad, so sad. I wanted to sob. Santigi who had always seemed to me to be so much of one piece, his whole body springing forward to run, to leap, to wrestle, to dance, Santigi was severed. Boy that I was, I understood that even as his head was separated from his body, his soul was separate from the body of his tribe. That, not his death, was the real horror of what I had seen.

I have no clear memory of how I stole back to Lamina's [a teacher of Modupe] hut. I must have managed it somehow in a daze of terror.

5

FROM

The Travels of Ibn Battuta

by Ibn Battuta

(1304–1368?)

The first four narratives have described tribal childhoods of recent times. While few records remain, an African childhood in earlier centuries must have been no less intriguing. In the Savannah area of West Africa, for instance (including the modern states of Mali, Upper Volta, eastern Senegal, northern Guinea, Niger, western Chad and northern Nigeria), a child of the 1300's grew up in a politically sophisticated empire. Although the nucleus of his state was tribal, many peoples lived under his sovereign's imperial rule.

In fact, in medieval times four notable empires emerged in West Africa—Ghana, Mali, Songhay, and Kanem-Bornu. The major reason for their rise was their geographical position on the trans-Saharan trade routes. By the ninth century an active trade in salt and gold had developed between North Africa and the forest regions of West Africa, and because of their intermediary position, these empires were able to act as middlemen.

In 1353 an Arab traveler, Ibn Battuta, visited one of these empires, Mali. Although by that year Mali was already in a period of decline, Ibn Battuta was still impressed by its efficient government and administration and its economic development.

Mali rose out of the ruins of the kingdom of Ghana in the early thirteenth century. Its founder, Sundiata, was a great warrior who succeeded in overrunning the declining Ghana in 1240. By his death in 1255 Sundiata had secured a large area of territory for his kingdom, the border of Mali ranging from the Senegal River in the west to the Niger in the east.

Mali reached its greatest splendor during the reign of Mansa Musa (1312–37) who continued Sundiata's imperial expansion and developed an impressive administrative structure. It was in his reign that Islam—originally imported by Arab travelers—became the official religion of Mali. Mansa Musa celebrated Islamic holy days, employed Muslim advisers, and in 1324 made the pilgrimage to Mecca.

When Ibn Battuta visited Mali during the reign of Mansa Sulaiman (1341–1360) Islam was firmly established, but as Ibn Battuta notes, the ruler continued to respect local customs. Ibn Battuta was particularly impressed by the ruler's court—which was as spectacular as any in Arabia or medieval Europe.

Here is an excerpt from Ibn Battuta's impressions of Mali. While not dealing specifically with childhood, his description does give the reader a vivid portrait of life in one of Africa's greatest empires.

WE set out thereafter from Karsakhú and came to the river of Sansara, which is about ten miles from Malli. It is their custom that no persons except those who have obtained permission are allowed to enter the city. I had already written to the white [Arab] community [there] requesting them to hire a house for me, so when I arrived at this river, I crossed by the ferry without interference. Thus I reached the city of Malli, the capital of the king of the blacks [the empire is also named Mali]. I stopped at the cemetery and went to the quarter occupied by the whites, where I asked for Muhammad ibn al-Faqíh. I found that he had hired a house for me and went there. His son-in-law brought me candles and food, and next day Ibn al-Faqíh himself came to visit me, with other prominent residents. I met the *qadi* [Muslim judge who interprets and administers the religious law of Islam] of Malli, 'Abd ar'Rahman, who came to see me; he is a negro, a pilgrim, and a man of fine character. I met also the interpreter Dugha [Dugha is a name of a kind of vulture and often given as a name to men], who is one of the principal men among the blacks. All these persons sent me hospitality-gifts of food and treated me with the utmost generosity—may God reward them for their kindness! . . .

On certain days the sultan [of Mali] holds audiences in the palace yard, where there is a platform under a tree with three steps; this they call the *pempi*. It is carpeted with silk and has cushions placed on it. [Over it] is raised the umbrella, which is a sort of pavilion made of silk, surmounted by a bird in gold, about the size of a falcon. The sultan comes out of a door in a corner of the palace, carrying a bow in his hand and a quiver on his back. On his head he has a golden skull-cap, bound with a gold band which has narrow ends shaped like knives, more than a span in length. His usual dress is a velvety red tunic, made of the European fabrics called *mutanfas*. The sultan is preceded by his musicians, who carry gold and silver guimbris [two-stringed guitars], and walks in a leisurely fashion, affecting a very slow movement, and even stops from time to time. On reaching the *pempi* he stops and looks round the assembly, then ascends it in the sedate manner of a preacher ascending a mosque-pulpit. As he takes his seat the drums, trumpets, and bugles are sounded. Three slaves go out at a run to summon the sovereign's deputy and the military commanders, who enter and sit down. Two saddled and bridled horses are brought, along with two goats, which they hold to serve as a protection against the evil eye. Dugha stands at the gate and the rest of the people remain in the street, under the trees.

The negroes are of all people the most submissive to their king and the most abject in their behaviour before him. They swear by his name, saying *Mansa Sulayman ki* [Emperor Sulayman has commanded in the local language, Mandingo].

If he summons any of them while he is holding an audience
in his pavilion, the person summoned takes off his clothes
and puts on worn garments, removes his turban and dons a
dirty skull-cap, and enters with his garments and trousers
raised knee-high. He goes forward in an attitude of humility
and dejection, and knocks the ground hard with his elbows,
then stands with bowed head and bent back listening to
what he says. If anyone addresses the king and receives a
reply from him, he uncovers his back and throws dust over
his head and back, for all the world like a bather splashing
himself with water. I used to wonder how it was they did not
blind themselves. If the sultan delivers any remarks during
his audience, those present take off their turbans and put
them down, and listen in silence to what he says. Sometimes
one of them stands up before him and recalls his deeds in
the sultan's service, saying "I did so-and-so on such a day"
or "I killed so-and-so on such a day." Those who have knowledge of this confirm his words, which they do by plucking the
cord of the bow and releasing it (with a heavy twang), just
as an archer does when shooting an arrow. If the sultan says
"Truly spoken" or thanks him, he removes his clothes and
"dusts." That is their idea of good manners. . . .

I was in Malli during the two festivals of the sacrifice and
the fast-breaking. On these days the sultan takes his seat on
the *pempi* after the midafternoon prayer. The armour-
bearers bring in magnificent arms—quivers of gold and
silver, swords ornamented with gold and with golden scab-
bards, gold and silver lances, and crystal maces. At his head
stand four *amirs* [variation of emirs, noblemen or chieftains]
driving off the flies, having in their hands silver ornaments
resembling saddle-stirrups. The commanders, *qadi*, and
preacher sit in their usual places. The interpreter Dugha
comes with his four wives and his slave-girls, who are about
a hundred in number. They are wearing beautiful robes,
and on their heads they have gold and silver fillets, with gold
and silver balls attached. A chair is placed for Dugha to sit
on. He plays on an instrument made of reeds, with some
small calabashes at its lower end, and chants a poem in praise
of the sultan, recalling his battles and deeds of valour. The

women and girls sing along with him and play with bows. Accompanying them are about thirty youths, wearing red woollen tunics and white skull-caps; each of them has his drum slung from his shoulder and beats it. Afterwards come his boy pupils who play and turn wheels in the air, like the natives of Sind. They show a marvellous nimbleness and agility in these exercises and play most cleverly with swords. Dugha also makes a fine play with the sword. Thereupon the sultan orders a gift to be presented to Dugha and he is given a purse containing two hundred *mithqals* [also mis-kal, any of various units of weight of Muslim countries] of gold dust, and is informed of the contents of the purse before all the people. The commanders rise and twang their bows in thanks to the sultan. The next day each one of them gives Dugha a gift, every man according to his rank. Every Friday after the *'asr* prayer, Dugha carries out a similar ceremony to this that we have described.

On feast-days, after Dugha has finished his display, the poets come in. Each of them is inside a figure resembling a thrush, made of feathers, and provided with a wooden head with a red beak, to look like a thrush's head. They stand in front of the sultan in this ridiculous make-up and recite their poems. I was told that their poetry is a kind of sermonizing in which they say to the sultan: "This *pempi* which you occupy was that whereon sat this king and that king, and such and such were this one's noble actions and such and such the other's. So do you too do good deeds whose memory will outlive you." After that, the chief of the poets mounts the steps of the *pempi* and lays his head on the sultan's right shoulder and then on his left, speaking all the while in their tongue, and finally he comes down again. I was told that this practice is a very old custom amongst them, prior to the introduction of Islam, and that they have kept it up. [It has been retained in some areas of West Africa to this day.]

The negroes disliked Mansa Sulayman [Mansa in Man-dingo means sultan; Sulayman is his name] because of his avarice. His predecessor was Mansa Magha, and before him reigned Mansa Musa, a generous and virtuous prince, who loved the whites and made gifts to them. It was he who gave Abu Ishaq as-Sahili four thousand *mithqals* in the course of a single day. I heard from a trustworthy source that he gave three thousand *mithqals* on one day to Mudrik ibn Faqqus, by whose grandfather his own grandfather, Saraq Jata, had been converted to Islam.

The negroes possess some admirable qualities. They are seldom unjust, and have a greater abhorrence of injustice than any other people. The sultan shows no mercy to anyone who is guilty of the least act of it. There is complete security in their country. Neither traveller nor inhabitant in it has anything to fear from robbers or men of violence. They do not confiscate the property of any white man who dies in their country, even if it be uncounted wealth. On the contrary, they give it into the charge of some trustworthy person among the whites, until the rightful heir takes possession of it. They are careful to observe the hours of prayer, and assiduous in attending them in congregations, and in bringing up their children to them. On Fridays, if a man does not go early to the mosque, he cannot find a corner to pray in, on account of the crowd. It is a custom of theirs to send each man his boy (to the mosque) with his prayer-mat; the boy spreads it out for his master in a place befitting him (and remains on it) until he comes to the mosque. Their prayer-mats are made of the leaves of a tree resembling a date-palm, but without fruit.

Another of their good qualities is their habit of wearing clean white garments on Fridays. Even if a man has nothing but an old worn shirt, he washes it and cleans it, and wears it to the Friday service. Yet another is their zeal for learning the Koran by heart. They put their children in chains if they show any backwardness in memorizing it, and they are not set free until they have it by heart. I visited the *qadi* in his house on the day of the festival. His children were chained up, so I said to him, "Will you not let them loose?" He replied, "I shall not do so until they learn the Koran by heart." Among their bad qualities are the following. The women servants, slave girls, and young girls go about in front of

everyone naked, without a stitch of clothing on them. Women
go into the sultan's presence naked and without coverings,
and his daughters also go about naked. Then there is their
custom of putting dust and ashes on their heads, as a mark of
respect, and the grotesque ceremonies we have described
when the poets recite their verses. Another reprehensible
practice among many of them is the eating of carrion, dogs,
and asses.

The date of my arrival at Malli was 14th Jumada I [seven
hundred and] fifty-three [28th June 1352] and of my departure from it 22 Muharram of the year fifty-four [27th
February 1353]. I was accompanied by a merchant called
Abu Bakr ibn Ya'qub. We took the Mima road. . . .

We halted near this channel at a large village which had
as governor a negro, a pilgrim, and man of fine character,
named Farba Magha. He was one of the negroes who made
the pilgrimage in the company of Sultan Mansa Musa. Farba
Magha told me that when Mansa Musa came to this channel
he had with him a *qadi*, a white man. This *qadi* attempted
to make away with four thousand *mithqals*, and the sultan,
on learning of it, was enraged at him and exiled him to the
country of the heathen cannibals. He lived among them for
four years, at the end of which the sultan sent him back to
his own country. The reason why the heathens did not eat
him was that he was white, for they say that the white is
indigestible because he is not "ripe" whereas the black man
is "ripe" in their opinion. . . .

I travelled next to the town of Mima and halted by some
wells in its outskirts. Thence we went on to Tumbuktu,
[Timbuktu] which stands four miles from the river. Most of
its inhabitants are of the Massufa tribe, wearers of the face-
veil [one of the principal tribes of the western Sahara, also
called Sanhaja]. Its governor is called Farba Musa. I was
present with him one day when he had just appointed one of
the Massufa to be *amir* of a section. He assigned to him a
robe, a turban, and trousers, all of them of dyed cloth, and
bade him sit upon a shield, and the chiefs of his tribe raised
him on their heads. In this town is the grave of the meritori-
ous poet Abu Ishaq as-Sahili, of Gharnata [Granada] who is

known in his own land as at-Tuwayjim [Little Saucepan].[1]

From Tumbuktu I sailed down the Nile [Niger] on a small boat hollowed out of a single piece of wood. We used to go ashore every night at the villages and buy whatever we needed in the way of meat and butter in exchange for salt, spices, and glass beads. I then came to a place the name of which I have forgotten, where there was an excellent governor, a pilgrim, called Farba Sulayman. He is famous for his courage and strength, and none ventures to pluck his bow. I have not seen anyone among the blacks taller or bulkier than him. At this town I was in need of some millet, so I visited him (it was on the Prophet's birthday) and saluted him. He took me by the hand, and led me into his audience hall. We were served with a drink of theirs called *daqnu*, which is water containing some pounded millet mixed with a little honey or milk. They drink this in place of water, because if they drink plain water it upsets them. If they have no millet they mix the water with honey or milk. Afterwards a green melon was brought in and we ate some of it.

A young boy, not yet full-grown, came in, and Farba Sulayman, calling him, said to me, "Here is your hospitality-gift; keep an eye on him in case he escapes." So I took the boy and prepared to withdraw, but he said, "Wait until the food comes." A slave-girl of his joined us; she was an Arab girl, of Damascus, and she spoke to me in Arabic. While this was going on we heard cries in his house, so he sent the girl to find out what had happened. She returned to him and told him that a daughter of his had just died. He said, "I do not like crying, come, we shall walk to the river," meaning the Nile [Niger], on which he has some houses. A horse was brought, and he told me to ride, but I said, "I shall not ride if you are walking," so we walked together. We came to his houses by the Nile, where food was served, and after we had eaten I took leave of him and withdrew. I met no one among the blacks more generous or upright than him. The boy whom he gave me is still with me.

[1] The poet as-Sahili met Mansa Musa at Mecca during the Pilgrimage, returned with him to Mali and was the architect of the mosques at Gao and Timbuktu. He died at Timbuktu in 1346.

6

FROM

"The Story of Rashid bin Hassani"

by Rashid bin Hassani as told to W. F. Baldock

As well as learning the ways and skills of their elders, some African children were confronted by the harshness of their environment and by man's inhumanity to man. Rashid bin Hassani, who grew up in the 1870's in what is presently Zambia, Southern Africa, had anything but a tranquil child-hood. Attacks by a lion and an enemy tribe violently disrupted his early years, although he can also recall many happy memories of his youth.

An interesting aspect of Rashid's youth is his contact with Arab and Muslim Africa. As early as the ninth century Arab travelers and settlers had introduced Islam to East Africa. By the nineteenth century many coastal Africans had converted to Muhammadanism—as slaves to Muslims, as in the case of Rashid bin Hassani, or as free men. In the 1800's an increasing number of Africans had economic contact with Islamic Africa. The development of sophisticated political organizations in the African interior made it possible for Arabs and coastal Africans to travel inland and trade with other African tribes. The coastal peoples exchanged firearms and manufactured goods for ivory and slaves. One of the major trade routes originated on the coast at Kilwa and penetrated across southern Tanzania. It is along this route that the Yao traders traded with the Bisa tribe and purchased Rashid bin Hassani.

As an adult Rashid bin Hassani served as a porter for the first British imperialists in East Africa. In the early 1930's, when he was an old man, he told his story to W. F. Baldock of the Forestry Department of Tanganyika, who recorded it for him.

MY name is Rashid bin Hassani, and I was born into the Bisa tribe beyond Lake Nyasa near Nakotakota and Kazungu in Northern Rhodesia [present-day Zambia, Southern Africa]. I was the tenth child of my mother; all the children before me had, however, died when quite young; after me my mother bore two more children, both girls. One of these died in the famine that came when she was about four; the other was killed by a spear during the Angoni raid when I was taken prisoner. My father had three wives; of the wives other than my mother, one had a boy and a girl, and one a baby girl, her firstborn. He had three huts, one for each wife, they lived separate lives and cooked separate food; my father ate and slept with each wife in turn for a week; the huts were round with low, mud walls and steep pointed, thatched roof; the doors were low and made of plaited withies, as planks were unknown.

The houses were in a group with other huts to the number of twenty, in a big clearing with other groups of huts to a total of nearly four hundred, including that of the Sultan. The whole clearing was divided into four areas occupied by different clans. It was situated in rolling orchard-like bush country in the valley of the Musora, which is a permanent river ten to twenty feet wide running into Lake Wemba (Tanganyika) in the Babembas' country, our neighbours and relations.

We had a certain amount of stock; to the ordinary man, about four or five head of cattle, ten sheep or goats and masses of fowls, with forty head of cattle to the Sultan. We had not more stock as the Angoni raided our cattle and took

them from us.[1] The stock was kept away from the village so
that the Angoni who raided at night often missed a head or
two, and if they did not catch the cattle by night the herd-boy
drove them into the forest or into the swamp on the Musora.

Our main crops were millet—both eleusine and sorghum.
Eleusine was the most dependable crop as it grew even in
years of bad rainfall. It was planted only in the ashes of the
burned orchard-bush or forest, fresh clearings of which were
made each year. After the harvest the trees of the bush
quickly re-established themselves, as their roots were not
killed by the fire, and many of the stumps which were cut
two or three feet from the ground sprouted at once. The
clearing was done by the men, usually helping each other:
a man would make beer and all his friends would help him
clear an area and next day they would all help somebody
else.

Sorghum was planted as many as five times in the same
area on wide raised beds about six feet wide and a foot high.
The sorghum was sown on the ridges of these beds and sometimes ground-nuts on the sides. In these millet-fields the beds
were made by the men and women working together with
iron hoes. Both sorghum and eleusine were attacked by
swarms of small birds, and constant watching by children
was necessary. By night the fields were liable to raids by elephant and pig and by day by baboons and monkeys. We had
no guns to scare or shoot elephants and we frightened them
with fire and sometimes shot one with poisoned arrows.

At the end of the harvest some of the grain was carried to
the village, but most was taken to islands in a papyrus swamp
in the Musora, where all the women and children and most
of the stock retreated to hide in times of Angoni raids.

In times of famine people used to eat fruits from the bush
and roots of plants that they dug up. Wild honey was a great
reserve in times of famine. If food was very scarce a man
would leave the village and take his family into the bush and

1 The Angoni were an African tribal group from Natal, South Africa, who
around 1820 fled to escape the rule of the African King Shaka and raged
northward into Zambia, Malawi, and Tanzania raiding cattle and pillaging.

build a grass shelter near a group of fruit-bearing trees and stay there till the planting season.

Hunting with bows and arrows and by pits and nets also helped us over the bad times to the next harvest. Besides elephant and pig there were rhinoceros, hippopotamus in the Musora, buffalo, eland, waterbuck, zebra and greater kudu in the forest and probably other game as well, but I do not remember well as I was only a child.

When I was about nine years old, I remember I was going with another boy about my own age to the millet-fields where my mother was working at collecting the millet already harvested to pack into baskets to be brought into the village. We stopped by some sweet-potato beds and started to dig out red moles so that we could tie them up and pretend they were cattle. My mother was about one hundred and fifty yards away when we heard two screams from her. My companion stood up and said:

'Look at that great dog.'

'Lion,' I replied, as I knew what it was, and we ran; we crossed an arm of the swamp and I started to shout for help and ran towards the village. We met my father running up the path with his bow and arrows, as he thought we had been stolen by some men. He asked what was the matter and we told him that my mother had been taken by a lion. Then two more men came running up and asked my father what had happened. When they were told, they asked him if he had seen the lion and he said 'No, but my son saw it, let us go after it,' but they hesitated and wanted help, so we returned to the village. Most of the men were out fetching millet from their fields but they came running in. Then we returned to the millet-fields and I was carried on a man's shoulder to show them the place. I showed them the place, and near by we found my mother's loin-cloth: I was then sent back to the village. Later I was told that they followed the trail and found my mother dead and her neck and shoulder eaten by two lions: the lions were on the body, and as they left it, one was shot by an arrow and the other got away. They waited till next day and found the wounded lion dead, and the other was never seen again. We did not bury people

killed by lions for fear the lions should kill more of us, so
my mother was left for the lions and hyaenas and next day
there was nothing left. The day she was killed everybody
came and helped carry in the millet and that field was
abandoned altogether.

After my mother's death, I continued to live in the same
hut with my sisters, and my grandmother looked after us. For
the next two or four years I lived the ordinary tribal life and
learnt to look after myself as my grandmother was old and
infirm.

In those days we traded cotton-cloth, beads, axes and hoes
with Yao traders [tribe of northern Mozambique, southeast
Africa] who worked in from the coast at Kilwa. They took
from us ivory and slaves.

There were also certain families that knew how to smelt
iron and make axes and hoes from the iron, and others
bought iron from the Yaos and made axes and hoes. The
iron-smelters made clay furnaces about ten feet high and
eight feet in diameter, converging into a funnel at the bottom, below which was a pit. The clay was well puddled with
water and built up quite wet, and the cracks were filled up as
they appeared in the drying till the sides were hard dry. Firewood cut in billets was stacked at the bottom of the furnace
and other alternate layers of ironstone and fuel were put in
till the furnace was full. It was then fired and the molten
iron ran into the pit at the bottom of the furnace; when
cool the clinkers and stones were removed and the furnace
reloaded; at each charge a lump of iron the size of a two-
pound loaf was made. One lump in every nine was taken to
Mtisa, the Sultan. Each lump of iron was put into a charcoal
fire blown with goatskin bellows, cut up into pieces and
beaten with a hammer into hoes, axes or arrowheads; the
bad parts of the metal and pieces of ash and charcoal were
burned off in the fire or flaked off as the metal was beaten
into shape.

We had no proper beds, but occasionally men made fixed
beds of sticks stuck in the ground with poles on the top and
then more cross-sticks, on which was spread a skin or a mat

plaited of split hippo grass. The women made cooking-pots and water-jars out of clay and burned them; some people did not know how to make them and bought them; the price was a fill of the pot with grain.

The full dowry paid for a girl was five hoes, four goats and a full load of tobacco, as well as some small symbolical and ceremonial gifts.

Marriages were arranged by the fathers when the boys were fourteen years old and the girls often only about four or five. A beer drink was arranged and a pot sent to the Sultan as evidence of the betrothal. A few beads were bought by the boy's father and given to the boy, who went with his friends to the girl's home, saluted the girl's mother and father and hung the beads round the girl's neck. Then they grew up side by side. The boy's father started to pay the dowry with occasional gifts of a hoe, joints of meat and loads of grain in times of good harvest. During this time the boy gave the girl any cloth or beads he could lay his hands on. When the girl came of marriageable age there was a dance for all the women and young girls, after which the bride was shut up in her hut for a year and did not see any men except her father. The mistress of the ceremonies, a kind of godmother, then instructed her in her duties as a wife and mother.

When the dowry had been paid and the girl's hair was long and her skin light from confinement in the dark, a final payment of a load of salt was made and the wedding proper took place.

A big dance and feast was held for the whole district. The bride with a small axe with metal inlaid in the handle, and her hair all dressed, plaited, oiled and decked with cowrie shells and with masses of beads round her neck and waist, wore nothing except a bark-cloth or cotton skirt. The bridegroom wore a loin-cloth and a quiver on his back, and bracelets of brass and ivory on his arms, with his bow in his hands. Thirty young unmarried youths followed the bridegroom and thirty girls the bride: they danced all day facing each other and holding hands and wriggling their shoulders and chest muscles. In the evening the bridegroom snatched the axe from the bride's hand and went for a young bull that had been prepared for the occasion. The bull had been tied up for two days without food and its tail and hind quarters pricked and inflamed with raw pepper. The bull was let loose at the bridegroom, who dodged its charge till he eventually succeeded in killing it with a blow of the axe between the eyes. Occasionally the bull was too quick or too strong and knocked the bridegroom down (a lasting disgrace), when one of the bride's brothers dashed up and shot the bull with an arrow. The older men and women sat further off and drank beer and helped eat the bull. When the meat was eaten, the bridegroom escorted the bride to his house and she was taken inside by all the girls, and young men danced outside half the night.

Generally a young man had no house of his own and the pair lived in a lean-to against the bride's mother's house till she was pregnant, when a house was built for her, and when the child was born she then started living in her own house with her own pots and hoes and other evidences of a separate establishment. The house was built on the strength of a beer drink with the help of their friends and relations.

A girl had the right to refuse to be married. Her father then had to repay the dowry, which he had generally used, so considerable pressure was put upon the girl unless she had a lover who could pay or agreed to pay the dowry and settle the matter that way. Girls usually married their betrothed, as they had received many presents and small favours from their young men: only if the young man was very notoriously unfaithful or lacking in his attentions and gifts did the girl refuse.

When a man died he was put in a round coffin made from a hollowed tree trunk or pieces of bark. He was not buried till all his relations had arrived; in the case of a Sultan this might not occur for a month.

Slaves were owned by the tribesman. They were either born as slaves or bought or made slaves as punishment for a crime or as compensation for the fault of one of their clan. Occasionally a man who was very hard up would sell himself into slavery to get food, but this was rare and only done by outcasts from their clan, as men of a clan always lent each other food in times of stress. Slaves married slaves and their children became slaves; the Sultan and other headmen had many slaves, and as these had children the numbers were always increasing.

Petty theft was uncommon, as members of a clan were generally willing to lend or give what nowadays is often stolen. Petty theft was settled by restitution or payment in stock or grain. Even murder was sometimes compounded, usually by payment of a son as a slave. The only kind of tax generally paid was the gift to the Sultan of one tusk of any elephant shot.

Sometimes when food was short, organized raids for food by peoples from a distance were carried out. A man would find the whole of his store of food looted in the night. He then went to the Sultan who investigated the matter. The Sultan called up his witch-doctor and told him of the theft. The witch-doctor made a fire on which he placed a large pot of water and added his medicine of a mixture of herbs and forest fruits and finally his medicine stone. The water was boiled and then allowed to cool. Meanwhile a large concourse of people had gathered to watch.

The medicine man then put his hand into the water and felt for the stone, and when he felt it he held it up for the people to see and everybody knew that the thief was not of the Sultan's people. The medicine stone was then replaced and the witch-doctor asked if the thief came from some neighbouring sultanate, and if he felt the stone and held it up everybody knew that the thieves did not come from that sultanate.

This went on until, when the witch-doctor put his hand into the pot, the water bubbled and boiled and he could not feel the stone which had hidden itself in the pot; the people then knew where thieves came from. The Sultan sent eight or ten men to this other Sultan with a message that his country had been named by the witch-doctor as containing thieves. The second Sultan sent his own messenger to the

first Sultan to ask whether the message was true and, when
it was confirmed, he allowed the witch-doctor to come and
smell out the thieves.

The witch-doctor came and brewed up his medicine and
put the stone in the pot. Then in his right hand he took a
zebra's tail and in his left hand a baobab gourd in which he
put the medicine stone. He waved the zebra-tail in a certain
direction, asked the stone if the thieves came from that direction and then smelled at the stone. If he smelled nothing
he knew that the thieves had not come from there. He tried
different directions till he smelled the stone and then knew
in what direction to go. He started off and at every cross-
roads or fork in the path he consulted the stone. When he
arrived at a village the headmen and all the village were
called up.

The witch-doctor brewed up his pot of medicine, put in
the stone and each man in turn had to come and stand with
his face over the pot and cough. If he coughed he was allowed
to go, but if he failed he was examined by the Sultan further
as to where he had been when the theft was committed. The
water was boiled up and his arm smeared with medicine and
he had to get the stone out of the pot. If he succeeded he was
guiltless, and the man who had accused him had to pay him
compensation, usually a goat for a false accusation.

If a man's child or wife or old mother died suddenly he
would suspect black magic and ask where the dead person
had last eaten food, and sometimes he would accuse the last
host of having bewitched the dead person. They would then
squabble and quarrel and eventually go to the Sultan. The
witch-doctor was called and he boiled up his medicine pot
until it bubbled and frothed, and then he put the stone into
the pot and if the accused man found it and fished it out he
was innocent and the accuser had to pay heavy compensation
—five head of cattle or a slave, as an accusation of black
magic was a very serious one. If, however, the man accused
failed to find the stone he was seized and string tied tightly
round his fingers till it cut the flesh to see if he would confess; his elbows were drawn together till they met behind his
back; pieces of bamboo were split and sharpened and fixed in

a kind of collar which was then put round his head and fore-head and pulled tighter and tighter till his eyes were ready to drop out of his head. He then named his associates, and all were sold as slaves to Yao safaris that came to trade guns, red cloth and beads for ivory and slaves. A gun, a barrel of powder and a box of caps went to the Sultan and the rest of the price was paid in beads that were distributed to the rest of the people of the district.

The accused might be taken out of the village into the forest with five or six men to guard him and everybody watching and himself made to cut firewood; this was stacked and a crib raised above it; he was put on the firewood and more wood above the crib. Then they made fire with sticks (they did not use fire from the village) and lit the small sticks and bark as kindling near his legs. When the fire burnt hot, it loosened his tongue and he confessed that he had be-witched the child, saying I did this and this. All his relatives, his whole clan, even if it were sixty people, were seized and sold as slaves.

We liked and respected our witch-doctors as they freed us of our enemies—those who practised black magic.

We had no formal religion, but we knew there was a God and had a word for him in our language. We were afraid of the spirits of our ancestors: if we did not mention their names and sing their praises or have beer drinks often enough in their honour, they would come and annoy us and we should be ill. We built miniature houses for them outside our villages or houses and put small earthenware pots in them in which we put offerings of meal or beer. If a man was ill he could propitiate the evil spirit by a big beer drink and dance. If a lion roared night after night we knew that the dead Sultan was angry (for some lions are sultans) and we poured beer on the Sultan's grave and slaughtered several oxen and held a big dance.

At the time that I was about twelve years old and was scaring and snaring birds in the crops, the Angoni, whose country was some way off, raided our country. I had heard of Angoni raids, but there had been none that I could remem-ber. I was told that my grandfather was killed by the Angoni and many other people at the same time. This raid probably took place about two years before I was born. My father at that time escaped to the swamp of the Musora, but he was nearly caught on account of a dog that I can well remember, called Mlengebera, the whisperer. My father and others were hidden in the swamp with the women when he missed his dog, and thinking that the Angoni had left as they had fired the village, he said he would go and look for it. He took his bow and arrows and returned towards the village calling the dog. The Angoni had hidden themselves near the village and when the dog left the village they followed. My father ran off to the Musora, pursued by the Angoni, swam the river and shot at the Angoni from the reeds on the bank till all his arrows were finished, when he made his way through the swamp to the others, taking two Angoni clubs that had been thrown at him as evidence that they were still in the village.

When I was captured it happened like this.

When evening came I went as usual to my grandmother's hut to get food and to sleep. I was asleep on a skin on the floor, when I was awakened by her. 'What is that?' She shook up the log, that lay smouldering as usual in the centre of the hut, till it burst into flames. As she did this there was the noise of shields rattling on doors all round us and ours was burst open: half the doorway was blocked by a shield of buffalo hide. The old woman ducked to run out of the door and an Angoni stabbed her in the ribs and she fell almost without a sound. I realized that these were Angoni that I had heard of and I thought I would run away: when I was clear of the door, I was swept by the warrior with his shield against his thigh and held there as his property and so that nobody else should stab me. My little sister started to scream and cry and another warrior grabbed her by the arm, held her up, and killed her with a blow of his throwing spear; he was afraid she would give the alarm in other parts of the village. I was too frightened to move or cry out. It was just getting light. All men who tried to come out of the doors were killed, but many burst through the walls of the hut and got away: these went off to the Sultan's.

I could see outside each hut two or three bodies were lying

and one or two Angoni warriors standing waiting. It was quite quiet as anybody who screamed was stabbed. My father I never saw and I do not know if he escaped or was killed; I believe his second wife was killed but I never saw her body; her elder child I saw taken away as a slave, but in another party, and I never spoke to him again. His youngest wife I saw standing with her baby at her breast and many of the younger women also. My captor went off to the next part of the village and to the Sultan's. The other prisoners and I were immediately taken off about two hours' walk to the Angoni camp in the bush; there were more than twenty of us, four tusks and all the axes, hoes and everything of value. When we got to the Angoni camp we saw the smoke of our village behind us.

The male prisoners were bound and fastened in pairs to wooden yokes; the women and children walked free but were tied up for the night to stop us running away. When we reached the Angoni camp we found thirty other prisoners from other Bisa villages and cattle from our village already there including two of my father's. The Angoni had already taken two other small villages without any resistance. We all stayed that night in their camp and they gave us food; they drew water from the Musora as there was none in the bush nearer their camp.

Each Angoni warrior had a shield of buffalo or ox hide, a stabbing spear and three small throwing spears with very sharp points and feathers on their butts, one or two clubs and sometimes a sword. They wore no clothes except a huge feather headdress; their shields were painted like those of the Masai [hunting tribal group of Kenya and northern Tanzania, East Africa]. The Angoni had no definite warrior organization or warrior class like the Masai, nor were they organized in definite fighting companies like the Masai.

The Babisa [Bisa] had only bows and arrows and small axes, but no spears or shields. Poison for the arrows was made from the bark of trees, which was boiled in special pots, and the men did not sleep with their wives for two months after making it.

The Angoni, having decided on a raid, made a main camp

near the borders of their own country and the warriors and women gathered in it; the women went on the raids to cook the food. They then moved rapidly four ordinary days' march in two days and made a camp in thick bush and were careful of their fires so that no smoke showed. They then sent out scouts to locate the villages to be raided and the paths to them; they also noted the position and number of any doors in stockades round villages or cattle kraals. After a couple of days they would move into the fields round a village at sun-set, and close in quietly all night, till at dawn they were waiting outside the doors. As it became light they would burst open the doors and take the village by surprise. If the Babisa saw the Angoni scouts, they warned all the villages and tried to find out which village the Angoni intended to attack: then everybody collected at that village, and in the evening the village would be abandoned and all the men would hide in shallow holes in the cultivated ground while the women and children were hidden in the bush. The men lay all night out in the fields and waited for the Angoni to pass inside them. When the Angoni were standing up and preparing to attack the village, the Babisa would shoot them with arrows from the rear or open side unprotected by the shield. Owing to their shields the Angoni were not easy to hit, and if you missed and an Angoni saw you, he would rush you and stab you before you could fit another arrow, unless your companion shot him from the uncovered side as he rushed. Our bows were poor and had only a short range.

The day after I was taken prisoner we were moved off to a camp which the Angoni had built of thorns near the Sultan's stronghold. The Angoni had not attempted to take the Sultan Mtisa's village by surprise and all his men, women, children, stock and ivory had been taken into his stronghold. This stronghold was on a steep rocky hill called Mkinga. The sides were in places almost precipitous and there was one narrow path up it which could be held by half a dozen men armed with loose stones. On the top of the hill was a plateau and in it a big cave in which the grain and ivory were stored, and the mouth of which could be blocked with a big stone. There was no permanent water on the plateau, but a spring at the foot of the hill; this spring the Angoni warriors seized, and they called to Mtisa, 'Have you any water?' 'Yes, rain water in the rocks.' We were in the camp and saw and heard all this as the camp was under the hill. The Angoni leader, named Kiliaonga, then called out, 'Shall we show you something?' 'Yes.' 'We will fetch it.' Mtisa then began to curse them and said, 'What do you thieves mean by coming and stealing my men and cattle?' We could see him sitting on a rock at the top of the cliff on the edge of the plateau. The Angoni came back to the camp and brought out his two daughters who had been living in another village which had already been captured. When he saw them, he stood up and seemed very surprised and shocked: he moved to another rock. Kiliaonga asked, 'Do you want your children?' 'Yes, I do.' 'Bring some goods.' 'I have none.' 'Bring some ivory.' 'Yes, I will bring the tusks tomorrow.' 'No, wait till our chief comes.' 'Who is he?' 'Mpeseni.' 'Mpeseni, is he there?' 'No, he is not, wait till he comes.' The Angoni leaders passed through the camp and disappeared into the bush, ostensibly to fetch Mpeseni. At 5 o'clock they came back and said, 'Bring the ivory tomorrow.' Mtisa replied, 'I will bring the ivory now. My children will be hungry.' 'No, we will give them food; are they not a sultan's children?' 'We will eat together tomorrow' (as a sign of friendship and submission). The Angoni returned to their camp and the children got meat and good food to eat and were told not to be frightened, as tomorrow they would go to their father.

In the night some Angoni warriors made their way up to the plateau and hid between the cave where Mtisa had shut himself in and the big rock where he came to speak with the Angoni below. In the morning he came out of the cave; the stone was not replaced, and he stood on the rock to speak to the Angoni not knowing he was surrounded by hidden warriors. The Angoni, unarmed, came up the path with his daughters and the ivory was carried down. When his children were near the top, the Angoni called, 'Are not these your daughters?' He stepped down to meet them, and there was a sudden shout and we saw him seized and his followers killed. They seized his gun and tore off his powder flask. He

was very angry and swore at them and told them to let him
alone and he would come and see Mpeseni, their Sultan.
They brought him down to the camp and told him that he
would be taken to Mpeseni. He replied, 'Who is this Mpeseni? Do you think I will go to him?' They argued with him
till sunset but he refused to go and said they had better kill
him as he refused to go. They then cut a pole about as thick
as my thigh and eighteen feet long, sharpened it to a very
sharp point and buried the other end in the ground; round
this pole they built a stage on four poles six feet high; they
then seized him and lifted him up: some held his arms and
others his legs till he was sitting on the point of the pole,
then they all pulled together: at the first heave, the pole
passed up into his stomach; at the second as far as his chest,
his head fell back and shook once or twice and blood and
entrails ran down the pole; at the third heave, the point
of the pole came out of his throat; he made no sound and
his children uttered no sound; everybody watched in amazement but dared do nothing. When he was dead the warriors
uttered one great yell. They left his body on the pole. So
died one of the finest men I ever saw. He was far larger than
anybody else in the tribe and had great authority. His
daughters were taken to Mpeseni who took them for his
wives.

When Mtisa was seized the stone was replaced at the
mouth of the cave and the women and children and those
who happened to be inside escaped.

Next morning we moved off to the Luangwa river, near
the Basenga's country; the next day we slept at a Senga
village, and here I was sold as well as many children too
young to go far. My father's younger sister who was a good-
looking girl was sold to the Sultan, Marama. The man who
bought me was called Kilole, and it was then millet harvest.
At the next planting season he sold me to a Yao safari, and
with me went fifteen others. This Myao's name was Chamba
and he treated me well; he gave me food and cotton cloth to
wear. He took me eventually to Kilwa and sold me to a
Manga Arab, Bwana Saidi, who lived in Zanzibar [coastal
island of Tanzania, East Africa]. He also bought six other

slaves and hid us in his house for two days for fear of the
European steamers which looked out for slave traders. At
the time there was only one European in Kilwa, a French
Father. We were taken on board a small open boat by night
and hidden under cloth and a coconut screen in the bottom
of the boat. We must have made a fast passage as the first
night we were run into a mangrove swamp and hidden: the
next night we were landed in Zanzibar and hidden in a coconut plantation at Fuoni, where we remained seven days.
Each day Saidi brought clothes and took two of us into the
town and to the market and handed us over to the market-
master, an Arab, called Saidi Ram. I stayed three days with
Saidi and then I saw a man wearing a turban come to the
market and say, 'Bibi Zem-Zem (the sister of Said Bargash,
the Sultan of Zanzibar) wants some slaves, go and pick some
out.' Perhaps twenty of us were picked out, taken to her
house and lined up. Here I was terrified and thought, 'Here
I shall be killed and eaten.' Out came an enormously fat
woman with gold ear-rings and gold nose-rings. I thought,
'She is as fat as that from eating men.' I did not then know
much Swahili but she said, 'Where are the slaves?' in a very
high voice. She picked out ten, saying 'That one, that one,
that one,' and counted up ten. Then she said, 'How much do
you want for these?' I was bought for 40 reales (60 rupees)
and others for 60 reales. When the deal was completed she
told a man to take us to her shamba. There her headman,
Nakoa Athmani, beat a drum and called all the slaves together from their houses on the shamba and said, 'Anybody
who has not got a child and wants one, can choose one from
this lot spawned by the old girl.' A woman named Mtondo
Msanja from the country south of Kilwa came and carried
me off and the others were similarly taken. When her husband came home he was told, 'I have got a child.' He was
called Hassani and that is why my name is Rashid bin Hassani; my tribal name was Kibuli bin Mchubiri. Here I remained three years, was circumcised and taught the Moham-
medan religion and to read the Koran. I was adopted as his
son but did no work in the shamba; he worked with a hoe
in the coconut shamba and on the cloves. On Thursdays he

worked on his own shamba of rice, maize and cassava for food, and Friday was his day of rest.

After three years Bibi Zem-Zem sent word to the plantation to look for slaves to work on a house. Five of us were produced and built houses for Indians and got eight pesas (pice) a day, but this Bibi Zem-Zem took. Each day we were fed and got one pice for ourselves.

7

"Song for the Dance of Young Girls"
(traditional: Didinga tribe of East Africa)

*As African boys learned the work of their fathers, so African
girls were trained to take over the role of mother and wife.
Among the Didinga of the eastern Sudan, East Africa, a
woman's tasks included the shaping of pottery. The dignity
of the woman's role and its continuity over the generations
is captured in this traditional verse. The song also reveals
the functional quality of music and dance in black Africa,
where children learned to chant and sing verses to accompany and complement their tasks of everyday life.*

> We mold a pot as our mothers did.
> The pot, where is the pot?
> The pot, it is here.
> We mold the pot as our mothers did.
>
> First, the base of the pot.
> Strip by strip, and layer by layer.
> Supple fingers kneading the clay,
> Long fingers molding the clay,
> Stiff thumbs shaping the clay,
> Layer by layer and strip by strip,
> We build up the pot of our mother.
>
> We build up the pot of our mother,
> Strip by strip and layer by layer.
> Its belly swells like the paunch of a hyena,

Of a hyena which has eaten a whole sheep.
Its belly swells like a mother of twins.
It is a beautiful pot, the pot of our mother.
It swells like a mother of twins.

8

FROM

Shinega's Village

by Sahle Selassie

(1936–   )

*The death of a child is a tragic event everywhere. In the
following account by Sahle Selassie the Guargé villagers of
central Ethiopia, East Africa, mourn the passing of Theresa,
a teen-age girl. The villagers blame the child's illness on an
evil eye, and they personify the figure of death. Their grief
and their mourning are poignantly human.*

Shinega's Village *is a description of life in Selassie's village
in the 1940's and 1950's. He wrote it in his native tongue,
Chaha, as a linguistic exercise for a professor of African
languages, and it was subsequently translated into English.
Selassie holds a master's degree in political science from the
University of California, Los Angeles, and is currently working for a government ministry in Ethiopia.*

ALL day and night the day Degemu [a family friend] left,
Theresa weakened. Her headache turned into some other
disease that no one could explain with certainty, and just
before dawn the next morning she died.

Shinega [Theresa's brother] had to go early to inform
Zemwet [Degemu's mother and close friend of Theresa]. She
was still asleep when he arrived, and he called to her.

"Sinega," Zemwet said, "why have you come so early?
Can it be for a good reason?"

"Mother told me to tell you that Theresa is very weak."

"O God! She isn't dead yet, is she?"

"Not yet," the boy lied. "But how much longer she will live is uncertain."

Zemwet broke into tears, for she had loved Theresa very much. At once she dressed and they hurried to Wardena [an Ethiopian village].

The people in the neighborhood of Bala's [Theresa's father] house were very busy when Shinega and Zemwet arrived. Kartchea, the Fuga, was in the eucalyptus grove felling trees and cutting them up for firewood for the funeral. The women were behind the house at work with their toothed mallets pounding the root of the false-banana plant to feed the mourners. Others, inside and outside the house, were already wailing. Kerwage [Theresa's mother] lamented in this way:

"Theresa, my daughter, you who had not reached woman's years, you so young; who looked upon you with the evil eye and caused your death?

"Theresa, my daughter, O bride, will you be able to warm your new dwelling-place alone?

"Theresa, my daughter, is it true that you have said good-bye forever?

"Theresa, my daughter, I believe you are still alive, I say you still live, you are only sleeping."

And Zemwet joined her, crying:

"Death, die in your turn, you separate mother and child.

"Death, die in your turn, you separate husband and wife.

"Death, die in your turn, you separate the one who loves and the one who is loved.

"O hero, rise and gird yourself

"O hero, take your shield.

"O hero, take down your spear.

"Death has come to your threshold

"Death has kidnapped your daughter

"Death has kidnapped your sister

"He has kidnapped your bride

"O hero, rise in your anger!

"Pierce and kill your enemy!

"So that he will not come back
"So that he will not take away your sister
"So that he will not take away the beloved one."

Each mourner lamented according to his sorrow. Some pounded their ribs with their elbows and some slapped their faces. Some leaped high and fell back upon the earth.

9

FROM

Baba of Karo

by Baba of Karo as told to Mary Smith

(1885?–1951)

*Before the arrival of Western missionaries, most tribal chil-
dren did not receive a formal education. Instead they learned
the skills and beliefs of their people by watching and imi-
tating their elders, by listening to their parents, and by
playing with their peers. Baba of Karo, a Hausa girl, was
born in 1885 in northern Nigeria, West Africa, and enjoyed
an ordinary childhood. Not long before she died, she gave an
account of her tribal life to Mary Smith, who recorded and
translated it. In this excerpt Baba of Karo shows how an
African girl in work and in play quite unconsciously receives
an important part of her learning.*

A Day in My Childhood

IN the morning when the sun got up our mothers would rise
and start making bean-cakes; we would get up and wash our
faces and put on our cloths and they would give us the
bean-cakes and we would go round the village selling them.
When we had sold them we came back and Mother gave us
some grain to grind. She did a lot and we did a little. We
sang our songs at the door of her hut, we were grinding away,
one of us would start the song and the others would
answer. . . .

When we had finished grinding we gave our mothers the

flour. They cooked a big pot of porridge and a pot of stew; then they would put out the porridge and pour the stew over it, 'Take this to so-and-so,' 'Take this to so-and-so.' We picked it up and took it to the men, and then we came back and ate ours with the other children; if we weren't full we got some more. When we were satisfied we put down our wooden bowls and calabashes (there were no enamel bowls then), then we ran off and played. At nightfall we came back and spread our mats in Mother's hut; the wife who was cooking that day went to the husband's hut, the maker of porridge took fire to the husband's hut, she drew water and she lit the lamp and took it. He would be at the house-door talking to his friends, when he came in he shut the door and went to his hut. The children filled up their mother's hut. In the morning she would wake us up and we all washed our faces.

The Children's Play-Associations at Zarewa

At Zarewa [town in northern Nigeria] we had titles among ourselves when we were young, the youths and the girls appointed their officials. The chief of the boys, *Sarkin Samari* [Sarkin means the chief or emir, and Samari means young man in Baba's native language, Hausa] was given a turban by the Chief of Zarewa and there were the chief's officials, Galadima, Ciroma, Madaki, Ma'aji, Magatakarda and Danmori. In my time there was Sarkin Samari Tanko and Sarkin Samari Bawa. The girls' chief was called Mama or chief of the girls, and the girls had other titled officials like those of the boys. One Friday in the dry season all the youths and girls would gather together in front of the Chief of Zarewa's palace, the boys in one place and the girls in another. The elders who appointed the Sarkin Samari sat with the Chief of Zarewa. Sarki [the chief of Zarewa] would instal the Sarkin Samari and give him a turban to wear. The young men selected their leader because he was popular and good-tempered, not because he was wealthy; when they had chosen him they would go to Sarkin Zarewa and say, 'We want so-and-so to be Sarkin Samari.' He would say, 'Very

well, we will instal him next Friday.' That boy would remain
chief of the young men for about four years, then when he
started to shave they would choose another one. We girls
used to go out and sing to the boys as they worked in the
fields, 'Work is new, Work is hard, We greet you at your
work . . .' The young men put on their ornaments, they
slung their hoes over their shoulders and we went with them
in our best clothes, then we would take food out to the
farms and give it to them.

When the boys' chief had been appointed, the boys and
girls went and toured the country round, singing songs, so
that everyone should see Sarkin Samari and Mama. Those
with titles mounted horses, as they do for a bridegroom, and
the rest went on foot round the wards of the town and out to
the hamlets. When they arrived in a place everyone dis-
mounted, stools were brought and millet-balls and sour milk,
everyone ate. That is, the hamlet recognized his rank. Sarkin
Samari and his titled officials sat on stools, and Mama sat on
a stool opposite to him; those who had no titles, the commoners, sat on the ground. Mama would send a girl over to
Sarki, she knelt down before him and said, 'May Allah pro-
long Sarki's life, I want to leave this place and go home.' He
would answer, 'No, we are going to stay here until tomorrow.' They did what Sarki said. When the people of the ward
brought porridge and kolanuts to Sarki and Mama he would
distribute them among his followers and she would distribute them among hers. Our Sarkin Samari was a son of
the onion-farmers and Mama was a daughter of the butchers;
they were both tall and very good-looking. At night the
young men would be shown a resting place in the forecourts
of the houses of the hamlet, and the girls would be shown a
resting place. Everyone chose the girl he liked best for
tsarance [institutionalized love making between unmarried
youths and girls]. They stroked one another and talked and
told stories, then they went to sleep. They don't do anything
more until they get married.

In the morning the girls washed and put on their fine
clothes, they all got up and the boys escorted their chief

while the girls escorted Mama,[1] and with the drummers and
praise-singers they returned to the town. Sarki had a body-
guard and attendants who walked in front of his horse,
everyone greeted him like a chief, 'May your life be long,
Sarkin Samari!' Mama had an attendant in front and one
behind, one on her left hand and one on her right, they
walked slowly while the drummers drummed:

> *See Mama, the chief's mother,*
> *See Mama, the chief's mother,*
> *See the chief, see the chief,*
> *See the chief, see the chief,*
> *See the chief, see Mama,*
> *See Mama, the chief's mother.*

For seven days after he was installed there would be dancing
and drumming, and after that Sarkin Samari's ceremony was
over. Every market-day there would be dancing to the large
deep drum. Sarki would come and take his place, Mama
would take hers, then the drummers drummed to them and
they got up and danced. We would all dance until dawn.

If someone called a farming bee he would tell the boys'
chief to bring his young men; the girls did not work, they
just put on their best clothes and followed the young men
to the farms, the young men went with their hoes and the
girls went too, singing farming songs and encouraging them
at their work.

Our parents forbade us to go to these girls' games, but we
went secretly and watched, we went secretly and danced.
They didn't approve, they said we were to play our own
games at home, Zarewa was too far away. But when we lived
in Zarewa, in the dry season our parents allowed us to go to
the dancing but they did not let us sleep with the boys. . . .

Girls' Trading Expeditions

The thing I remember best before I was married was our
girls' trading expeditions. We took our money and our big
calabashes, we went to Doka and bought yams, we went to

[1] Earlier Hausa chiefs always had an official 'mother' who had certain important political functions.

Fillata and got groundnuts, we went and bought sweet potatoes from our hamlet, Karo, and from Dankusuba, Sundu,
Wawaye, Guga. . . . When we had been to a lot of different
villages and bought things, we came home and cooked them.
When they were ready we took them to market. This had
nothing to do with our parents, we went and sold our goods
and put by our money. In the dry season we traded like this.
When we had been to market in the morning with our
mothers' cakes, eight or ten of us, we would meet our friends
and come back, twenty of us, all singing, crowds of girls.
Then we would put our heads together, we would go on an
expedition. 'Are you coming?' 'Yes, I'm coming.' In the
morning we got up early and we went along singing, twenty
of us, thirty of us. When we arrived at a village we would go
to the market and see things for sale. 'Oh, look at that! It's
cheap, we'll go and make a profit.' And we bought it. One
girl would buy groundnuts, one would buy yams, one sweet
potatoes—each one bought her own produce. The little girls
came along too with little loads, about three-pennyworth.
We older ones took about a shillingsworth. The country
people said, 'Welcome, daughters of the village, welcome!'
We said 'M-hm.' Then the country people would laugh, 'Ha!
ha! ha!', they never laugh softly. We weren't exactly village
children, we used to live in the town. They were country
bumpkins, they hadn't got much sense, they weren't used to
seeing a lot of people.

When we got back home we would cook the food we had
bought, and next day we sold it in the market. The third
day we returned to the hamlets. We were traders all right!
For instance, if you got something for sixpence you would
sell it for a shilling—but it was in our old kind of money,
cowries. Then at night you danced and gave the praise-
singers money, you danced and gave the drummers cloths.
Next day you would go to your mother and say, 'I haven't any
money, I spent it all on the praise-singers!' If she is annoyed
she says, 'I haven't got any money.' Then you say, 'Give me
some, I'll return it to you.' Then she gives it to you and you
go to market, you make a profit and come home and give her
money back to her. When you hear drumming, you hear the

deep drum and you hear the praise-singers—you'll give them money! One girl would give them a cloth, then they would go on singing about her until she gave them another, and she has to go seeking for one to wear. But they don't do that nowadays. . . .

Bori

In Zarewa we used to watch the *bori* dancers [children of the bori is the Hausa term for a cult of spirit possession]. One day I was watching and one of the dancers became possessed by Dandambe, the Boxer. She bound up her hand in a cloth as boxers do, and she came over to me, singing. She liked me. She was handsome in her fine clothes. The Boxer's song is:

> *Whoever succeeds takes something to his sarki,*
> *Also if he wins he takes something to Baba.*
> *I am Madambaci, son of the Boxer,*
> *I am Madambaci the Boxer's son.*

The onlookers gave him money and he gave it to me, then when the spirit had left the dancer I gave the money to the praise-singers. Then I went home.

I often saw *bori* dancing at the compound of Magajiya, the head of the prostitutes [a profligate person of either sex], they were the *bori*-dancers. Among married women you would find one here and there, but most dancers were prostitutes. At Zarewa when we were young there were many prostitutes, they had their large huts in Magajiya's house. A man who went to their compound would take one of them home with him, and in the morning he would give her a little money and she would return to Magajiya's compound. There was Lemo's compound, Magajiya's and Auta's in the Butchers' Ward, they were all houses of prostitutes. The prostitutes came to the town and stayed two or three nights, then they went and some others came. We used to see their huts full of men and women. At night if a thief had stolen something he would sleep with a prostitute and give her money, then he would flee so as not to be caught; but the prostitutes didn't steal.

Some prostitutes were the daughters of *malams* [Muslim scholars], some were the daughters of noblemen, some were the daughters of commoners; if their parents had arranged marriages for them against their will they ran away and became prostitutes. Then and now, it's all the same; there have always been prostitutes. Magajiya is their mother, when any of them get money they take her a little. A man will come to Magajiya and say, 'I desire your daughter.' She says, 'Bring your money.' If he hasn't any money, she says, 'She does not desire you.' If he has enough money she will desire him. If a prostitute comes to her house without anything, Magajiya will help her. Lemo and Auta had prostitutes in their compounds, too. The men were always coming, they had their wives, they had their concubines, then they went out and had prostitutes too.

Sometimes a wife, if her husband is away, will steal her own body[1] and go off to other men; whoever sees her going along the road desires her, he sends a message by an old woman: 'I have come to greet you. How is the master of the house?' 'He is very well thank you, he has gone away to work.' 'When will he return?' 'Tomorrow.' 'Ap. See, here are some kolanuts, here is some money, so-and-so sent them to you.' 'I'll come tonight.' Then quickly, quickly the wife pays her visit and returns. In the compound of his bond-friend the man will borrow a hut and take her in; his own wives would beat the woman if they saw her in his compound! If the faithless wife has a co-wife she will say to her, 'I am going to visit my family.' The co-wife will keep her secret. A married woman may have ten lovers, or even twenty —then or nowadays. She will go and tell her *kawa* [a woman's female friend] about it. They desire men and they desire money. I never behaved like that.

In the old days *bori*-dancing was prostitutes' work, but there were some men dancers, too; there were two in my family, Dogo and Dan Auta, my father's 'younger brother,' a son of Malam Bawa. Their *bori* was good, but there are more women than men.

I remember when I was about ten years old, after my

---

[1] A linguistic expression of the fact that at marriage a Hausa woman surrenders the rights over her body and its issue to her husband.

mother had died, a prostitute was chosen to be Magajiya and she was installed in front of the chief of Zarewa's palace; we went and watched. The prostitutes all danced in the morning, then they went to the house of Sarkin Zarewa, where he gave her a turban and appointed her Magajiya. He said that if any man took a prostitute to his house and did not give her any money, she was to take a complaint to Magajiya, who would make the man pay the woman her money and also fine him. That is, he gave her authority to do this.

We used to go to their compound and watch the dancing, their ward of the town was near to ours. When they were dancing at night their drumming prevented us from sleeping. In Zarewa when I was eight or nine years old, there was Dandaudu's compound in Illalawa Ward, there was Auta's house at the North Gate, Lemo's at the South Gate and Magajiya's near the Butchers' Ward. *'Yandauda* [male homosexuals] aren't healthy, they are men but they become like women, some of them even put on women's clothes. They build women's huts for rent in a compound of prostitutes. The prostitutes give them a little money. I remember Danjuma, Citama, a son of the blacksmiths, Balarabe and Dandaudu; there they were, very beautiful to look at, like women. But they had no health, they could not go to women or to men. They put on fine clothes and ate nice food, that's all. The prostitutes would hire huts from them and pay them money, and in the day they would go to market and sell farm produce on commission, as the Chief Food-broker does here —but he's healthy all right, there's nothing wrong with him, he's always out hunting women!

10

"Circumcision Songs"

(traditional: Bangi tribe of Central Africa)

*Many African tribes celebrate the abandonment of child-
hood and the formal acceptance of adult responsibilities by a
puberty or circumcision rite. Besides the actual operation,
the rite is both a joyful celebration and a somber ceremony.
It celebrates the youngsters' coming of age and initiates them
into the beliefs and responsibilities of tribal membership.
Among the Bangi tribe of Central Africa, both girls and boys
participate in the rite. They sing the songs recorded below
before the operation. The songs also celebrate their tribal
affiliation, for the words are passed from generation to generation and are identical to those the children's ancestors
have sung and those their unborn children will yet learn.*

1.

(*Before the operation*)
Today is a great day
For us, the youth
Among us no girl can be found,
We have nothing to do with love today.

Tonight our sweetheart will be alone in her house.
Whoever lay down in the village
Will sleep tonight in the forest,
And the beloved will cry for her lover.

2.

(*After the operation*)
Once I said, "There are no initiates,"

But now I have seen the knife
I have seen the knife and I was not afraid,
For, when the knife cuts, that is good,
If it does not cut, that is not good,
For all men would jeer at you
And say that you are like a woman.

Once when I went hunting,
The men laughed at me,
But now they will no longer jeer at me.
Young boys are not circumcised,
But you, you are now one of the elect,
You will no longer be their comrade,
For I would be ashamed of you.

1.

(By the female elder who officiates)
Once we were playmates
But today I take command over you,
For, you see, I am a man,
I have a knife in my hand
And I am going to operate upon you.
Your clitoris which you guard so jealously
I shall cut off
And cast upon the ground,
For today I am a man.
I have a cold, cold heart,
Otherwise I could not operate upon you.
Afterwards your wound will be dressed,
And I shall be aware of many things:
I shall know who takes care of herself
And who does not.

2.

(By those about to be initiated)
Your words produce great fear within us,
But we cannot run off.
Yet you, you once were also an initiate

And obviously you are not the least bit dead:
So we too shall not die.

3.

(By one of the initiates)
Do not speak thus, my sisters,
My heart is much too heavy
And my fear is great.
Ah, if I could change myself into a bird,
Oh, I would fly away quickly.

4.

(By another)
To be afraid is disgraceful,
So much the worse if we die,
We must be brave.

5.

(By all)
Today I am going to be an initiate,
I shall leave the house of my mother,
I shall no longer see
Either my father or my brothers:
Who then will bring them water?
Who will prepare their meals?
Who will sweep their house?

11

FROM

The African Child (or *The Dark Child*)

by Camara Laye

(1924–   )

In Africa many children belong to an age group, a group of children of similar age, which acts as a unit on all important occasions from childhood to manhood. These events include participation in tribal initiation, circumcision rites, and entrance into the warrior class.

In the following passage from Camara Laye's autobiography, The African Child, *the author describes his age group's initiation rites. Although the Guinean novelist remembers the ceremony with a great deal of humor, he recognizes the importance of the event as "that occasion when every boy has the opportunity to overcome his fear and his own baser nature." Laye wonders if modern Africans are not losing an important part of their heritage as they depart from time-honored traditions.*

I WAS growing up. The time had come for me to join the society of the uninitiated. This rather mysterious society— and at that age it was very mysterious to me, though not very secret—comprised all the young boys, all the uncircumcised, of twelve, thirteen and fourteen years of age, and it was run by our elders, whom we called the big *Kondens*. I joined it one evening before the feast of Ramadan [feast for Muslims after their month of fasting during the ninth month of their calendar year].

As soon as the sun had gone down, the tom-tom had begun to beat. Even though it was being played in a remote part of the concession, its notes had roused me at once, had struck my breast, had struck right at my heart, just as if Kodoke, our best player, had been playing for me alone. A little later I had heard the shrill voices of boys accompanying the tom-tom with their cries and singing. Yes, the time had come for me.

It was the first time I had spent the feast of Ramadan at Kouroussa. Until this year, my grandmother had always insisted on my spending it with her at Tindican. All that morning and even more so in the afternoon, I had been in the state of great agitation, with everyone busy preparing for the festival, bumping into and pushing each other and asking me to help. Outside, the uproar was just as bad. Kouroussa is the chief town of our region, and all the canton chiefs, attended by their musicians, make it a custom to gather here for the festival. From the gateway to the concession I had watched them pass by, with their companies of praise-singers, balaphonists and guitarists, drum and tom-tom players. Until now I had only been thinking of the festival and of the sumptuous feast that awaited me—but now there was something quite different in the wind.

The screaming crowd that surrounded Kodoke and his famous tom-tom was getting nearer. Going from one concession to another, the crowd would stop where there was a boy of an age, to join the society, and take him away. That is why it was so slow in coming, yet so sure, so ineluctable. As sure, as ineluctable as the fate that awaited me.

What fate? My meeting with Konden Diara!

Now I was not unaware of who Konden Diara was. My mother had often talked of him, and so at times had my uncles and whoever else had authority over me. They had threatened me only too often with Konden Diara, that terrible bogeyman, that "lion that eats up little boys." And here was Konden Diara—but was he a man? Was he an animal? Was he not rather half-man, half-animal? My friend

Kouyate believed he was more man than beast—here was
Konden Diara leaving the dim world of hearsay, here he was
taking on flesh and blood, yes, and roused by Kodoke's tom-
tom was prowling around the town! This night was to be the
night of Konden Diara.

Now I could hear the beating of the tom-tom very plainly
—Kodoke was much nearer—I could hear perfectly the
chanting and the shouts that rose into the dark. I could make
out almost as distinctly the rather hollow, crisp, well-marked
beats of the *coros* that are a kind of miniature canoe, and are
beaten with a bit of wood. I was standing at the entrance to
the concession, waiting. I, too, was holding my *coro*, ready to
play it with the stick clutched nervously in my hand. I was
waiting, hidden by the shadow of the hut. I was waiting,
filled with a dreadful anxiety, my eyes searching the blackness.

"Well?" asked my father.

He had crossed the workshop without my hearing him.

"Are you afraid?"

"A little," I replied.

He laid his hand on my shoulder.

"It's all right. Don't worry."

He drew me to him, and I could feel his warmth; it
warmed me, too, and I began to feel less frightened; my
heart did not beat so fast.

"You mustn't be afraid."

"No."

I knew that whatever my fear might be I must be brave.
I wasn't to show fright or to run off and hide. Still less was
I to resist or cry out when my elders carried me off.

"I, too, went through this test," said my father.

"What happens to you?" I asked.

"Nothing you need really be afraid of, nothing you can
not overcome by your own will power. Remember: you have
to control your fear; you have to control yourself. Konden
Diara will not take you away. He will roar. But he won't do
more than roar. You won't be frightened, now, will you?"

"I'll try not to be."

"Even if you are frightened, do not show it."

He went away, and I began waiting again, and the disturbing uproar came nearer and nearer. Suddenly I saw the crowd emerging from the dark and rushing towards me. Kodoke, his tom-tom slung over one shoulder, was marching at their head, followed by the drummers.

I ran back quickly into the yard, and, standing in the middle of it, I awaited the awful invasion with as much courage as I could manage. I did not have long to wait. The crowd was upon me. It was spreading tumultuously all around me, overwhelming me with shouts and cries and beating tom-toms, beating drums. It formed a circle, and I found myself in the center, alone, curiously isolated, still free and yet already captive. Inside the circle, I recognized Kouyate and others, many of them friends of mine who had been collected as the crowd moved on, collected as I was to be, as I already was; and it seemed to me they were none of them looking very happy—but was I any more happy than they? I began to beat my *coro,* as they were doing. Perhaps I was beating it with less confidence than they.

At this point young girls and women joined the circle and began to dance; young men and adolescents, stepping out of the crowd, moved into the circle too and began to dance facing the women. The men sang, the women clapped their hands. Soon the only ones left to form the circle were the uncircumcised boys. They too began to sing—they were not allowed to dance—and, as they sang, sang in unison, they forgot their anxiety. I too sang with them. When, having formed a circle again, the crowd left our concession, I went with it, almost willingly, beating my *coro* with great enthusiasm. Kouyate was on my right.

Toward the middle of the night our tour of the town and the collection of uncircumcised boys were finished. We had arrived at the farthest outskirts of the concessions, and in front of us lay only the brush. Here the women and young girls left us. Then the grown men left. We were alone with the older boys, or should I say "delivered over" to them— for I remember the often rather disagreeable natures and rarely pleasant manners of those older ones.

The women and young girls now hurried back to their

dwellings. Actually, they can not have been any more at ease than we were. I know for a fact that not one of them would have ventured to leave town on this night. Already, they found the town and the night sinister. I am certain that more than one who went back to her concession alone was to regret having joined the crowd. They took courage only after they had shut the gates of their concessions and the doors of their huts. Meanwhile, they hurried on and from time to time cast unquiet looks behind them. In a short while, when Konden Diara would begin to roar, they would not be able to stop shaking with fright; they would all shake uncontrollably. Then they would run to make sure the doors were all properly barred. For them, as for us, though in a much less significant way, this night would be the night of Konden Diara.

As soon as our elders had made sure that no intruder was present to disturb the mysteriousness of the ceremony, we left the town behind and entered the bush by a path which leads to a sacred place where each year the initiation takes place. The place is well known: it is situated under an enormous bombax tree, a hollow at the junction of the river Komoni and the river Niger. At normal times it is not forbidden to go there; but certainly it has not always been so, and some emanation from the past I never knew still seems to hover around the huge trunk of the bombax tree. I think that a night such as the one we were going through must certainly have resurrected a part of that past.

We were walking in silence, closely hemmed in by our elders. Perhaps they were afraid we might escape? It looked like it. I do not think, however, that the idea of escape had occurred to any of us. The night, and that particular night, seemed impenetrable. Who knew where Konden Diara had his lair? Who knew where he was prowling? But was it not right here, near the hollow? Yes, it must be here. And if we had to face him—and certainly we had to face him—it would surely be better to do so in a crowd, in this jostling group that seemed to make us all one, and seemed like a last refuge from the peril that was approaching.

Yet for all our nearness to one another and for all the

vigilance of our elders, our march—so silent after the recent uproar—through the wan moonlight, far from the town, frightened us. And we were filled with terror at the thought of the sacred place toward which we were going, and the hidden presence of Konden Diara.

Were our elders marching so closely beside us only to keep watch over us? Perhaps. But it is likely that they too felt something of the terror which had seized us. They too found the night and the silence disturbing. And for them, as for us, marching close together was a means of allaying terror.

Just before we reached the hollow we saw flames leap from a huge wood fire previously hidden by bushes. Kouyate squeezed my arm, and I knew he was referring to the fire. Yes, there was a fire. There too was Konden Diara, the hidden presence of Konden Diara. But there was also a reassuring presence in the depth of the night: a great fire! My spirits rose—at least they rose a little—and I squeezed Kouyate's arm in return. I quickened my steps—we all quickened our steps—and the crimson radiance of the fire enveloped us. We had a harbor now, this kind of haven from the night: a huge blaze, and, at our backs, the enormous trunk of the bombax tree. Oh! It was a precarious haven! But, however poor, it was infinitely better than the silence and the dark, the sullen silence of the dark. We assembled beneath the bombax tree. The ground beneath had been cleared of reeds and tall grasses.

Our elders suddenly shouted: "Kneel!"

We at once fell to our knees.

"Heads down!"

We lowered our heads.

"Lower than that!"

We bent our heads right to the ground, as if in prayer.

"Now hide your eyes!"

We didn't have to be told twice. We shut our eyes tight and pressed our hands over them. For would we not die of fright and horror if we should see, or so much as catch a glimpse of the Konden Diara? Our elders walked up and down, behind us and in front of us, to make sure that we

had all obeyed their orders to the letter. Woe to him who
would have the audacity to disobey! He would be cruelly
whipped. It would be a whipping all the more cruel because
he would have no hope of redress, for he would find no one
to listen to his complaint, no one to transgress against custom. But who would have the audacity to disobey?

Now that we were on our knees with our foreheads to
the ground and our hands pressed over our eyes, Konden
Diara's roaring suddenly burst out.

We were expecting to hear this hoarse roar, we were not
expecting any other sound, but it took us by surprise and
shattered us, froze our hearts with its unexpectedness. And
it was not only a lion, it was not only Konden Diara roaring:
there were ten, twenty, perhaps thirty lions that took their
lead from him, uttering their terrible roars and surrounding
the hollow; ten or twenty lions separated from us by a few
yards only and whom the great wood fire would perhaps not
always keep at bay; lions of every size and every age—we
could tell that by the way they roared—from the very oldest
ones to the very youngest cubs. No, not one of us would
dream of venturing to open an eye, not one! Not one of us
would dare to lift his head from the ground; he would
rather bury it in the earth. And I bent down as far as I
could; we all bent down further; we bent our knees as much
as we could; we kept our backs as low as possible. I made
myself—we all made ourselves—as small as we could.

"You mustn't be afraid!" I said to myself. "You must
master your fear! Your father has commanded you to!"

But how was I to master it? Even in the town, far away
from this clearing, women and children trembled and hid
themselves in their huts. They heard the growling of Konden Diara, and many of them stopped their ears to keep it
out. The braver arose—that night it took courage to leave
one's bed—and went again and again to check the doors and
see that they were shut tight. How was I to stave off fear
when I was within range of the dread monster? If he pleased,
Konden Diara could leap the fire in one bound and sink his
claws in my back!

I did not doubt the presence of the monster, not for a single instant. Who could assemble such a numerous herd, hold such a nocturnal revel, if not Konden Diara?

"He alone," I said to myself, "he alone has such power over lions. . . . Keep away, Konden Diara! Keep away! Go back into the bush! . . ." But Konden Diara went on with his revels, and sometimes it seemed to me that he roared right over my head, right into my own ears. "Keep away, I implore you, Konden Diara!"

What was it my father had said? "Konden Diara roars; but he won't do more than roar; he will not take you away. . . ." Yes, something like that. But was it true, really true?

There was also a rumor that Konden Diara sometimes pounced with fearsome claws on someone or other and carried him far away, far, far away into the depths of the bush; and then, days and days afterwards, months or even years later, quite by chance a huntsman might discover some whitened bones.

And do not people also die of fright? Ah! how I wished this roaring would stop! How I wished I was far away from this clearing, back in the concession, in the warm security of the hut! Would this roaring never cease?

"Go away, Konden Diara! Go away! Stop roaring." Oh! those roars! I felt as if I could bear them no longer.

Whereupon, suddenly, they stopped! They stopped just as they had begun, so suddenly, in fact, that I felt only reluctant relief. Was it over? Really over? Was it not just a temporary interruption? No, I dared not feel relieved just yet. And then suddenly the voice of one of the older boys rang out: "Get up!"

I heaved a sigh of relief. This time it was really over. We looked at one another: I looked at Kouyate and the others. If there were only a little more light. . . . Yes, we were afraid. We were not able to conceal our fear.

A new command rang out, and we sat down in front of the fire. Now our elders began our initiation. For the rest of the night they taught us the chants sung by the uncircumcised. We never moved. We learned the words and tunes as we heard them. We were attentive as if we had been at school, entirely attentive and docile.

When dawn came, our instruction was at an end. My legs and arms were numb. I worked my joints and rubbed my legs for a while, but my blood still flowed slowly. I was worn out, and I was cold. Looking around me, I could not understand why I had shaken with fear during the night: the first rays of dawn were falling so gently, so reassuringly, on the bombax tree, on the clearing. The sky looked so pure! Who would have believed that a few hours earlier a pack of lions led by Konden Diara in person had been raging fiercely in the high grass and among the reeds, and that they had been separated from us only by a wood fire which had just now gone out as dawn came? No one. I would have doubted my own senses and set it all down as a nightmare if I had not noticed more than one of my companions casting an occasional fearful glance in the direction of the highest grass.

But what were those long white threads which hung from, or, rather, waved from the top of the bombax tree and which appeared to write on the sky the direction in which the town lay? I had not time to wonder very long at this: our elders were regrouping us; and, because most of us were almost sleep-walking, the operation was carried out with difficulty, with shouts, and with some rough treatment. Finally we started off back to the town, singing our new songs, and we sang them with unbelievably carefree abandon: as the steed that scents the approaching stable suddenly quickens his step, however weary he may be.

When we reached the first concessions, the presence of the long white threads struck me once more: all the principal huts had these threads on the very tops of their roofs.

"Do you see the white threads?" I asked Kouyate.

"I can see them. They are always there after the ceremony in the clearing."

"Who puts them there?"

Kouyate shrugged his shoulders.

"That's where they come from," I said, pointing to the distant bombax tree.

"Someone must have climbed up."

"Who could possibly climb a bombax tree?"

"I don't know."

"Could anyone possibly get his arms around such a huge trunk?" I said. "And even if he could, how could he hoist himself on bark all covered with all those thorns? You're talking nonsense. Can't you imagine what a job it would be just to reach the first branches?"

"Why do you expect me to know more about this than you do?" asked Kouyate.

"Because this is the first time I have taken part in the ceremony, while you—"

I didn't finish my sentence. We had reached the main square of the town. I stared in amazement at the bombax trees in the market place. They too were ornamented with the same white threads. All but the humblest huts, indeed, and all the big trees were tied to one another by these white threads whose focal point was the enormous bombax tree in the clearing, the sacred place marked by the bombax tree.

"The swallows tie them on," said Kouyate suddenly.

"Swallows? Are you crazy?" I said. "Swallows don't fly by night."

I questioned one of the older boys who was walking beside me.

"It is our great chief who does it," he said. "Our chief turns himself into a swallow during the night. He flies from tree to tree and from hut to hut, and all these threads are tied on in less time than it takes to tell."

"He flies from tree to tree like a swallow?"

"Yes. He's a real swallow and as swift. Everyone knows that."

"Isn't that what I told you?" asked Kouyate.

I did not say another word. The night of Konden Diara was a strange night, a terrible and miraculous night, a night that passed all understanding.

As on the previous evening, we went from one concession to another, preceded by tom-toms and drums, and our companions left us one after another as they reached their homes. Whenever we passed a concession where someone whose

courage had failed him had refused to join us, a mocking
chant rose from our ranks.

I arrived at our concession completely exhausted but very
satisfied with myself: I had taken part in the ceremony of the
lions! Even if I had not put up much of a show when Konden Diara was roaring, that was my own affair; I could keep
that to myself. I passed triumphantly over the threshold of
our concession.

The festival of Ramadan was beginning. In the yard, I saw
my parents, who were dressed to go to the mosque.

"Here you are at last," said my mother.

"Here I am," I said proudly.

"What kind of time is this to come home?" she said,
pressing me to her bosom. "The night is over, and you
haven't had a bit of sleep."

"The ceremony did not finish until break of day," I said.

"I know, I know," she said. "All you men are mad."

"What about the lions?" asked my father. "What about
Konden Diara?"

"I heard them," I replied. "They were very close; they
were as near to me as I am to you now. There was only the
fire between us."

"It's crazy," said my mother. "Go to bed, you're dropping
with sleep." She turned toward my father: "Now, where's
the sense in all that?"

"Well, it's the custom," said my father.

"I don't like such customs," she said. "Young boys should
not have to stay awake all night."

"Were you afraid?" asked my father.

Should I admit that I was very frightened?

"Of course he was afraid," said my mother.

"Only a little," said my father.

"Go to bed," ordered my mother. "If you don't get some
sleep now you'll fall asleep during the feast."

I went inside to lie down. Outside I heard my mother
quarreling with my father. She thought it stupid to take
unnecessary risks.

Later I got to know who Konden Diara was, and I learned

these things when the time had come for me to learn them. As long as we are not circumcised, as long as we have not attained that second life that is our true existence, we are told nothing, and we can find out nothing.

We begin to have a vague understanding of the ceremony of the lions after we have taken part in it many times. But even then, we are careful to share our knowledge only with those companions who have had the same experience. And the real secret lies hidden until the day when we are initiated into our life as men.

No, they were not real lions that roared in the clearing, for it was the older boys, simply the older boys. They created the roaring sound with small boards, thick at the center, sharp at the edges: the edges were all sharper from having such a thick center. The board was ellipsoidal in shape and very small. There was a hole on one side that permitted it to be tied to a string. The older boys swung it around like a sling, and, to increase the speed of the gyrations, they too turned with it. The board cut through the air and produced a sound like a lion's roar. The smallest boards imitated the roaring of the lion cubs; the biggest ones the roaring of full-grown lions.

It was childishly simple. What was not so childish was the effect produced at night on someone who did not expect it: the heart froze! If it had not been for the far greater fear of finding themselves lost in the bush, the terror it created would have made the boys run away. The bombax tree and the fire which had been kindled near it made a kind of haven which kept the uninitiated from running away.

But if Konden Diara's roaring is easily explained, the presence of the long white threads binding the great bombax tree in the sacred clearing, to the tallest trees and the principal houses of the town, is less easily explained. For my own part, I never succeeded in obtaining an explanation: at the time when I might have obtained it, that is, when I should have taken my place among the older boys who conducted the ceremony, I was no longer living at Kouroussa. All I know is that these threads were spun from cotton and that bamboo poles were used to tie them to the tops of the huts.

What I don't know is how they were attached to the tops of the bombax trees.

Our bombax trees are very big, and it is difficult to imagine poles sixty feet high. Such structures would certainly collapse, no matter how carefully they had been put together. Moreover, I do not see how the summit of these thorny trees could be reached by climbing. There is of course a kind of belt which tree-climbers use. It is tied around the tree and the climber gets inside it, placing the belt against the small of his back, then climbs by a series of jerks, pressing against the trunk with his feet. But such a procedure is quite preposterous given the enormous size of the trunks of our bombax trees.

Or why not plainly and simply use a sling? I do not know. A good slinger can work miracles. Perhaps it is this sort of miracle which would most easily explain the inexplicable presence of white threads at the summit of the bombax trees. But I can come to no final decision about it.

I do know that the men who tie the threads to the rooftops have to take great care not to mislay the bamboo poles. Things must not be revealed in that fashion. For it would take only one mislaid pole to start the women and children on the way to discovering the secret. That is why, as soon as the threads are tied, the poles and boards are removed. The usual hideouts are thatched roofs and secret places in the bush. And so nothing escapes about these manifestations of the power of Konden Diara.

But what about the men? What about those who *do* know?

They won't breathe a single word about it. They keep their knowledge a close secret. Not only do they keep women and children in a state of uncertainty and terror, they also warn them to keep the doors of their huts firmly barred.

I know that such conduct must appear strange, but it is absolutely true. If the ceremony of the lions has the character of a game, if it is for the most part pure mystification, yet it has one important feature: it is a test, a training in hardship, a rite; the prelude to a tribal rite, and for the present that is all one can say. . . . It is obvious that if the secret were to be given away, the ceremony would lose much of its power.

Certainly the teaching which follows the roaring of Konden
Diara would remain the same. But nothing would remain of
the trial by fear, that occasion when every boy has the opportunity to overcome his fear and his own baser nature.
Nothing would remain of the necessary preparation for the
painful tribal rite of circumcision. But, at the moment of
writing this, does any part of the rite still survive? The secret.
. . . Do we still have secrets?

11

COLONIAL CHILDHOOD:

CONTACT WITH THE WEST

DURING classical times occasional Roman and Greek vessels reached Africa, but these voyages were rare. Much more important for West Africa was its trans-Saharan trade with Arab itinerants, and East Africa's main outside contact was the Omani Arabs with whom the coastal Africans maintained close trading ties. In fact, by the fifteenth century Arab settlers had intermarried with East Africans and had established prosperous coastal city-states; and Arabs and Berbers were regular and important visitors of the West African kingdoms.

In the late 1400's the West through Portugal began to take an interest in Africa. Mercantile activity was expanding rapidly in late medieval Europe, and Portugal was one of the leading sea powers. The Portuguese were particularly drawn to Africa because of Moorish tales of Africa's wealth in gold and because of a desire to break the Muslims' economic hold on Africa and the Orient. The best-known patron of Portuguese expansion was Prince Henry the Navigator, the youngest son of the Portuguese King, John I. After 1420 Henry regularly despatched Portuguese ships along the African coast. In 1448 a ship reached the Gambia, West Africa; in 1462, Sierra Leone, West Africa; in 1488, the Cape of Good Hope, South Africa; and in 1499 East Africa and India.

A lucrative trade developed between the coastal African kingdoms and the Portuguese. In West Africa the Portuguese established several trading posts and bartered for gold and slaves. In East Africa they overran most of the city-states and by 1600 established a coastal ascendancy.

The Portuguese impact on African kingdoms was not long-lasting, however. In East Africa their control never spread inland, and by 1700 the indigenes with support from Oman had expelled them from East Africa. In West Africa their trade had drastically declined by the 1530's, and although they did establish an alliance with the kingdom of the Congo, Central Africa, and had control of Angola, Southwestern Africa, their large volume of slave raiding quickly devastated these areas.

In the late 1600's and 1700's a more important Western contact developed among the African states—first with Dutch and then French and British traders. Commercial activity was particularly active in West Africa. The trade commodity was slaves for American plantations. In the 1800's the West African slave trade declined, but an illegal East African trade directed by Arabs flourished until the 1870's.

Even with the decline of the slave trade, European interest in Africa continued to grow. The industrial powers in search both of raw materials and markets for their manufactured goods saw a potential in Africa. In the 1860's the Niger delta, West Africa, seemed particularly promising because of its supply of palm oil which was used in the production of soap. Then in the 1880's gold was discovered in the Transvaal of South Africa.

In addition to traders, missionaries of the 1840's also became intrigued by the possibilities of African converts. And Africa began to fascinate such explorers as Heinrich Barth who traveled in central and western Sudan during the 1850's and David Livingstone who explored East and Central Africa from the 1850's to the 1870's.

To ease tension among trading nationalists and to ensure the safety of other citizens penetrating inland, the major European powers (Britain, France, Germany, Belgium, and Portugal) met in 1884 in Berlin and carved up the map of Africa among them. Britain gained control over most of Southern Africa and Nigeria, Gambia, and the Gold Coast in West Africa, and Kenya and Uganda in East Africa; France took most of West Africa and North Central Africa, while Portugal claimed Mozambique in Southeast Africa and Angola in Southwest Africa; King Leopold of Belgium obtained the Congo in Central Africa, and Germany Tanganyika in East Africa, Southwest Africa, and Togo and the Cameroons in West Africa.* (France and Britain took over these German colonies after World War I.)

While the two-century-long slave trade had ravaged Africa, the imperial division of Africa was even more devastating. European slavers had taken Africans away from their continent, but they themselves had not ventured inland. European colonialists, on the other hand, not only penetrated Africa but conquered its peoples and remolded their societies to fit European economic, social, and cultural standards.

The lives of Africans were drastically affected by the colonial takeover. After the 1880's they were no longer responsible to their own chiefs but to the colonial governor. The education they needed was not the trade of their fathers but Western education, and even the values they held were vigorously questioned.

The childhood of a colonial African was no longer spent in the peaceful and secure womb of the village, but rather in the harsh sunlight of the colonial awakening of Africa. The conditions children encountered in the communities in which they were reared varied according to the tribe they belonged to, the number of white settlers present, and the goals and administrative structure of their colonial overlord.

* See Map of Africa in 1914.

Whatever their environment, their youth in colonial times was still markedly different from the childhood of their fathers and grandfathers. For the most part it was less fulfilling.

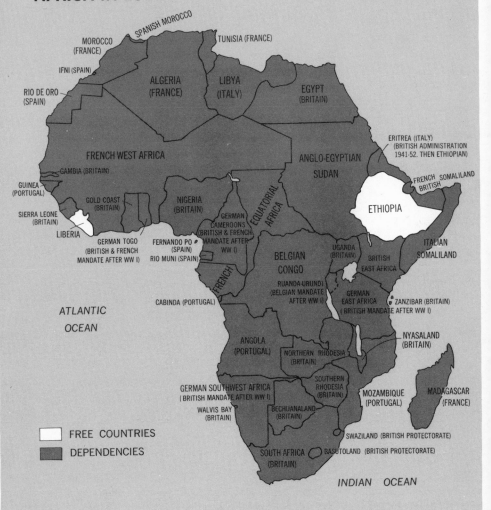

AFRICA IN 1914

MOROCCO (FRANCE)

SPANISH MOROCCO

TUNISIA (FRANCE)

IFNI (SPAIN)

RIO DE ORO (SPAIN)

ALGERIA (FRANCE)

LIBYA (ITALY)

EGYPT (BRITAIN)

FRENCH WEST AFRICA

GAMBIA (BRITAIN)

GUINEA (PORTUGAL)

SIERRA LEONE (BRITAIN)

GOLD COAST (BRITAIN)

LIBERIA

NIGERIA (BRITAIN)

GERMAN TOGO (BRITISH & FRENCH MANDATE AFTER WW I)

GERMAN CAMEROONS (BRITISH & FRENCH MANDATE AFTER WW I)

FERNANDO PO (SPAIN)

RIO MUNI (SPAIN)

EQUATORIAL AFRICA

FRENCH

CABINDA (PORTUGAL)

ANGLO-EGYPTIAN SUDAN

ERITREA (ITALY) (BRITISH ADMINISTRATION 1941-52. THEN ETHIOPIAN)

FRENCH SOMALILAND BRITISH

ETHIOPIA

BELGIAN CONGO

UGANDA (BRITAIN)

BRITISH EAST AFRICA

ITALIAN SOMALILAND

RUANDA-URUNDI (BELGIAN MANDATE AFTER WW I)

GERMAN EAST AFRICA (BRITISH MANDATE AFTER WW I)

ZANZIBAR (BRITAIN)

ATLANTIC OCEAN

ANGOLA (PORTUGAL)

NORTHERN RHODESIA (BRITAIN)

NYASALAND (BRITAIN)

GERMAN SOUTHWEST AFRICA (BRITISH MANDATE AFTER WW I)

SOUTHERN RHODESIA (BRITAIN)

WALVIS BAY (BRITAIN)

BECHUANALAND (BRITAIN)

MOZAMBIQUE (PORTUGAL)

MADAGASCAR (FRANCE)

SWAZILAND (BRITISH PROTECTORATE)

SOUTH AFRICA (BRITAIN)

BASUTOLAND (BRITISH PROTECTORATE)

INDIAN OCEAN

☐ FREE COUNTRIES

■ DEPENDENCIES

1

FROM

The Interesting Narrative
of the Life of Olaudah Equiano

by Olaudah Equiano

(1745?–1797)

From the seventeenth and eighteenth centuries an important European influence impinged itself on tribal communities. This influence was the prosperous Atlantic slave trade. Cheap labor was needed for American plantations, and European and American slavers could easily obtain this supply from Africa. The slave traders would arrive on an African coast, and African chiefs would provide them with their human cargoes, usually criminals or prisoners captured in tribal wars. A conservative estimate of the number of Africans who were victims of this trade is ten million men, women, and children.

The personal hardship and heartbreak of those captured and separated from their homeland can never be completely documented. Equiano, an eighteenth-century Ibo from eastern Nigeria, West Africa, does, however, provide us with one account. Equiano, who was born near Onitsha in the 1740's, was captured at the age of eleven by local raiders in search of slaves. The horror of his trip from his homeland to the sea contrasts sharply with the tranquillity and security of most of the tribal childhoods included in this volume.

On the coast his introduction to the white man's world was even more brutal. On shipboard he met the English sailors, "white men with horrible looks, red faces and loose hair," men whom Equiano described as savage and whom he feared were cannibals. Ironically, the same whites who thought Africans were savage were rather more justifiably considered uncivilized by black men.

His experiences during the Middle Passage—during his Atlantic voyage—were typical. Slaves were crowded into such cramped quarters that a large number of them invariably died en route. If the slaves refused to eat, they were regularly flogged, and if one of their number became ill, he was often thrown overboard.

In 1807 the British Parliament outlawed the slave trade, but the trade continued and even increased in volume until the cessation of the American Civil War. Although the British navy sent out patrols to capture slave ships, they were of limited efficacy. Slavers merely employed smaller rigs which could evade the British, and if they were in fear of being captured, they could throw their human cargo overboard or could wage battle with the cruiser.

Equiano was more fortunate in the New World than were most slaves. Eventually he obtained his freedom. Originally brought to Barbados, he was then taken to Virginia where a British naval officer bought him and took him to England. He served in the British navy in the Seven Years War and in 1763 was taken to the West Indies and resold. A Quaker merchant from Philadelphia purchased him, and Equiano became an assistant to the captain of one of his ships. By engaging in petty trade he was able to save £40 and in 1776 at the age of thirty-one bought his freedom. He then returned to London and worked as a valet. His slave masters had taught him to read and write, and in 1789 at the age of forty-four he published his autobiography, an immediate best seller. He became an active participant in the antislavery movement and played a significant role in establishing the colony of Sierra Leone—a British-governed West African haven for slaves whom the patrol had liberated from the Middle Passage.

MY father, besides many slaves, had a numerous family of which seven lived to grow up, including myself and a sister who was the only daughter. As I was the youngest of the sons I became, of course, the greatest favourite with my mother and was always with her; and she used to take particular pains to form my mind. I was trained up from my earliest years in the art of war, my daily exercise was shooting and throwing javelins, and my mother adorned me with emblems after the manner of our greatest warriors. In this way I grew up till I was turned the age of 11, when an end was put to my happiness in the following manner. Generally when the grown people in the neighbourhood were gone far in the fields to labour, the children assembled together in some of the neighbours' premises to play, and commonly some of us used to get up a tree to look out for any assailant or kidnapper that might come upon us, for they sometimes took those opportunities of our parents' absence to attack and carry off as many as they could seize. One day, as I was watching at the top of a tree in our yard, I saw one of those people come into the yard of our next neighbour but one to kidnap, there being many stout young people in it. Immediately on this I gave the alarm of the rogue and he was surrounded by the stoutest of them, who entangled him with cords so that he could not escape till some of the grown people came and secured him. But alas! ere long it was my fate to be thus attacked and to be carried off when none of the grown people were nigh. One day, when all our people were gone out to their works as usual and only I and my dear sister were left to mind the house, two men and a woman got over our walls, and in a moment seized us both,

and without giving us time to cry out or make resistance
they stopped our mouths and ran off with us into the nearest
wood. Here they tied our hands and continued to carry us
as far as they could till night came on, when we reached a
small house where the robbers halted for refreshment and
spent the night. We were then unbound but were unable to
take any food, and being quite overpowered by fatigue and
grief, our only relief was some sleep, which allayed our misfortune for a short time. The next morning we left the house
and continued travelling all the day. . . .

When we went to rest the following night they offered us
some victuals, but we refused it, and the only comfort we
had was in being in one another's arms all that night and
bathing each other with our tears. But alas! we were soon
deprived of even the small comfort of weeping together. The
next day proved a day of greater sorrow than I had yet experienced, for my sister and I were then separated while we
lay clasped in each other's arms. It was in vain that we besought them not to part us; she was torn from me and immediately carried away, while I was left in a state of distrac-
tion not to be described. I cried and grieved continually,
and for several days I did not eat anything but what they
forced into my mouth. At length, after many days' travelling,
during which I had often changed masters, I got into the
hands of a chieftain in a very pleasant country. This man had
two wives and some children, and they all used me extremely
well and did all they could to comfort me, particularly the
first wife, who was something like my mother. . . .

[After a month with them, however] I was again sold. I
was now carried to the left of the sun's rising, through many
different countries and a number of large woods. The people I was sold to used to carry me very often when I was
tired either on their shoulders or on their backs. I saw many
convenient well-built sheds along the roads at proper dis-
tances, to accommodate the merchants and travellers who lay
in those buildings along with their wives, who often accompany them; and they always go well armed.

[After travelling for some time] I was again sold and carried through a number of places till, after travelling a con-

siderable time, I came to a town called Tinmah in the most beautiful country I had yet seen in Africa. It was extremely rich, and there were many rivulets which flowed through it and supplied a large pond in the centre of the town, where the people washed. Here I first saw and tasted coconuts, which I thought superior to any nuts I had ever tasted before; and the trees, which were loaded, were also interspersed amongst the houses, which had commodious shades adjoining and were in the same manner [as] are ours, the insides being neatly plastered and whitewashed. Here I also saw and tasted for the first time sugar-cane. Their money consisted of little white shells the size of the finger-nail. I was sold here for 172 of them by a merchant who lived and brought me there. I had been about two or three days at his house when a wealthy widow, a neighbour of his, came there one evening, and brought with her an only son, a young gentleman about my own age and size. Here they saw me; and, having taken a fancy to me, I was bought of the merchant, and went home with them. Her house and premises were situated close to one of those rivulets I have mentioned, and were the finest I ever saw in Africa: they were very extensive, and she had a number of slaves to attend her. The next day I was washed and perfumed and when meal-time came I was led into the presence of my mistress, and ate and drank before her with her son. This filled me with astonishment; and I could scarce help expressing my surprise that the young gentleman should suffer me, who was bound, to eat with him who was free; and not only so, but that he would not at any time either eat or drink till I had taken first, because I was the eldest, which was agreeable to our custom. Indeed everything here, and all their treatment of me, made me forget that I was a slave. The language of these people resembled ours so nearly that we understood each other perfectly. They had also the very same customs as we. There were likewise slaves daily to attend us, while my young master and I with other boys sported with our darts and bows and arrows, as I had been used to do at home. In this resemblance to my former happy state I passed about two months; and I now began to think I was to be adopted into the family, and was beginning to be reconciled to my situation, and to forget by degrees my misfortunes, when all at once the delusion vanished; for without the least previous knowledge, one morning early, while my dear master and companion was still asleep, I was wakened out of my reverie to fresh sorrow, and hurried away even amongst the uncircumcised. . . .

All the nations and people I had hitherto passed through resembled our own in their manner, customs, and language: but I came at length to a country the inhabitants of which differed from us in all those particulars. I was very much struck with this difference, especially when I came among a people who did not circumcise and ate without washing their hands. They cooked also in iron pots and had European cutlasses and crossbows, which were unknown to us, and fought with their fists amongst themselves. Their women were not so modest as ours, for they ate and drank and slept with their men. But above all, I was amazed to see no sacrifices or offerings among them. In some of those places the people ornamented themselves with scars, and likewise filed their teeth very sharp. They wanted sometimes to ornament me in the same manner, but I would not suffer them, hoping that I might some time be among a people who did not thus disfigure themselves, as I thought they did. At last I came to the banks of a large river, which was covered with canoes in which the people appeared to live with their household utensils and provisions of all kinds. I was beyond measure astonished at this, as I had never before seen any water larger than a pond or a rivulet: and my surprise was mingled with no small fear when I was put into one of these canoes and we began to paddle and move along the river. We continued going on thus till night, and when we came to land and made fires on the banks, each family by themselves, some dragged their canoes on shore, others stayed and cooked in theirs and laid in them all night. Those on the land had mats of which they made tents, some in the shape of little houses: in these we slept, and after the morning meal we embarked again and proceeded as before. I was often very much astonished to see some of the women, as well as the men, jump into the water, dive to the bottom, come up

again, and swim about. Thus I continued to travel, sometimes by land, sometimes by water, through different countries and various nations, till at the end of six or seven
months after I had been kidnapped I arrived at the sea coast.

The first object which saluted my eyes when I arrived on
the coast was the sea, and a slave ship which was then riding
at anchor and waiting for its cargo. These filled me with
astonishment, which was soon converted into terror when I
was carried on board. I was immediately handled and tossed
up to see if I were sound by some of the crew, and I was now
persuaded that I had gotten into a world of bad spirits and
that they were going to kill me. Their complexions too dif-
fering so much from ours, their long hair and the language
they spoke (which was very different from any I had ever
heard) united to confirm me in this belief. Indeed such were
the horrors of my views and fears at the moment that, if ten
thousand worlds had been my own, I would have freely
parted with them all to have exchanged my condition with
that of the meanest slave in my own country. When I looked
round the ship too and saw a large furnace or copper boiling
and a multitude of black people of every description chained
together, every one of their countenances expressing dejection and sorrow, I no longer doubted of my fate; and quite
overpowered with horror and anguish, I fell motionless on
the deck and fainted. When I recovered a little I found some
black people about me, who I believed were some of those
who had brought me on board and had been receiving their
pay; they talked to me in order to cheer me, but all in vain.
I asked them if we were not to be eaten by those white men
with horrible looks, red faces, and loose hair. They told me
I was not, and one of the crew brought me a small portion of
spirituous liquor in a wine glass, but being afraid of him
I would not take it out of his hand. One of the blacks therefore took it from him and gave it to me, and I took a little
down my palate, which instead of reviving me, as they
thought it would, threw me into the greatest consternation
at the strange feeling it produced, having never tasted such
any liquor before. Soon after this the blacks who brought
me on board went off, and left me abandoned to despair.

I now saw myself deprived of all chance of returning to my native country or even the least glimpse of hope of gaining the shore, which I now considered as friendly; and I even wished for my former slavery in preference to my present situation, which was filled with horrors of every kind, still heightened by my ignorance of what I was to undergo. I was not long suffered to indulge my grief; I was soon put down under the decks, and there I received such a salutation in my nostrils as I had never experienced in my life: so that with the loathsomeness of the stench and crying together, I became so sick and low that I was not able to eat, nor had I the least desire to taste anything. I now wished for the last friend, death, to relieve me; but soon, to my grief, two of the white men offered me eatables, and on my refusing to eat, one of them held me fast by the hands and laid me across I think the windlass, and tied my feet while the other flogged me severely. I had never experienced anything of this kind before, and although, not being used to the water, I naturally feared that element the first time I saw it, yet nevertheless could I have got over the nettings I would have jumped over the side, but I could not; and besides, the crew used to watch us very closely who were not chained down to the decks, lest we should leap into the water: and I have seen some of these poor African prisoners most severely cut for attempting to do so, and hourly whipped for not eating. This indeed was often the case with myself. In a little time after, amongst the poor chained men I found some of my own nation, which in a small degree gave ease to my mind. I inquired of these what was to be done with us; they gave me to understand we were to be carried to these white people's country to work for them. I then was a little revived, and thought if it were no worse than working, my situation was not so desperate: but still I feared I should be put to death, the white people looked and acted, as I thought, in so savage a manner; for I had never seen among my people such instances of brutal cruelty, and this not only shewn towards us blacks but also to some of the whites themselves. One white man in particular I saw, when we were permitted to be on deck, flogged so unmercifully with a large rope near the foremast that he died in consequence of it; and they tossed him over the side as they would have done a brute. This made me fear these people the more, and I expected nothing less than to be treated in the same manner. I could not help expressing my fears and apprehensions to some of my countrymen: I asked them if these people had no country but lived in this hollow place (the ship): they told me they did not, but came from a distant one. 'Then,' said I, 'how comes it in all our country we never heard of them?' They told me because they lived so very far off. I then asked where were their women? had they any like themselves? I was told they had: 'and why,' said I, 'do we not see them?' They answered because they were left behind. I asked how the vessel could go? They told me they could not tell, but that there were cloths put upon the masts by the help of the ropes I saw, and then the vessel went on; and the white men had some spell or magic they put in the water when they liked in order to stop the vessel. I was exceedingly amazed at this account and really thought they were spirits. I therefore wished much to be from amongst them for I expected they would sacrifice me: but my wishes were vain, for we were so quartered that it was impossible for any of us to make our escape. While we stayed on the coast I was mostly on deck, and one day, to my great astonishment, I saw one of these vessels coming in with the sails up. As soon as the whites saw it they gave a great shout, at which we were amazed; and the more so as the vessel appeared larger by approaching nearer. At last she came to an anchor in my sight, and when the anchor was let go I and my countrymen who saw it were lost in astonishment to observe the vessel stop, and were now convinced it was done by magic. Soon after this the other ship got her boats out, and they came on board of us, and the people of both ships seemed very glad to see each other. Several of the strangers also shook hands with us black people, and made motions with their hands signifying I suppose we were to go to their country; but we did not understand them. At last, when the ship we were in had got in all her cargo, they made ready with many fearful noises, and we were all put under deck so that we could not see how they managed the vessel. But

this disappointment was the last of my sorrow. The stench of
the hold while we were on the coast was so intolerably loathsome that it was dangerous to remain there for any time, and
some of us had been permitted to stay on the deck for the
fresh air; but now that the whole ship's cargo were confined together it became absolutely pestilential. The close-
ness of the place and the heat of the climate, added to the
number in the ship, which was so crowded that each had
scarcely room to turn himself, almost suffocated us. This
produced copious perspirations, so that the air soon became
unfit for respiration from a variety of loathsome smells, and
brought on a sickness among the slaves, of which many died,
thus falling victims to the improvident avarice, as I may
call it, of their purchasers. This wretched situation was again
aggravated by the galling of the chains, now become insup-
portable, and the filth of the necessary tubs, into which the
children often fell and were almost suffocated. The shrieks
of the women and the groans of the dying rendered the
whole a scene of horror almost inconceivable. Happily perhaps for myself I was soon reduced so low here that it was
thought necessary to keep me almost always on deck, and
from my extreme youth I was not put in fetters. In this situation I expected every hour to share the fate of my companions, some of whom were almost daily brought upon
deck at the point of death, which I began to hope would soon
put an end to my miseries. Often did I think many of the
inhabitants of the deep much more happy than myself. I
envied them the freedom they enjoyed, and as often wished
I could change my condition for theirs. Every circumstance
I met with served only to render my state more painful, and
heighten my apprehensions and my opinion of the cruelty
of the whites. One day they had taken a number of fishes,
and when they had killed and satisfied themselves with as
many as they thought fit, to our astonishment who were on
the deck, rather than give any of them to us to eat as we
expected, they tossed the remaining fish into the sea again,
although we begged and prayed for some as well as we could,
but in vain; and some of my countrymen, being pressed by
hunger, took an opportunity when they thought no one saw

them of trying to get a little privately; but they were discovered, and the attempt procured them some very severe floggings. One day, when we had a smooth sea and moderate wind, two of my wearied countrymen who were chained together (I was near them at the time), preferring death to such a life of misery, somehow made through the nettings and jumped into the sea: immediately another quite dejected fellow, who on account of his illness was suffered to be out of irons, also followed their example; and I believe many more would very soon have done the same if they had not been prevented by the ship's crew, who were instantly alarmed. Those of us that were the most active were in a moment put down under the deck, and there was such a noise and confusion amongst the people of the ship as I never heard before, to stop her and get the boat out to go after the slaves. However two of the wretches were drowned, but they got the other and afterwards flogged him unmercifully for thus attempting to prefer death to slavery. In this manner we continued to undergo more hardships than I can now relate, hardships which are inseparable from this accursed trade. Many a time we were near suffocation from the want of fresh air, which we were often without for whole days together. This and the stench of the necessary tubs carried off many. During our passage I first saw flying fishes, which surprised me very much: they used frequently to fly across the ship and many of them fell on the deck. I also now first saw the use of the quadrant; I had often with astonishment seen the mariners make observations with it, and I could not think what it meant. They at last took notice of my surprise, and one of them, willing to increase it as well as to gratify my curiosity, made me one day look through it. The clouds appeared to me to be land, which disappeared as they passed along. This heightened my wonder, and I was now more persuaded than ever that I was in another world and that everything about me was magic. At last we came in sight of the island of Barbados, at which the whites on board gave a great shout and made many signs of joy to us. We did not know what to think of this, but as the vessel drew nearer we plainly saw the harbour and other ships of different kinds and sizes, and we soon anchored amongst them off Bridgetown. Many merchants and planters now came on board, though it was in the evening. They put us in separate parcels and examined us attentively. They also made us jump, and pointed to the land, signifying we were to go there. We thought by this we should be eaten by these ugly men, as they appeared to us; and when soon after we were all put down under the deck again, there was much dread and trembling among us, and nothing but bitter cries to be heard all the night from these apprehensions, insomuch that at last the white people got some old slaves from the land to pacify us. They told us we were not to be eaten but to work, and were soon to go on land where we should see many of our country people. This report eased us much; and sure enough soon after we were landed there came to us Africans of all languages. We were conducted immediately to the merchant's yard, where we were all pent up together like so many sheep in a fold without regard to sex or age. As every object was new to me everything I saw filled me with surprise. What struck me first was that the houses were built with storeys, and in every other respect different from those in Africa: but I was still more astonished on seeing people on horseback. I did not know what this could mean, and indeed I thought these people were full of nothing but magical arts. While I was in this astonishment one of my fellow prisoners spoke to a countryman of his about the horses, who said they were the same kind they had in their country. I understood them though they were from a distant part of Africa, and I thought it odd I had not seen any horses there; but afterwards when I came to converse with different Africans I found they had many horses amongst them, and much larger than those I then saw. We were not many days in the merchant's custody before we were sold after their usual manner, which is this: On a signal given, (as the beat of a drum) the buyers rush at once into the yard where the slaves are confined, and make choice of that parcel they like best. The noise and clamour with which this is attended and the eagerness visible in the countenances of the buyers serve not a little to increase the apprehensions of the terrified Africans, who may well be supposed to consider them as the ministers of that destruction to which they think themselves devoted. In this manner, without scruple, are relations and friends separated, most of them never to see each other again. I remember in the vessel in which I was brought over, in the men's apartment there were several brothers who, in the sale, were sold in different lots; and it was very moving on this occasion to see and hear their cries at parting. O, ye nominal Christians! might not an African ask you, Learned you this from your God who says unto you, Do unto all men as you would men should do unto you? Is it not enough that we are torn from our country and friends to toil for your luxury and lust of gain? Must every tender feeling be likewise sacrificed to your avarice? Are the dearest friends and relations, now rendered more dear by their separation from their kindred, still to be parted from each other and thus prevented from cheering the gloom of slavery with the small comfort of being together and mingling their sufferings and sorrows? Why are parents to lose their children, brothers their sisters, or husbands their wives? Surely this is a new refinement in cruelty which, while it has no advantage to atone for it, thus aggravates distress and adds fresh horrors even to the wretchedness of slavery.

2

"Martyr"

by David Diop

(1927–60)

Although the slave trade was no longer in existence by the late nineteenth century, the Africans' contact with the white man became no more benign. By the 1890's most of Africa had been conquered or claimed by France, Britain, Germany, and Portugal.

In the following poem, David Diop presents a childlike view of the coming of European colonialism. Even for a child, colonialism was not merely a defeat of blacks by whites. The Europeans did not just conquer the Africans and proclaim political hegemony over them. They also insisted that the Africans' way of life was savage, that their customs were barbaric, and that their skin color alone relegated them to the position of the white man's hewer of wood and drawer of water. In short, the whites completely disregarded the black man's humanity.

Diop was born in 1927 in Bordeaux, France, of a Senegalese father and Cameroonian mother. He published a small volume of verse and was one of West Africa's most promising poets when he was killed in a plane crash in 1960.

> The White Man killed my father,
> My father was proud.
> The White Man seduced my mother,

My mother was beautiful.
The White Man burnt my brother
            beneath the noonday sun.

My brother was strong.
His hands red with black blood
The White Man turned to me;
And in the Conqueror's voice said,
"Boy! a chair, a napkin, a drink."

3

FROM

Awo: the Autobiography
of Chief Obafemi Awolowo
by Chief Obafemi Awolowo

(1909–   )

African children in the early 1900's were often born into a
society in flux. Their tribes still tried to maintain their own
traditions, but·the presence of Westerners threatened the
tribes' traditions, values, and stability.

West Africans were more fortunate than inhabitants of
other areas of Africa. Because of the inclement weather few
Europeans settled in West Africa, and the colonial admin-
istrators usually remained in the larger towns. As a result
many West Africans had almost no contact with whites.
Nevertheless their communities were affected by the colonial
presence. Even in the isolated villages the white man even-
tually established control, and although no settlers arrived,
the imposition of colonial authority radically changed the
tribes' law and their traditional hierarchy of power and
prestige.

Chief Obafemi Awolowo was born in 1909 in Western
Nigeria, West Africa. In the following selection from his auto-
biography he describes his impressions as a twelve-year-old
boy of the early tensions between traditional and colonial
Africa.

Later Awolowo earned a law degree from London University, and became active in Nigerian politics. In 1944 he founded a Western Nigerian tribal society, the Egbe Omo Oduduwa, and in 1947 organized it into a regional political party from which he launched the Action Group, a nationalist party. As leader of the Action Group he was elected to the Western Region House of Assembly, Nigeria, in 1951, and in 1959 to the Nigerian Federal House of Representatives. He was imprisoned in 1962 by the Nigerian Federal Government on a charge of treasonable felony, and was pardoned by General Gowon, head of the Nigerian Federal Military Government, in 1966.

THE society into which I was born was an agrarian and peaceful society. There was peace because under the Pax Britannica there was a total ban on intertribal as well as intratribal war, and civil disturbances of any kind and degree were severely suppressed and ruthlessly punished. There was peace because there was unquestioning obedience to constituted authority. There was peace because the people lived very close to nature, and she in her turn was kind and extremely generous to them. And there was peace because the family life was corporate, integrated and well regulated. The order of precedence in the family and in the community as a whole was essentially in accordance with age. The little ones were given every legitimate indulgence. The parents, grand-parents, and, more often than not, the great grand-parents, were all there—living in one and the same compound, sometimes under one and the same roof—to pet them. Discipline, when occasion called for its application, was severe and spartan. The sturdy members of the family were also there to cater for the aged parents or grand-parents as the case might be. The land was fertile, and the rains fell in their due season. At that time there was more than enough land for everybody. Land was and still is owned not by the individual but by the family. This is the custom in Ijebu as well as in other parts of Yorubaland [Western Nigeria].

Every member of the family is entitled to cultivate any portion of his family land either on the paternal or maternal side. Because of the fertility and sufficiency of farmland, only a minimum amount of effort was required to satisfy the sparse wants of the individual. Until western civilization began to make its inroad into the lives of the people, it did not require too much exertion to provide food, shelter and clothing. Food was obtained with the minimum of effort from the farms. Shelter was easily provided by erecting mud walls and covering them with thatch or certain kinds of leaves for a roof. Friends and relatives usually helped one another in building one another's houses in turn. It was one of the obligatory duties of a son-in-law to help build the house of his father-in-law, and annually to help repair the roof thereof. The amount of clothing required was limited to the demands of a peasant farming life and of the annual festivities. There were many annual festivals, all of which were and still are held during the period of harvest. There was plenty of leisure.

Notwithstanding its ostensible mirth, peace and tranquility, the society into which I was born was one which was riddled with fear, uncertainty and suppression. There was the fear of the white man who was the supreme lord of any area placed under his jurisdiction. His word was law, and his actions could never be called in question by any member of the community. Those Africans who dared to criticise the white man lived in Lagos, and they went by the un-Biblical English names of Williams, Macauley, etc. There were one or two westernised and politically conscious individuals in Ijebu Remo who played the role of champion and defender of the people's rights. But apart from being somewhat oppressive themselves, they were not quite so effective. The barriers between the people and the white official were language, and the latter's undisguised aloofness. The sources of the people's fear of him were his strange colour, his uncanny power to shoot people down at long range, and his obvious unimpeachable authority. There was the fear of the white man's carriers and messengers who were a law unto themselves.

There was the fear of the local chieftains who were more or less the agents of the British Government, and who, as a result, acquired new status, prestige and power. The form and the system of government in Ijebu Remo, before the advent of British rule, were respectively monarchical and gerontarchal. At the head of each town in Ijebu Remo, as in other parts of Yorubaland, there was a king. Under British rule all the Yoruba kings were designated Obas, since there could only be one reigning monarch at one and the same time in the Empire. The fact remains, however, that the English equivalent for 'Oba' is 'King.' Apart from the Oba, there are Chiefs in each town. It is the prerogative of the Oba, in consultation with his Chiefs, to confer a chieftaincy title on any citizen who in his judgement possesses the necessary qualities. The candidate for a chieftaincy title must be an outstanding person in the community, possessing good character and integrity, and fairly well-to-do. It is a maxim among the Ijebus that 'A rascal or a poverty-stricken person is not qualified for a chieftaincy title.' He must also have a reputation for tact and wise counsel. He must be of a very ripe age. The appointment of educated, enlightened, well-to-do or prominent young persons as Chiefs is a modern innovation, and it is an eloquent proof of the importance attached to western education and culture in present-day Yoruba society.

The affairs of each town were administered by the Oba and his Council of Chiefs, subject to such checks and balances as were provided by the reactions of the populace to any given measure. In the days before British rule, an unpopular Council would not remain long in office. In Ijebu, the younger elements under the Balogun would attack the houses of the guilty Chiefs and completely destroy them. If the Oba was the guilty party, he would be advised by the Chiefs to retire, and this might take one of two forms: suicide or voluntary exile.

Under British rule, these methods were no longer applicable, and as there were no popularly elected Councils at the time, the Oba and Chiefs, instead of regarding themselves as being responsible to their people as before, considered themselves responsible to the white man who in the view of the people was unapproachable as well as unassailable and invincible. In due course, therefore, the word of the Oba and his Chiefs also became something of a law. If they chose to be tyrannical there was nothing that anyone could do about it, unless there was an educated or semi-educated person around to advise on and help in writing a petition to the white man. But it required a good deal of guts to write petitions criticising the Oba and his Chiefs. It was regarded by many white men, then in the Administrative Service, as gross impudence bordering on sedition to write critical letters, petitions, or remonstrances about an Oba. During the first five years of this century, two educated citizens of Ijebu Remo who summoned up enough courage to call attention in a petition to what they regarded as glaring cases of injustice and misrule on the part of one of the Remo Obas, were arrested, tried summarily, and sent to gaol for some months for their impertinence.

There was the fear of innumerable gods, and of the medicine-men who claimed and were credited with all manner of supernatural and magical powers. Every natural phenomenon, like drought, unusual flood, or thunder, was attributable to the anger of one of the gods. Every serious ailment or disease or organic disorder like severe headache, ulcer, tuberculosis, elephantiasis, barrenness, or mental malady, never happened to man save through the agency of an irate god or a malevolent and offended medicine-man. Whenever someone had fallen on bad times, or was seriously ill, it had always been because he had offended one or more of the gods or medicine-men in some inexplicable manner. The well-known remedy in any one of these cases was the offering of sacrifices as prescribed by the medicine-man who was the earthly accredited intermediary between a given god and mortal beings, supported by the taking by the patient of an indiscriminate quantity of various assortments of herbal preparations and medicinal powder.

The newly converted Christians were in a quandary. They believed in one God as against a multiplicity of gods; they believed that all the graven images or idols which they previously worshipped were nothing but the blind, deaf and dumb things that they really are; they believed in Jesus Christ as a Saviour and Redeemer and as an Intercessor between them and God; they believed also in hell with its brimstone and unquenchable fire; and in short they believed in the Apostle's Creed, and in as much of the teachings of Christ as were imparted to them. But in spite of their belief, they suffered from serious ailments and diseases whose causes were unknown to them, in the same way as the pagans. At best, they ascribed the cause in each instance to the work of Satan, whose agents, according to them, the medicine-men were. They believed in the efficacy of certain herbs in the cure of ailments and diseases, but their belief in this connection had not always been justified by results. They believed in the potency of prayer.

In a society where most people did not have anything at all like a bath more than half-a-dozen times in a year, the Christians were in a class by themselves. They cultivated the habit of having a really good bath, and of putting on their best apparel, at least every Sunday. Christian men and women had to cooperate in maintaining the church and the Mission House in a state of perfect cleanliness. This in its turn had some influence on the way the Christians looked after their own houses. As time went on, the Christians looked cleaner because they lived more hygienic lives, and in consequence many of them and their children became immune from some diseases like yaws. In this, they saw some evidence of the triumph of their faith. But as they still suffered from other diseases in the same manner as the pagans; as there were no hospitals and trained doctors around; and as the medicine-men continued blatantly and garrulously to claim to possess the power of dealing with such diseases, the occasions when the faith of a new Christian convert was shaken were much more numerous than now.

They were, however, immensely sustained in their faith by the activities of the missionaries of those days. These Christian missionaries were intrepid pioneers, and conscientious and selfless evangelists of a great doctrine. They reflected the spirit and teachings of Christ as much as any hu-

man being could, in their day-to-day contact with their new
flock. They lived more or less with the people, and conducted constant visitations. They cared for the flock in sickness, helped them in times of trouble, and, through the in-
strumentality of the administrative authorities, protected
them against attacks or unnecessary buffetings and threats
from the pagan elements. In spite of the prevailing fears,
therefore, I was made to realise quite early in life that Christianity was, of a surety, superior in many respects to pagan-
ism.

Until I visited Abeokuta [Western Nigerian city] in 1921, I
had thought that the white man was a superman. To me, his
colour symbolised delicacy, innocence and purity, because it
resembled very much the colour of Ikenne children [Western
Nigerian] at birth. Why he remained white and we grew
black beat my little imagination. I don't think I saw more
than half-a-dozen white men before I went to Abeokuta.
There was a Rev. G. Henry Lester—a Wesleyan minister of
religion. I saw him fairly often—on Empire Days and when,
during my pupillage at the Wesleyan School, Ikenne, he
came there for inspection. There was a Rev. L. C. Mead—
another Wesleyan minister. I saw him only once, but I vividly
remember him. He came in the company of the Rev. Lester
to inspect our school.

On a number of occasions, I saw white officials who passed
through Ikenne at different times. The first white official I
saw was carried in a hammock by two hefty Nigerians. His
luggage was carried by a number of Nigerian carriers. He
was ministered unto by a number of messengers and police
constables. We were told that a white man used to sleep in
the hammock in the course of the journey. But the one I saw
did have an open book on his chest whilst he was being carried through Ikenne. Presumably he had been reading the
book before he reached our town. Almost all the little
urchins in the town flocked around to have a glimpse of him.
What a mighty man I thought he was, so specially favoured
by God to have a white skin and to occupy such a position
of exalted superiority. The second one I saw spent about two

days in Ikenne. His tent was pitched in the market place. The children—particularly school children—were there to have a look at him and his carriers, messengers, police constables and interpreter. A few days before his arrival, the Oba of Ikenne had caused a public proclamation to be made for firewood, yams, chickens, water and other necessaries to be provided in plenty in the market place for the use of the Ajele (Administrative Officer). Certain specified age-groups were saddled with the responsibility. But apart from the Oba and his chiefs (aged people all of them) who must visit the Ajele to pay their respects, no other adult or able-bodied person—man or woman—would dare to come too near to the Ajele, especially when his carriers and messengers were about to depart, or when they were actually on their journey. It was the practice for the messengers and carriers to impress anyone forcibly into the service of the Ajele as a relief for themselves. Those who had the misfortune of falling into their hands had been forced to carry the Ajele's luggage until the messengers and carriers could get hold of other persons as substitutes, or until they were about to reach their destination. The forced carriers were entitled to neither money nor thanks for their labour.

4

"Song"

(traditional: Nyasa tribe of Southern Africa)

To many African children the Europeans with their strange clothing and haughty manners must have seemed peculiar indeed. The Nyasa children of Malawi, Southern Africa, sing the following ditty about the white man. In the words of critic Ulli Beier, the song "expresses the bewilderment of the child at the purposelessness of the behavior of Europeans."

> Europeans are little children.
> At the river bank they shot an elephant.
> Its blood became a canoe, and it sank;
> and it sank oars and all.
> I collected wild sorghum for Miss Mary.

5

FROM

The African

by William Conton

(1925–   )

Toward the end of the eighteenth century an evangelistic crusade to convert non-Christian peoples gained momentum in Europe. By the 1870's the missionary movement in Africa had made an impressive impact. The missionaries' influence on Africans was not limited to the spiritual realm. Besides preaching the Bible, men of the cloth introduced modern agricultural techniques, Western concepts of society, commercial connections, and most important, Western education. Although the colonial powers were able to lure a substantial number of Africans to their schools only after they had established political hegemony, then their schools were very successful. They did not just present new sources of knowledge to the African but also provided him with the one avenue to success in a Western-oriented colonial regime.

A schoolboy's arrival at school could be a moment of great excitement for him. For Kisimi Kamara, William Conton's central figure in his novel The African, *it was particularly meaningful, for it was his first journey to the fictional West African city Sagresa and the beginning of his first stay away from his village and tribe.*

Conton attended school in Sierra Leone, West Africa, and later at Durham University. He served as headmaster of

Accra High School, Ghana, and principal of the Government
Secondary School in Bo, Sierra Leone. He is presently senior
officer of the Ministry of Education, Freetown, Sierra Leone.
His publications include The African *and* West Africa in
History.

IT was a very wet day at the beginning of the rainy season
when my father, Miss Schwartz (who had recently returned
from furlough in the United States) and I climbed aboard
the lorry which was to take me on my first journey away from
the village where I was born and which had thus far contained my entire experience of life. My friends and relatives
all gathered to see me off, and my mother's eyes shone with
pride and her voice shrilled with excitement as she and my
father enlarged to the company on the future they saw ahead
for me. Strong muscles glistened in the driving rain. I
manoeuvred my solitary soap box of luggage into such a
position on the floor of the crowded lorry as would enable
my father to sit on it in relative dryness and comfort during
the journey, and then squatted on the tailboard to exchange
final farewells with the chattering group on the muddy road-
side. I suddenly realized to what extent I had now become
the focus of the hopes and ambitions of practically everyone
in my village. There was now more than mere envy of my
good fortune. In my departure for secondary schooling in
Sagresa, Lokko [fictional West African village] saw both a
recognition of its own growing importance, and an opportunity to accelerate still further that growth. More, much
more, than good wishes were going with me. Everything that
could be done by way of ritual and ceremony, to assure the
success of the venture on which I was now launching, had
been done. If some of the ritual was non-Christian, this was
my people's way of splitting the risks.

The lorry driver and his numerous assistants finished their
ministrations under the bonnet, and the engine sprang suddenly, noisily, and smokily to life. Feeling very far from tears,
and elated with excitement, I saw Miss Schwartz put her
head round the side of the driver's cab (she was travelling

first class). I heard her say, with a smile almost as pleased and happy as mine must have been, 'You're on your way, Tom Brown!' My father and I exchanged final shouted remarks with the others on the road, the gears grated, the lorry lurched and lumbered wheezily off; and distance, dust, and exhaust smoke soon swallowed up the little group which to me represented home, love, security.

I do not remember very much about the journey itself, except that at one point the road ran parallel to a railway line for a few hundred yards, and, to my great delight, I caught my first glimpse of a train. My first sight of the snorting, sparking, clanking engine and its short crocodile of swaying carriages whistling along the shining track was a token of wonders yet to come. I must have gaped and goggled at it quite unrestrainedly; for my interest in it provoked a stream of information, most of which I later found completely inaccurate, about railways and how they worked. Then suddenly the rattling and bouncing ceased, the red road turned black, and the lorry shook off its cloak of dust. It ran humming along now, down a steep slope to a little bridge across a stream; and then up the other side of the gorge. Halfway up, the note of its engine, which had gradually been dropping down the scale, coughed out, brakes were hastily applied, and we all had to get out and walk up the rest of the slope, while our vehicle dragged its lightened bulk up in front of us. At the top we clambered aboard again and resumed our journey; and soon afterwards the closing gap between the enormous houses, which receded from my view, told me that we were entering the capital. In a few minutes we were outside the mission house, and I was forced to give all my attention to the task of unloading Miss Schwartz's luggage, my father's, and my own.

I was soon an interested bystander at an interpreted interview between my father and the general superintendent of the mission. I learned that I was to be prepared during the course of the next few months to sit the entrance examination to one of the secondary schools in Sagresa. If successful, as everyone seemed confident I would be, I was to enter the school as a boarder. My father appeared to be highly

satisfied with these plans. He thanked the missionary pro-
fusely for his kindness, presenting him with the gifts we had
brought down specially from our village for this moment—
an enclosed basket containing three live fowls, and an open
one containing a generous and varied collection of fresh
fruit. These gifts were received with a warmth of gratitude
to match my father's; and we were then shown the cupboard
under the staircase where I was to sleep and keep all my be-
longings (a considerable improvement, I realized at once,
on the open veranda corner I had used in the missionary
bungalow at Lokko). Having bundled my sleeping mat and
my box into my snug little boudoir, I went out with my
father to have my first good look at Sagresa.

My recollection of that first walk through those crowded
streets is confused. One or two impressions persist—of large
numbers of people in the markets, most of them speaking
a language which was neither English nor Hausa. The houses
were mostly made of stone or wood, many of them appearing
to have a kind of enclosed veranda running along the front
of the first floor. There appeared to be a fair number of
white faces to be seen behind the counters of shops and the
windscreens of cars. I had not yet learned to distinguish between the Syrian and the European white faces, so I was
much impressed at the enlarged opportunities I imagined I
would now have of listening to and learning good English—
to me then the very purpose of existence.

Then there was the sea. As to any schoolboy anywhere,
people and the works of people's hands were of more immediate interest and concern to me than the works of nature.
But my first glimpse of the sea at the end of one of the streets
leading to the harbour filled me with awe and wonder. I had
seen nothing in the way of natural scenery other than the
landscape around my village. But I knew at once that this
was something romantic and unordinary, and that it would
win my heart. Throughout the years since, I have heard
travellers to West Africa, usually disgruntled servicemen who
had the misfortune of being casseroled in a troopship in a
harbour for days on end, refer only to the heat of this love-
liest of coasts. But their view is understandably jaundiced;

for to judge fairly it is necessary to put oneself to the trouble of going ashore and getting away from the town, away to the hills and to the villages, whose quiet, unhurried charm would escape only the most insensitive of souls. Then one needs to go down to the coves and beaches where the surf creams endlessly and the cocoanut palms droop trembling fronds from arching stems.

But these were later discoveries. For the present the wideness of the sea and the greenness of the sloping land filled my eyes; and as I curled up that night outside the entrance to my cupboard (which my father was occupying for the night) they also filled the background of my dreams. And the sky which roofed them over contained no cloud that my young eyes could see.

Next day I said good-bye to my father and watched the lorry carry him away, with a lot of noisy hooting, down narrow Prince Henry Street and away toward the long brown dusty road. I suddenly realised as the lorry disappeared round a corner that that road was now my only visible link with my village. I felt more exhilarated than anything else at the thought. Rather than return to the mission house immediately, I decided to take advantage of this new and stimulating sense of personal freedom by exploring Sagresa and its vicinity on my own.

I first discovered a vast building with thick walls on the shore, and guessed from the soldiers standing at the gates in uniforms of storybook splendour that this was where the Governor himself must live. I went as close as I dared to the forbidding cannon guarding the walls, approached one of the sentries, and looked admiringly at the shining rifle he carried. I had read a lot about guns, and had seen many home-made hunting guns in the village. I thought, disappointedly, that his looked decorative and unbusinesslike. Something in the sentry's face prompted me to speak to him in Hausa; and, to my great delight, I found he was of my tribe. Without moving his head or body, and in low undertones, he asked me what village I was from, and what I was doing alone so far from home; and in return he answered my eager questions. Had he ever fought in a war?—No. Had any

of the other soldiers?—No. Were many of them Hausas?—
Yes, most of them were Hausa-speaking. Could I come and
talk to him and the others now and then?—Yes, but only
when they were off duty.

And with that I had to be content. But my pleasure at
finding one of my own people in what was for me a completely new world was proof that, below all my excitement,
nostalgia and homesickness were merely lying dormant,
awaiting a convenient opportunity to assert themselves. Later, of course, I found many others of my tongue in Sagresa,
but the Governor's soldiers never lost their place in my affec-
tions as both my first heroes and my first friends, in a town
big and strange and altogether different from anything I had
known before.

6

FROM

"Some Contexts of Blackness"

by Sillaty K. Dabo

(1937–   )

Missionary education, indeed colonial education, was im-
bued with cultural and religious chauvinism. Many mis-
sionaries were distrustful of non-Christian religions, just as
European educators were disdainful of non-European so-
cieties and cultures. African schoolboys in French West
Africa, for instance, were taught to recite the Bourbon king
chronology but learned nothing about the many great Afri-
can kings.

Here, Sillaty K. Dabo, a Muslim from Sierra Leone, West
Africa, recounts his unhappy encounter with Sierra Leone
missionary education of the 1940's. Later he studied com-
parative literature at the Sorbonne, the University of Mont-
pellier, and Oxford University, and is now a member of the
Education Department in Sierra Leone.

TAKE the case of old Father Davis, of the Roman Catholic
School at Mbekor [in Sierra Leone], the Poor Man! Not that
I really liked him or the Headmaster at the time. In fact if
anything, I think I hated them both, though I must confess
that theirs was a difficult task. How I would have liked to
see them carry out their threats. I wonder whoever gave these
two the brilliant idea of compelling Muslims to go to church
on Sundays or, failing this, to give them half-a-dozen lashes

every Monday morning? Of course it seemed then a clever
solution (a very easy and pleasant one for the African Headmaster, who could be seen every Monday morning with a list
of absentees from Sunday School, and holding in his left
hand, TERROR, his long whip) to the problem of the
propagation of Christianity in the middle of the Dark Continent.

I don't suppose the blame was one-sided. My parents too
should share some of it. I do not think that I should have
become a Christian if Dad had let me go to church on Sundays. He would have probably allowed me to go, but I don't
believe some of the other members of the family would have
approved of this. However, not satisfied with the six lashes
they gave us every Monday morning, our two friends hit
upon a more brilliant idea. I am almost certain this was the
Headmaster's idea: all Muslims were going to be dismissed
from the school, and none would be admitted in future unless they became converts!

How I wish they had consulted me. It never occurred to
them that Dad would take them on their word, or that there
was a fairly large number of Muslims in the school. The
only other probability is that they were just making an
empty threat to see whether our parents could be frightened
and brought to their knees. Anyway, we stayed at home for a
day or two, and both the threat and corporal punishment
were withdrawn. I was very grateful. I must point out also
that it is most unlikely that Dad would have allowed any
of the children from the neighbouring villages, who were
staying in our compound, to go to church on Sundays. If they
had, he would have probably punished them or sent them
away from the compound. The need did not arise, however,
because their parents had previously been converted to Islam
by my father.

None of these things would have made me detest Father
Davis and the Headmaster if they had not gone to extremes
in their hatred of Muslims, and of my family in particular.
My brother and some friends were walking a long distance
on the motor road when a van came up the road. Who else
could be the occupants but Father Davis, the Headmaster,

and another Reverend Father? They gave a lift to all but my brother. I was very angry when I heard this, and my brother certainly dramatized the situation a little.

Now that I know the reasons for what seemed to be a total lack of generosity, I have long since modified my views. It happened that two days before, Father Davis and the Head-master (from now on referred to as H.M.) had called on Dad asking to be allowed to build a school in another village in the District. Dad seems to have been willing to grant them permission but promised to discuss the matter over with my brother. Father Davis and the H.M. were to return the fol-lowing morning. The next day Dad did not give them permis-sion to build the school. The permit was given to the Method-ist Mission, where the question of church services was never seriously discussed.

I think this was one of the many reasons why Father Davis and his party did not give a lift to my brother. I wonder who is to blame? None of them forgave the other when he should have. I think they were both too strict, and this, in my view, is probably not in the interest of any of the great religions they stand for. One must of course allow for the spirit of the age and environment, and in the middle of the Dark Con-tinent at the time, this attitude on the part of each is under-standable.

7

FROM

Kossoh Town Boy

by Robert Wellesley Cole

(1907–   )

The settlers of Sierra Leone and Liberia had unusual colo-
nial experiences. Sierra Leone was founded as a haven for the
poor blacks of England, and later prospered as a colony for
liberated slaves; Liberia was founded as a back-to-Africa
answer for the blacks of the United States. Thus, in both
cases the incoming colonists were Africans who had been
separated from their tribal communities. In some instances,
in fact, the colonists had been born abroad. While each
group in many ways reassimilated into African culture, both
quite naturally developed societies which were more similar
to Western communities than were any of the African tribes
of their origin. The black colonists had undergone the
trauma of slavery; they were no longer supported by their
own people but by a Western power; they received their
education from Western missionaries and many material
goods from Europe. Naturally, as time went by the colonists'
children and grandchildren became more and more Western-
ized.

One of the colonists' descendants was Robert Cole, who
was born in Freetown, Sierra Leone, in 1907. His father
being a successful water engineer, Cole enjoyed a carefree
childhood which was quite similar to that of a middle-class

British or American boy. He received a medical degree in
England, and is now a health officer in Nottingham.

I WAS born at no. 15, Pownall Street, in the Kossoh Town
District of the Eastern Ward of Freetown, capital city of
Sierra Leone. The number was later changed to no. 13. The
day was 11 March, a Monday.

In Freetown all the street names are British. As if to em-
phasise this incongruity, nothing could be less British and
more African than the street scenes. Pownall Street lies practically at the centre of Kossoh Town. Kossoh Town, Fula
Town, Cline Town, Fourah Bay, Mende Town, Bambara
Town, Kru Town, and other such names, are all districts of
Freetown. In most cases the names refer to the people who
were originally settled in each district after Freetown was
founded.

Many of those settlers were free and self-respecting Africans who in the bad days of the first half of the last century,
when slavery had been banned by the British Parliament but
was still a profitable trade, had been tricked by their own
kinsmen and sold to the white slavers. They had, however,
been rescued by British warships on the high seas and taken
to Freetown, where they became free once more and were
given British citizenship, education, a new religion, and new
life. They were termed 'Liberated Africans.' They should
have been termed 'Reborn Africans.'

Between 1807 when the slave trade was outlawed and 1863
when the last slaving ship was captured some 50,000 Africans
were released and set free in Freetown. Many returned home,
but many also remained in Freetown, where they formed a
polyglot community, hailing from every part of the African
coast, from Cape Verde [West Senegal Africa] to the Congo
[Central Africa] and from as far inland as Timbuktu [Mali,
West Africa], and Sokoto in Northern Nigeria [West Africa].

In addition to the 'Liberated Africans' there were the
Maroons, or freed slaves from Jamaica, the Nova Scotians, or
remnants of American Negro slaves who had fought on the
side of the British in the American War of Independence,
and a few of the descendants of the original band of two

hundred freed slaves who had gone out with white 'wives'
from the streets of London, in 1787, under the auspices of
the British philanthropist Granville Sharp, to found the
new colony of Freetown. In addition there were a number of
primitive natives who technically had not been exported as
'slaves' nor 'liberated,' but who were drawn to the new town
from the hinterland and from neighbouring countries.

A sample study of the voices heard in the streets of Freetown in 1849 showed no less than ninety languages and dia-
lects. From this motley they rapidly settled down to become
the people now known as Krios, with distinctive customs and
a language of their own. Any Kossohs in Kossoh Town had
long cast off their original tribalism and become Krios by the
time I was born. Krio, pronounced 'cree-oh,' is African for
Creole.

This transformation took place in less than a single cen-
tury. But so definite and striking were the people so born, so
'British' were the Krios in outlook and sympathy, that Queen
Victoria called their country her 'Ancient and Loyal Sierra
Leone'. . . .

Our day started with family prayers. Our grandmother and
aunts usually joined us upstairs, and so did the foster brothers
and sisters. We sat round the room, and, after the word of
grace from father, each read in turn a verse from the portion
allotted for the day in the Scripture Union card.

Almost unique among all the peoples of West Africa,
practically all Krios are literate. The poorest family would
die rather than not send its children to school even for a
year, so that they could read. It is considered a disgrace
among them for a child to be illiterate.

This, together with such distinguishing features as dress,
language, Christian religion, English or anglicised names,
the acceptance of monogamy, and even the type of their
houses, all stemmed from the fact that the Krios of Sierra
Leone started life as a settler community under Christian
British influence.

Krio baby boys are circumcised when a week old. Baby
girls have their ears pierced at the same age for ear rings.
The Krios, like their main ancestors the Yorubas of Nigeria,

look to the East for their basic origin. But where the Yoruba
ancestors thought of Yemen, Arabia, and Mecca, the Christian Krios think of the stories of the Old Testament.

Among them, a mother, after giving birth to a child, is
churched, before she can go out and resume her social activities. Each time any of my brothers or sisters was baptised,
the family attended morning service at St Philip's, with
mother dressed all in white. After the service the family
moved up near the choir, and mother knelt at the steps of
the chancel, where our pastor read the service for the
Churching of Women, and purified and blessed her. Then
followed the baptism of the baby.

Christianity was the central force of our home. But
though a strict disciplinarian, father was not a bigot. Those
foster children who were not Christians he left alone. They
were not forced to attend family prayers nor to attend
church. And when one after the other they asked to join us,
and to go to church with us, he sent for their parents, and
discussed the matter fully with them; and it was only after
the latter had given their consent that he took steps to have
them instructed in Christianity, and prepared for baptism.
I can remember one of them, who at the time would be in
his late teens, being baptised at the same ceremony as one of
my baby brothers.

All this fitted in with the family prayers at home every
morning and evening. On Sundays we had singing of hymns
and psalms at home as well. It was a great day when I too
was able to read my share of the verses of scripture with the
rest of the family. Later on I became the family organist,
and accompanied the singing (hymns and psalms) on the
family harmonium (American organ).

But it was playtime in the afternoon and evening that
meant so much to me in those early days. I looked forward
to three o'clock. Although I could not tell the time, I could
sense when the hour approached, and would hover at the
gate peering out for my foster 'cousins' to return home from
school.

I can remember a long bench which stood against one
wall of the house, in the yard. Round this we would sit or

stand, and take part in all those pastimes which, all the world over, fill in the period between coming home from school and going to bed. Along another wall of the house were flowering shrubs.

Those afternoon play sessions in the yard must have done much to help me develop normally. As most of my brothers and sisters were not then born, but for this companionship of foster children I would for some years have been more or less a lonely child, a phenomenon which is rare in African society. As it was I grew up instead in the fold of young people.

Apart from this I also played with boys of my own age in our street. There was cricket, not to mention top spinning, hoop trundling ('gig running'), kite flying, and other activities.

When sent on an errand down the street I would debate whether to take my hoop or a top. If the hoop, I trundled it all the way by the simple method of hitting it with a short piece of stick in a straight line. This was the quickest method of getting to my destination.

On the other hand the top was a more interesting if leisurely and erratic way of going on an errand. I would spin the top and lash it with the cotton thong tied to the end of a short piece of stick. On its flat surface I would make marks with chalk, and these would join into lovely patterns as the top spun. Thus I would progress sideways, with my jutting posterior describing little horizontal arcs like a waddling duck, as I lashed the top on its spinning course.

What different techniques were applied to this simple pastime! At times a gentle stroke with the whip, and the top would hum forward a couple of feet or so, either in a straight line or off zigzag. There it would continue to spin. Sometimes I would let it alone until it was almost spent, and then coax it once more into animated life; then again suddenly I would go berserk, leap into the air, and give it a terrific wham with the thong, and the top would shoot up and glide in a graceful curve to land on its spinning point several feet ahead.

We often had competitions to see who could hit his top furthest in one hop. Needless to say, on such occasions the concentration was so intense that we were lost to the outside world. Once my attention was so occupied that I did not see a pedestrian coming, and I mistakenly hit his ankle, hard. He was a large man. . . !

Eastertime was kite-flying season, and long before then we would get our coloured tissue papers from the shops, and the special bamboo canes with which kites of different kinds were made. These varied from the simple skate design most commonly in use, to the powerful giant *Ognos* (Krio for hog's snout). This takes its name from the open triangular top segment of this hexagonal kite with its often double tail, altogether a ferocious-looking object.

Competitions were often held as to whose kite would rise the highest, or perform the most intricate loops in the sky. Sometimes this friendly rivalry would take the form of a cold war. A boy would deliberately get his *Ognos* to loop and entangle his opponent's kite. Sometimes the lead twine would snap, and we would all run excitedly to recover the errant kite, often over fields, and across several streets and properties, before the kite was caught, or fell to the ground, or more probably became entangled in the top of some trees and had to be abandoned.

As for cricket, we used the base of the street lamp post for stumps, or if we played in our yard we used an upturned pail or wicker basket (*blai*). The bat was a curved blade shaped from the giant petiole of the compound coconut leaf. As a result the commonest stroke was the hook, and the usual method of dismissal was by the catch. This was no disgrace, as usually it was the result of a hefty swipe which might send the ball soaring to the roof of the house, from which it would bounce and roll down into the patient hands of a waiting fielder!

This ball was made from one of mother's black stockings, the toe being rammed with soft cotton waste, tied hard at the neck, then turned inside out and tied tight again, the process repeated until the whole stocking had been taken up;

then the edges were sewn to the surface. A well-hit ball has
been known to stay lodged on the roof or in the branches
of a tree. Then the game was abandoned as a draw.

Similarly, if a serious dispute arose among the players,
each boy would walk off with his ball, bat, wicket, or whatever part of the gear belonged to him.

I cannot recall having many girl playmates in those very
early days. I think in their early days boys tend to mix with
boys. Possibly also our parents had something to do with it,
for on one occasion I remember one of the little girls coming
to play with us. When father came home in the evening he
sent her away, and did not seem pleased. And as the eldest of
my sisters was not born until I was seven years old, when I
had started school, in those earliest years mine was a man's
world.

At home, among the young people, we all called each
other 'cousins.' But among the servants they were all
'brothers.'

There were the four 'hammock boys,' who carried father
to and from work and on his various tours of inspection of
water-works installations in the peninsula. There was the
'lunch boy' who called at eleven to fetch father's hot lunch
(this was called 'breakfast') and take it to the office at the
Water Works headquarters on Tower Hill, and brought the
remains back in the afternoon. There was another 'boy,'
somewhat younger, who did much of the heavy work and
ran errands, when the others had gone to school.

But over and above this there was the 'head boy.' I cannot clearly recall what were his precise duties. He was a
majordomo, a butler, foreman, or chargehand, rolled into
one. He was treated with respect, and he saw to it that the
others reported for duty regularly and did their jobs well.

One day he came up and said to papa:

'Masa, a de go kontri.'

(Please, master, I have come to say goodbye. I am going
back to my country.) Papa wished him God-speed and inquired when he would be returning.

'Waka gud! Ustem yu de cam bak?'

But Sori, who had been with us so long that he was part of

the family, had suddenly grown tired of life in the city. He
wanted to go back to his people, marry and farm his land.
But he was not leaving his master in the lurch; instead, he
said:

'*Dis na mi broda!*' (I've brought you my brother), intro-
ducing another and somewhat younger man.

'But every time you bring a man for a job, you say he is
your brother,' countered my father, eyeing the newcomer
carefully.

'Yes, master,' Sori answered, speaking in Krio, which was
the only language he knew apart from his own native Limba.

'Yes, master, we are all brothers. Same country. Same
chief. But this man, he is my real brother. Same mother.'
The new man took over the majordomo-ship, and when
years afterwards he too left he first brought a 'brother' to
take over his place.

Father abhorred smoking, and the servants would hide in
all sorts of corners in the yard or in the garden to light their
little short-stemmed white clay pipes. This they did by the
simple method of tamping down the tobacco in the pipe
bowl, tossing on top of it a piece of live coal from the fire,
and making a run for it as far away as possible from the
house and father's sharp nostrils. Sometimes there seemed
to be in the pipe nothing but the lump of coal; but they
would suck away at it, like babies at their dummy teats. Invariably if father caught them he would confiscate the pipe.

My father was six feet one and a half inches tall, and slim.
Rather ascetic looking, with lean features, high forehead,
strong cuboid chin, and a trimmed moustache across the
whole length of his upper lip. Often, having ridden on his
hammock all day, he would prefer to walk on the way home.
He took deceptively long strides, stooping slightly forward,
marching ahead of the men, who, even with only the lightened hammock to carry, would have to run, in order to keep
up with him.

Certainly my brother Arthur and I had great difficulty in
keeping up with him, years afterwards when we were young
men in our late teens.

'Come on, men, don't fall asleep,' he would say to us, as

we marched manfully on, slightly irritated that we could not keep up with 'the old man.' Indeed there was another sore point with us, concerning our father. We never grew taller than he! However much we measured our heights Arthur and I never exceeded six feet!

8

"To a Farm in the White Highlands"

by Solomon Kagwe

(1935–   )

The childhood memories of most East Africans are less tranquil than those of Sierra Leonean Robert Cole. Many East African children were raised as sons of squatters or tenant farmers. In colonial Kenya only whites were allowed to buy the best farm land, and blacks in need of money were forced to work as wage laborers for the whites. As described in this selection, the East African wage-labor system and the conditions under which the Africans worked are strikingly similar to the migrant and tenant-farmer arrangements in America.

Solomon Kagwe was born in the Nyeri district of Kenya in 1935. In 1964 he received his B.A. in English, history, and political science from Makerere College, Uganda. "To a Farm in the White Highlands" has been broadcast by the BBC and Radio Uganda.

THE basic economy of Kenya depends on agriculture in the White Highlands. Nearly all commodities for export, such as maize, coffee, pyrethrum and wheat are grown in this area. The best butter in East Africa also comes from the White Highlands. There is no doubt, therefore, that the farms in the settled area command a wide interest not only from those people whose homes are in Kenya but also from those in foreign countries. It would be useful and interesting for you to visit a typical farm belonging to Mr. Brown, where I was born and brought up and which I visit regularly to see my relatives. But before you go there, it is important, if you are an African, that you change any smart clothes you may have and put on dirty ones. If they are ragged, the better. You may resent this but there is no alternative. Mr. Brown knows the educated people by the way they dress and does not allow these people 'from the town' to visit his farm. He says that they suffer from chronic infectious laziness and that they have strange ideas which his workers do not desire.

When you look around his big farm, you start wondering where his workers live. All you see are small mud-and-wattle huts huddled together and perhaps you may think that these are stables. You would be mistaken, for these are workers' houses. A barbed-wire fence and a big trench surround these huts. Mr. Brown has told the workers that this is necessary to keep thieves away. Opposite this village, as these huddled huts are usually called, is Mr. Brown's house which is a quarter of a mile away. But it has no fence around it.

The farm, which covers about a thousand acres, has many good and fat cows, sheep and pigs. Some other parts of the farm are devoted to coffee, pyrethrum and tea.

When you go there, you meet bare-footed people who are thin and hungry-looking. They are all invariably in soiled and tattered clothes. Let them learn that you come from the town and that you have a little education. At first they will be surprised at your ragged clothes. They always expect a person from the town to be in a suit. They will then show you their hospitality. You will be led to one of their huts. On seeing the inside of the hut you cannot help being moved to pity and sympathy. At the same time, you will be astonished to learn that some human beings can live in conditions which you never dreamt of. The hut is their kitchen, dining-room, bedroom, bathroom. All members of the family sleep there. In a typical hut, you will see a bed for the mother and another one for the father. All children sleep on the bare floor together with fleas and sheep. But these people appear happy. The boys sing and play during the day and the evening time. You would never think that they will go to sleep on the floor where about four of them will share one blanket. They do not go to school for there is not one. Mr. Brown thinks that these boys should grow up to replace their parents when they retire from working for him. In his belief that education makes a person lazy, he has resisted all attempts by his workers to build a Village School. The workers will tell you how they like meeting people from the towns. You will have noticed this long before they say it. They welcome you to their houses smiling, and give you the best stool in the hut, specially for visitors. The mother of the hut will busy herself preparing porridge while the children stand gazing at you admiringly. The neighbours of your host come to greet you and express pleasure at your visiting them. Their appearance, their smiling faces and their pleasant gestures will make you think they are happy; but in this village during a working day you will wonder whether some people do not need hell's fire to make them look unhappy.

They wake up at 4:30 a.m. They prepare themselves for work. The mothers cook for their children and then all go to the farm at about 6 a.m. leaving their young ones behind. No sooner do they reach their places of work than they meet Mr. Brown and his overseers. Watch these people clearing and digging a new area for plantation and you see what a mighty job they have to do. The women clear the bush. The men follow them, digging, while the young boys break the large lumps of soil. As soon as a boy is over five years old he goes to do this job. Mr. Brown says that this is the best age for offering young boys the earliest opportunity of apprenticeship to the job they hope to do, that of digging and harvesting his crops.

All the workers do their job without rest—not because they do not know the dangers of overwork but because the prospects of being seen standing idle are not pleasant. A slight pause is enough to make the angry Mr. Brown decide not to give a person his day's wages. In the absence of Mr. Brown, his wife takes over. She is not the sort of person either who would get tired of watching the workers. Go near where they work. The earth shakes under men's heavy hoes. They do this job without break up to 8 p.m. in the evening, with only fifteen minutes at 12 o'clock when they can snatch their lunch. This consists of porridge and one or two sweet potatoes. You wonder whether this is sufficient when you consider the amount of work they have to do but Mr. Brown will tell you that a person who eats much grows lazy and that is why he gives them fifteen shillings a month. After 12:15 p.m., all, including children, resume their work, now in the blazing afternoon sun. Men and boys remove their shirts. The former continue breaking the ground as before. You can see swift streams of sweat running down their slender bodies. Their faces become wet with perspiration. Often they use their torn handkerchiefs to dry themselves. But they do not spend a minute to do this. The Browns or their obsequious overseers are quick at seeing 'lazy' people.

While working, these people keep away tedium by singing as soldiers do in order to elevate their spirits and courage. It is interesting to notice a verse of one of these songs which runs as follows:

> Since you erred, Adam,
> We've got to sweat
> And like tractors work
> For all our lives
> To earn our living.

Mr. Brown knows that his workers are simple and religious people who are not aware that they have rights. That is why he works them from 6 a.m. to 8 p.m.

After work at 8 p.m. the people wearily plod their way homewards. The mothers start the tiring business of cooking while the hard-worked men relax on their hard stools. The mothers first of all cook light food for their hungry, crying children, who have not been with their parents all the day long. They cry because they have not had enough food during the day. If you have been to a cattle *boma* (a Swahili word for a cattle dwelling) and have heard the clamour that calves make in the evening while waiting for their mothers, then you know what to expect in this village.

After they have had their supper, the tired workers go to bed and then start their dreary routine at 4:30 a.m. the following morning.

9

FROM

Tell Freedom

by Peter Abrahams

(1919–   )

South Africa's colonial experience began earlier than that of East or West Africa.

In 1652 Dutch colonialists landed at the Cape of Good Hope to establish a watering station for ships traveling to India. Soon more Dutch colonists arrived, and many families ventured inland. The story of their trek is similar to the tale told of the American pioneers—except that, instead of fighting Indians, the Boers fought Africans.

In the nineteenth century many British settlers arrived in South Africa, and after the British defeated the Dutch settlers in the Boer War of 1899–1902, the English government established hegemony over all of South Africa. The government, immediately faced with the problem of dealing with the many black residents, gradually developed the system of apartheid. In theory, apartheid is a scheme of separate race development through which blacks and whites live separately but equally. In practice, however, it is a method by which a small number of whites—one fifth of the population of South Africa—dominates a large number of blacks. In 1961 the South African government proclaimed its country an independent republic, and to this day only whites can vote and can hold certain jobs, and not even whites enjoy freedom

*of speech, press, or assembly. Other African countries which
are still ruled by white racist regimes include Portuguese
Guinea in West Africa, Southwest Africa, Rhodesia, Mozambique, and Angola, all of Southern Africa.*

*Perhaps the most shattering experience for a black South
African youth is his discovery that the barriers imposed upon
him are based on the arbitrary distinction of race. Peter
Abrahams' discovery of this bitter truth as a young child
came about through a scuffle with a gang of white boys.*

*Abrahams was a Cape Colored boy—a mulatto—and born
to a colored mother and an Ethiopian father. He spent his
earliest years in the slums of Vrededorp in Johannesburg,
South Africa, but in 1924 on the death of his father was sent
to Elsburg, South Africa, to live for a year with his aunt and
uncle. He then returned to Vrededorp where he was educated
at St. Peter's School. In 1939 he left South Africa and spent
two years as a seaman before settling in Britain. In 1957 he
moved to the West Indies where he is present editor of the*
West Indian Economist. *His publications include* Mine Boy,
Path of Thunder, Wild Conquest, Tell Freedom, Return to
Goli, Jamaica, An Island Mosaic, A Wreath for Udomo, *and*
A Night of Their Own.

I WALKED down Nineteenth Street with the strange
woman. And as we went, I became aware of a noise. I tried to
place it, but it was everywhere. A continuous deep rumble
pervaded the world. It seemed to come from the bowels of
the earth, to reach down from the spaces of the heavens.
What was it? Where did it come from? Why?

"Hear the noise?" I said to the woman.

"What noise?" She was not interested.

I felt homesick suddenly and looked back. I looked for our
house but could not identify it. Each house looked like the
next, all strange. And the people about me were all strangers.
I panicked. I tried to pull free of the woman's grip.

"Where are we going?" I asked.

"To the station." Her voice was more kindly.

"Why?"

"We are going to Elsburg."

I began to whimper. "I want to go home. I want my mother."

The woman spoke soothingly and quieted me down. About me was the big world. There was so much of it. Motors flashed by. Trams rumbled along. Large horses dragging huge carts pranced up and down the wide Delarey Street. Shop windows were filled with new and interesting things. My head jerked from left to right. I forgot my home and my mother. All this was new, excitingly new.

At Fordsburg Station our train was on the point of departure. We scrambled on. The train moved off. The engine puffed and screamed a shrill warning. We found a place near the window. The woman sat on the hard wooden seat. I stood with my nose pressed against the dirty windowpane, watching the world go by.

The engine puffed and snorted. Every now and then, when the train curved round a bend, it screamed its shrill warning. And the wheels, under me, whispered: "On a-w-a-y. O-n a-w-a-y. O-n a-w-a-y." Then they said: "On away. On away. On away." Then they said: "On away, on away, on away." And after that, for nearly all the time, they said: "On-awayonawayonawayonawayonawayonawayonaway."

Soon the houses and other buildings were far behind. The land came rushing up, only to rush away again: vast stretches of green land, and brown land; land rising and falling. Sometimes hills and mountains flashed by. Sometimes we went through a mountain and were in darkness. And the engine would scream its warning and we would come out of the mountain. Tall telegraph poles came up to meet us, then rushed away with clock-like regularity. And all the time the wheels said: "Onawayonawayonawayonawayonawayonaway-onawayonawayonaway," till I was drunk with it all.

I was hazy and sleepy and very tired when we stepped off the train at the little gravel siding at Elsburg. The sun had

gone down. There was a softness over the land. It made
everything more beautiful than it really was.

The woman took my hand and we set off on our four-mile
walk through the beautiful land. When we got to her house
at the location, I was asleep on my feet. Vrededorp was far
away and I was happy and tired, so I tumbled into a strange
bed and slept deeply.

I woke in a strange place. Fear took hold of me. I longed
for the familiar, for my mother and for the home I knew.
For days, till I grew used to the people with whom I lived
and familiar with the place, I was miserable and painfully
homesick.

In time the woman became Aunt Liza to me, a person
with a name. And there was comfort in her having a name.
Her husband, whom I had hardly noticed the night before,
was Uncle Sam.

When I got up, Uncle Sam had already gone to his work.
In common with all the men, as well as some women, of Elsburg location, he worked on one of the white farms near by.
The routine of my days at Elsburg began that morning. I
made my bed. Then I went outdoors to the sunny side of the
house with a small bowl of cold water and a piece of home-
made soap. There I washed. Then I went in to breakfast.
This was a plate of mealie pap. Maize is crushed to a powder
slightly coarser than flour. A saucepan of salted water is
brought to the boil, then the required amount of maize is
added and stirred continuously. It is cooked in about fifteen
minutes. The result is mealie pap. For breakfast it is thinned
down to a runny liquid. A plateful of that and a mug of
black coffee were my breakfast. I had the choice of having
two teaspoons of sugar either in my coffee or over my pap.
I elected to have one over the pap and one in the coffee. The
coffee remained bitter and I could hardly taste the sugar
over the pap.

After breakfast I had five minutes to myself. I sat in the
warmest and most protected spot I could find. I took stock of
the place that was now my home.

The houses were built in two lines, as they would be on

either side of a wide road, each line facing the road. Only there was no road. What could have been the road was a strip of land dotted with mounds and potted with holes. Here and there footpaths had worn the grass away; here and there children, by constant playing on the same spot, had created patches of dusty sand. The location stood on a rising between a valley on one side and a river on the other. To the east and west the land sloped away gently.

On windy days the sand patches were stirred to life and everything, all in all the houses, was coated with the fine, gritty sand that hung like a thick mist over the place. In the rainy season the pot-holes in what might have been the wide street were filled and became stagnant pools. When the rainy season passed, the children fished for tadpoles in those pools. If the wet spell had been long, we often found frogs in the mud after the water had seeped away.

The houses were usually two-roomed. Here and there a smaller room had been added to the back. But where that had been done there was not the bit of land left on which to grow a few green vegetables, for each house stood in a small piece of fenced-off land. And the land belonged to the farmers for whom the people of the location worked. And behind the fenced-off little plots, spreading in all directions, were vast stretches of rolling land.

The houses were made by those who lived in them. And because they had no security of tenure, few took pride in what they put up. The walls were of unbaked mud bricks held together by straw. The roofs were sheets of corrugated iron nailed or screwed together over rafters. And the holes and open spaces were stopped up with sacking and pieces of canvas. Neither cold nor wet was ever effectively kept out.

The place itself seemed to fit into the bleak austerity of the land about it. There was not a tree in the valley below. To the east and west there was just the harshness of the sloping land under the curving sky. Even the sky seemed cold and remote and very far away.

Only the river promised a touch of softness in this hard place. A line of willows marked the course it took. They were the only trees in all the land about. I would go there,

I promised myself. I would go down to the river and look at the trees.

Aunt Liza came out of the house. My five minutes were up. She gave me two pails.

"The well is up the street."

I took the pails and marched out of the gate. Women and children were already at the well. I was the stranger and everyone turned to look at me. I looked steadily at the ground. A little boy, no bigger than myself, arrived after me.

At last all the others had their water and went and only the boy and I were left. It was my turn, but I did not know how to work the well. I looked at the boy.

"You go first," I said.

He started towards the handle, then changed his mind.

"No. It is your turn."

I had hoped to watch and learn from him.

The bucket stood on the edge of the well. It was weighted with an iron bar. I took hold of the handle and began to unwind the rope.

"The bucket," the boy said.

It was still on the mouth of the well. A long strand of the rope dangled down into the darkness of the well. I let go of the handle, leaned forward, and pushed the bucket in. As I straightened up, the rope jerked taut, the handle swung in a downward arc. It struck me flush on the mouth, then on the upper part of my chest. I fell flat on my back. My jaw was paralysed. I swallowed blood. Above me the handle whirled dangerously. As suddenly as it had started, the handle stopped. I got up slowly. My chest and jaw were beginning to hurt.

The boy was holding his sides, laughing. Then he saw the blood dripping from my mouth. He looked frightened suddenly. His eyes opened wide.

"Are you going to die?" he whispered.

Aunt Liza stalked up to the well, raging at the top of her voice.

"The first damn thing you'll learn here is that time's not to be wasted! I'll take the skin off your damn back if you play around when I send you for something! When'll I finish all that damn washing? You'll have to learn or I'll damn kill you!"

Neighbours pushed their heads out of doors to see what the storm was about. When Aunt Liza saw my face, concern replaced her rage.

"What happened?"

I tried to speak, but could not. I was too hurt to cry. In her anxiety she shook me.

"What happened?"

The frightened boy whispered: "Is he going to die, Auntie?"

Aunt Liza turned to him. And he told her what had happened. He ended with his big question:

"Is he going to die, Auntie?"

"Of course not, Andries!" Aunt Liza snapped.

"But I saw a dog bleeding and he died," Andries said anxiously.

"Of course you didn't know," Aunt Liza said to me. "Why didn't I think of that?" Her brow creased in a worried frown.

Andries' mother, our next-door neighbour, came cursing to the well, promising hell and damnation to Andries for being so long about the water. She, too, was silenced by my bleeding mouth.

Aunt Liza put her arm about my shoulders and hurried me down to the house.

From across the way someone called: "Wash his mouth with salt! That'll do it!"

When you have a cut, it is bathed with salt water. They say the sting of it is good. They say it kills the pain. When your nose bleeds, you inhale salt water up the nostrils. They say it will stop the bleeding. When you have ear-ache you bathe your ear with warm salt water. When you have a sore throat, you gargle with salt water. If your eye is inflamed and sore, salt water eases it. When you have toothache you fill your mouth with hot salt water and let it soak into the aching tooth. If you have stomachache, a large mug of warm salt water is the best cure. It either drives the sickness down or brings it up. . . . Salt was the greatest cure-all of my childhood days. And it nearly always worked!

I washed my mouth repeatedly with salt water till the bleeding stopped. The intense pain soon passed. The inside of my mouth was sore, one of my teeth was loose, my lips were badly swollen, but no real damage had been done. And I was soon fit to go back to the well.

With the help of Andries, who became my friend once he was sure I was not going to die, I learned how to handle the well. Together we carried a relay of pails, first for Aunt Liza, then for his mother.

It was washing day for Aunt Liza. I was to discover that every day was washing day for Aunt Liza. And nearly all afternoons and nights were given up to ironing. Uncle Sam brought home a huge bundle of dirty laundry each night, and took away a neat bundle each morning. For a long time this was a mystery to me. Then I discovered it was the laundry bundle of the white people for whom Uncle Sam worked.

Aunt Liza had two tubs out in the yard. A string of drying-lines criss-crossed so that every inch of space was used when the lines were full. One of the tubs stood on stones over an open fire built in a scooped-out hollow of the ground. Near it was a huge pile of pieces of dried cow dung. She fed the fire with these.

When we had brought enough water for her washing needs, we filled the rusty rain-water tank. Then two pails filled the drinking-bowl inside the house. The water I poured into the drinking-bowl was yellow, almost opaque. I watched the sediment settle. When it was clear, I saw a black water-spider moving slowly over the sediment. Other signs of tiny life wriggled about as well. I told Aunt Liza. She laughed.

"You'll get used to it. They haven't killed me. Just don't drink the water at the bottom. They stay there. Now go with Andries and find some manure, and be quick because I'm short. You'll find the sacks in the corner. There's a piece of bread in the bin."

I found the sacks, and a hard crust in the bin. I hurried out to Andries.

"Come!" he chanted.

He dashed away. I followed. We streaked across the virgin fields, veering slightly to the east so that, if we kept that course, we would reach the river a long, long way farther on. He was getting farther away from me, so I called: "Hey, Andries!"

He eased up a little. With a burst of speed I caught up with him.

"Don't run so fast."

"We must."

"Why?"

"Others will get all the dung."

"Where are they?"

"Must be nearly there."

"Where?"

"Where we get the dung, silly!"

"Where is that?"

"Shut up and come on. You'll see."

"I'm tired."

"Come on!"

"Let's walk a little."

"Want Auntie Liza to lick you?"

"Why?"

"If you walk now, there'll be nothing when you get there. You'll go home with empty sacks. And, man, will she lick you! Seen how thick her arms are? My mother's thin, but she licks like hell. Auntie Liza with her thick arms will kill. Come on!"

"But I'm tired."

He shot away again. I had not noticed Aunt Liza's arms, but thinking of them, they became huge clubs swinging at me. I shot across the veld after Andries, forgetful of my tiredness. The space between us narrowed gradually. By the time we topped the rising of the land, we were running side by side.

"There!" Andries cried.

Far ahead, a cluster of children walked across the veld, playing as they went. We eased the pace a little and trotted steadily across the wide green valley. Some way ahead, be-

yond the children, a herd of cows grazed under the gentle
sun.

We caught up with the others. Andries was soon drawn
into the play and banter. I was left on the outside. I was the
new boy, the stranger. I had still to earn the right to be one
of them.

Where we walked, the grass was lush and taut. I could feel
its sharpness on my feet where my canvas shoes had split. A
little below us, to the left, in the direction of the river, were
willow trees. They were stunted and their leaves were pale
and transparent. They grew in two lines that were more or
less straight. That they were there suggested that where we
walked had been the bed of a wide, shallow river in times
long gone.

The morning sun was getting warmer. The land seemed
vast, unending, and very quiet. And we, the children and
the cattle, were the only living creatures on the earth, owned
it and the sky, belonged to earth and sky. The light breeze
that was about us carried the voices of the children to the
cows. The cows turned their heads ponderously. One or
two opened their mouths and hailed us with a placid
"Mooooo. . . ."

A cross-eyed boy who seemed to command universal respect raised his hand. We all stopped.

Andries ran to me and said: "When he says go, you go
looking for dung. Quickly."

I thought of Aunt Liza's arms. I did not want the weight of
those arms on my body. But I was worried about the cows.
Did they bite?

"Do they bite?"

"Who?"

"Those things." I pointed.

Andries doubled up with laughter. He turned to the
others.

"Hey! He wants to know if cows bite!"

They joined in the laughter.

"He's just a dumb towny," someone called out.

"Shut your trap!" the cross-eyed boy called. "Go!"

They forgot my ignorance. We streaked off in all direc-

tions searching for the precious dung. Dung makes the fire
that cooks the food. Dung is the fire that fights off the cold.
Dung boils the washing that brings the money that pays for
our bread.

We darted here and there, grabbing the dried flat cakes
and shoving them into our sacks. We were not children at
play. This was serious. Life depended on this. To the left of
me, two boys argued over a piece of dung both had spotted
at the same time. They soon came to blows. The rest were
too concerned with finding dung to stop and look. I lost my
nervousness of the cows and darted among them, grabbing
pieces of dung. I saw a huge piece and dashed for it. Another boy had seen it at the same time. We glared at each
other—two savage dogs over a bone. I remembered I was
the stranger. I had to install myself before I could expect to
fight on terms of equality. I veered away and left the precious
piece to him.

I filled one sack and started on the next. But now the dung
became more rare. Competition became fierce. There were
more dog-fights. I passed a boy on his knees, blood dripping
from his nose. Two little girls were pulling each other's hair.
I bumped into a boy. He pushed me over. I jumped up. He
waited, his fists bunched, ready for the fight. I looked into his
eyes and it seemed he was as frightened as I was. Somehow,
seeing fear in his eyes made me feel less of an outsider. I
turned my back on him. I heaved the full sack onto my back
and trotted away scanning the grass. I was beginning to
recognize the cakes at quite a distance. The boy cursed me,
a frustrated desperation in his voice.

All about me, each with sacks on his or her back, children
ran; they darted first this way, then that; they stooped,
grabbed, shoved dung into their sacks, and were off again.
The area of search widened till we ceased to be a group, till
we lost contact with one another.

When I had filled both my sacks the sun was high and I
was alone in a hollow strip of land. I flopped down on the
ground and leaned against the sacks. I was utterly wearied.
It was not just tiredness. There had been a tight desperation

in the search, a nervous tension. Now that it was over, I felt listless.

After a while I got up. I now had to find my way home. There was not a person in sight. If I faced about, the river would be on my right. If I kept walking with the river on my right, and if I veered slightly to the left, I would be going in the general direction of home.

I heaved the sacks onto my back and climbed out of the hollow strip. I walked steadily, anxiously, yet wearily, till I topped a slight rising. The cows grazed in the valley below. I was right. That was the way home. And down there, among the cows, were some of the children. To the left, some way behind me, were others. Yet others were far ahead, on their way home. I trudged down into the valley. I met up with some of the children and we walked in silence, each bent under the weight of dung.

Ahead of us, children walked in twos and threes. Others came behind us. Hardly a word was spoken on the journey back. The listlessness that was on me seemed on everyone else as well.

We soon left the valley of the cows and walked where everything was sombre and hard, where even the grass was stunted. We crossed deep dongas of eroded and eroding soil. We passed barren patches where no blade of grass grew and the earth had turned to a fine, dusty sand. The way seemed infinitely longer returning than it had been going. And the sacks on my back grew heavier with each step I took.

I reached home near sunset. Aunt Liza was still at her washtub. She straightened her back painfully. I dumped the sacks near the fire. Though the day was not hot, sweat dripped from her face. Her eyes were bloodshot. The top of her dress clung damply to her body and was wet under her arms. I noticed the thickness of her arms, and her big hands, which were pitted from being in water the whole day, white as a sheet and swollen to twice their size. A tired smile softened her face.

"Tired?"

I nodded.

"First time's always the worst," she said.

She put an arm about my shoulders and pressed me against her body. I felt strangely comforted and rewarded. The dull ache seemed to go from my back.

"Let's have some coffee," she said.

She warmed up the remains of the breakfast coffee.

"When do we eat, Aunt Liza?"

"When Uncle Sam comes home."

We drank our coffee. Aunt Liza went back to her tub. I found the warmest corner of the house and squatted. The coffee rumbled in my stomach. I felt warm inside and out. I leaned back against the wall and closed my eyes. . . .

Journeying from a great distance, I became aware of Aunt Liza. She shook my shoulder.

"Wake up!"

I opened my eyes.

"Come on," Aunt Liza said.

She moved slowly, heavily; only the strength of her will seemed to hold her big body together.

The huge bundle of washing was done. The little yard was filled with clothes drying on the lines. The whites gleamed cleanly. And in the tub was a huge pile waiting to go on the lines.

I shivered and got up. I followed her out of the gate, up the wide strip of field that might have been a road, past the well, across the veld. We walked till the location was out of sight. We made for a cluster of hillocks on the other side of a valley. She stooped and picked some broad leaves that grew among the grass. She gave them to me.

"It is called moeroga. Look at them carefully. You'll come by yourself tomorrow. They grow among nettles."

I studied the leaves of wild spinach. Aunt Liza made a carrier of her apron. Deftly, quickly, she plucked the leaves. The nettles did not bother her. I worked more slowly, more clumsily. I tried to avoid the nettles, but my hands were soon purple and stung as though on fire.

At last the hollow of her apron filled. We turned back. Night was nearly on us. A fine mist hung over the veld. It grew cold. Night had fallen when we reached home.

"Build up the fire," Aunt Liza said.

I squatted close to the fire and piled it high with dung. As the dung caught, light, bluish smoke with a fragrant sweetness about it spiralled up to the misty sky. Aunt Liza came and squatted beside me. Catching some of the warmth of the fire, she prepared the moeroga. I watched her work, and became aware of my gnawing hunger.

"Aunt Liza—"

"Heh?"

"When does Uncle Sam come home?"

"Very hungry?"

"Yes."

"Soon now."

My front was warming; my back was freezing.[1] I thought about Uncle Sam. I had not really seen him the night before. I had been too tired and worked up. What was he like? Aunt Liza had become a person to me. When I thought of her my mind said: two huge arms that terrified Andries; a gruff but gentle voice; two bloodshot eyes in a coarse reddish-brown face; a broken left-front upper tooth when she smiled; great tiredness; the comfort of her rough embrace. A person. And Uncle Sam? I tried to build an image from what I had seen last night. Nothing came. Just a name: Uncle Sam.

Well, he would soon be home now. I would eat. And I would see him.

Aunt Liza crammed the moeroga into a huge pot and put a stone on the lid to keep it down. I moved back from the fire. The heat was burning my face. My behind was numbing with cold. The fire gave off less smoke now. The dung glowed more brightly. And about me, in the darkness, were the noise of the cricket, the croak of the frog, and a thousand other noises I could not name. When had these begun? One moment the world had been silent, the next I was aware of all these noises. I looked into the darkness and saw the flickering lights of glowworms go on and off continuously.

_____

[1] In parts of South Africa the temperature drops well below freezing during their winter, which is at the same time as our summer.

When the fire glowed at its brightest and gave off no smoke, we carried it into the kitchen and shut out the cold, the night, and the noises of the veld. I made myself comfortable on a sack in a corner on the floor and watched Aunt Liza prepare the evening meal.

She cooked a thick, lumpy mealie pap. When it was nearly done, she added a blob of fat. She put two iron bars across the fire, moved the pap to the very edge, and put on the moeroga.

Uncle Sam arrived. He flung open the kitchen door and brought in a gust of cold night air. He was very tall; his head was up among the rafters near the roof. But this was an illusion. I was seeing him from ground-level and he only seemed tall. In reality he was no taller than Aunt Liza. He was very thin. His face showed up the rise and fall of every bone of his skull, like skin drawn tight over a skeleton head. His eyes, small, were set deep in their sockets. They were stern, forbidding eyes. And the curve of his mouth made him the most forbidding man I had ever seen. He carried a sack slung over his shoulder.

"Hello, Sam," Aunt Liza said.

"Liz . . ." His voice was harsh.

He put the sack on the table, shut the door, hung his hat on the nail behind it, and looked at me. I lowered my eyes quickly.

"How's he?"

"Near killed himself at the well," Aunt Liza said. "But he picks up fast."

"Done anything?"

"A good bit. Get the things?"

"Yes. Our debt's up to a pound." His voice was bitter.

"Brought the washing?"

"It's outside." To me he said: "Bring it in."

"Let it be," Aunt Liza said. "I'm fed up with their dirt."

I settled back in my corner. Uncle Sam sat on the bench near the fire and stared moodily into it. Aunt Liza took the moeroga off. From the cupboard she got three pieces of crackling. When a pig is killed, it is skinned. The thick skin is fried to a crisp brown. This is cut into square pieces and sold as crackling. There was a pig farm near Elsburg siding where the people of the location bought their crackling. Aunt Liza warmed up the three pieces. The meal was ready. She dished it into three tin plates. A dollop of pap, a spoonful of moeroga, and a piece of crackling. She sat on the bench beside Uncle Sam. He said grace:

"Thank You for the food we are now going to eat, God. Amen."

We ate.

While we ate, four irons warmed on the fire. I marvelled at how the moeroga had shrunk: so much had gone into the pot, so little came out. And it was the most tasteful part of the meal. When I finished, Aunt Liza said: "You can scrape the pot."

With a knife I scraped the brown crust from the bottom of the pap pot. I discovered a delicacy, crisp and crunchy, and the tastiest part of the pap.

My last chore of the day was washing up. While I did it, Aunt Liza prepared my bed in the corner on the floor. Uncle Sam sat staring into the fire, picking his teeth with a used matchstick. On the fire, beside the irons, the coffee-pot brewed Uncle Sam's good-night cup. I put the dry crocks away and went back to my corner.

I took off my canvas shoes. They would last another day at most; then I would have to get used to going about barefooted. Next I took off my khaki shorts. Draughts suddenly stung my bare bottom and thighs. I hurried under the protection of the blankets. The flame from the thick home-made tallow candle fluttered. Aunt Liza poured Uncle Sam's good-night coffee. Then she cleared the table and began to iron.

I glanced furtively at Uncle Sam. The last sound he had made was to say grace. He sat, the mug of coffee in his hands, his face expressionless, his eyes fixed on one spot of the fading fire. I closed my eyes. I still had no picture of Uncle Sam. He was still not a person. He was just a name, a being, and silence. I felt afraid of him because I did not understand anything about him.

I dozed off, then woke. Aunt Liza was still ironing. Uncle Sam still sat staring fixedly at the fading fire. I dozed and

woke again. Uncle Sam had gone. Aunt Liza was still ironing. The candle was nearly burnt out. The saucer on which
it stood was gutted with molten tallow.

"In a minute, Sam," Aunt Liza called.

I fell asleep.

The pattern of my days was set. Each day I would perform
the tasks I had performed this day; eat the meals I had eaten
this day. With skill and speed, I would perform my chores
more quickly and earn time, later, for a daily visit to the
river. On Sundays there would be a small piece of meat to
vary the diet. Often there was a piece of bread at midday to
take the edge off my hunger. Each day Aunt Liza washed;
each night I fell asleep while she ironed. In time I lost my
fear of Uncle Sam's silence. There was, of course, variety;
but the basic pattern of my days was as this first day had
been.

Wednesday was crackling day. On that day the children of
the location made the long trek to Elsburg siding for the
squares of pig's rind that passed for our daily meat. We collected a double lot of cow dung the day before; a double lot
of moeroga.

I finished my breakfast and washed up. Aunt Liza was at
her washtub in the yard. A misty, sickly sun was just showing. And on the open veld the frost lay thick and white on
the grass.

"Ready?" Aunt Liza called.

I went out to her. She shook the soapsuds off her swollen
hands and wiped them on her apron. She lifted the apron
and put her hand through the slits of the many thin cotton
dresses she wore. The dress nearest the skin was the one with
the pocket. From this she pulled a sixpenny piece. She tied it
in a knot in the corner of a bit of coloured cloth and handed
it to me.

"Take care of that. . . . Take the smaller piece of bread
in the bin, but don't eat it till you start back. You can have
a small piece of crackling with it. Only a small piece, understand?"

"Yes, Aunt Liza."

"All right."

I got the bread and tucked it into the little canvas bag in which I would carry the crackling.

"Bye, Aunt Liza." I trotted off, one hand in my pocket, feeling the cloth where the money was. I paused at Andries' home. . . .

We hurried . . . to the distant shed where a queue had already formed. There were grown-ups and children. All the grown-ups and some of the children were from places other than our location.

The line moved slowly. The young white man who served us did it in leisurely fashion, with long pauses for a smoke. Occasionally he turned his back.

At last, after what seemed hours, my turn came. Andries was behind me. I took the sixpenny piece from the square of cloth and offered it to the man.

"Well?" he said.

"Sixpence crackling, please."

Andries nudged me in the back. The man's stare suddenly became cold and hard. Andries whispered into my ear.

"Well?" the man repeated coldly.

"Please *baas*," I said.

"What d'you want?"

"Sixpence crackling, please."

"What?"

Andries dug me in the ribs.

"Sixpence crackling, please, *baas*."

"What?"

"Sixpence crackling, please, *baas*."

"You new here?"

"Yes, *baas*." I looked at his feet, while he stared at me.

At last he took the sixpenny piece from me. I held my bag open while he filled it with crackling from a huge pile on a large canvas sheet on the ground. Turning away, I stole a fleeting glance at his face. His eyes met mine, and there was amused, challenging mockery in them. I waited for Andries at the back of the queue, out of the reach of the white man's mocking eyes.

The cold day was at its mildest as we walked home along

the sandy road. I took out my piece of bread and, with a small piece of greasy crackling, still warm, on it, I munched as we went along. We had not yet made our peace, so Andries munched his bread and crackling on the other side of the road.

"Dumb fool!" he mocked at me for not knowing how to address the white man.

"Scare arse!" I shouted back.

Thus, hurling curses at each other, we reached the fork. Andries saw them first and moved over to my side of the road.

"White boys," he said.

There were three of them, two of about our own size and one slightly bigger. They had school bags and were coming towards us up the road from the siding.

"Better run for it," Andries said.

"Why?"

"No, that'll draw them. Let's just walk along, but quickly."

"Why?" I repeated.

"Shut up," he said.

Some of his anxiety touched me. Our own scrap was forgotten. We marched side by side as fast as we could. The white boys saw us and hurried up the road. We passed the fork. Perhaps they would take the turning away from us. We dared not look back.

"Hear them?" Andries asked.

"No." I looked over my shoulder. "They're coming," I said.

"Walk faster," Andries said. "If they come closer, run."

"Hey, *klipkop*!"

"Don't look back," Andries said.

"Hottentot!"

We walked as fast as we could.

"Bloody Kaffir!"

Ahead was a bend in the road. Behind the bend were bushes. Once there, we could run without them knowing it till it was too late.

"Faster," Andries said.

They began pelting us with stones.

"Run when we get to the bushes," Andries said.

The bend and the bushes were near. We would soon be there.

A clear young voice carried to us: "Your fathers are dirty black bastards of baboons!"

"Run!" Andries called.

A violent, unreasoning anger suddenly possessed me. I stopped and turned.

"You're a liar!" I screamed it.

The foremost boy pointed at me. "An ugly black baboon!"

In a fog of rage I went towards him.

"Liar!" I shouted. "My father was better than your father!"

I neared them. The bigger boy stepped between me and the one I was after.

"My father was better than your father! Liar!"

The big boy struck me a mighty clout on the side of the face. I staggered, righted myself, and leaped at the boy who had insulted my father. I struck him on the face, hard. A heavy blow on the back of my head nearly stunned me. I grabbed at the boy in front of me. We went down together.

"Liar!" I said through clenched teeth, hitting him with all my might.

Blows rained on me—on my head, my neck, the side of my face, my mouth—but my enemy was under me and I pounded him fiercely, all the time repeating:

"Liar! Liar! Liar!"

Suddenly stars exploded in my head. Then there was darkness.

I emerged from the darkness to find Andries kneeling beside me.

"God, man! I thought they'd killed you."

I sat up. The white boys were nowhere to be seen. Like Andries, they'd probably thought me dead and run off in panic. The inside of my mouth felt sore and swollen. My nose was tender to the touch. The back of my head ached. A trickle of blood dripped from my nose. I stemmed it with

the square of coloured cloth. The greatest damage was to my
shirt. It was ripped in many places. I remembered the
crackling. I looked anxiously about. It was safe, a little off
the road on the grass. I relaxed. I got up and brushed my
clothes. I picked up the crackling.

"God, you're dumb!" Andries said. "You're going to get
it! Dumb arse!"

I was too depressed to retort. Besides, I knew he was right.
I was dumb. I should have run when he told me to.

"Come on," I said.

One of many small groups of children, each child carrying
his little bag of crackling, we trod the long road home in the
cold winter afternoon.

There was tension in the house that night. When I got
back, Aunt Liza had listened to the story in silence. The
beating or scolding I expected did not come. But Aunt Liza
changed while she listened, became remote and withdrawn.
When Uncle Sam came home she told him what had happened. He, too, just looked at me and became more remote
and withdrawn than usual. They were waiting for something; their tension reached out to me, and I waited with
them, anxious, apprehensive.

The thing we waited for came while we were having our
supper. We heard a trap pull up outside.

"Here it is," Uncle Sam said, and got up.

Aunt Liza leaned back from the table and put her hands
in her lap, fingers intertwined, a cold, unseeing look in her
eyes.

Before Uncle Sam reached the door, it burst open. A tall,
broad, white man strode in. Behind him came the three
boys. The one I had attacked had swollen lips and a puffy
left eye.

"Evening, *baas*," Uncle Sam murmured.

"That's him," the bigger boy said, pointing at me.

The white man stared till I lowered my eyes.

"Well?" he said.

"He's sorry, *baas*," Uncle Sam said quickly. "I've given
him a hiding he won't forget soon. You know how it is,

baas. He's new here, the child of a relative in Johannesburg, and they don't all know how to behave there. You know how it is in the big towns, *baas.*" The plea in Uncle Sam's voice had grown more pronounced as he went on. He turned to me. "Tell the *baas* and young *basies* how sorry you are, Lee."

I looked at Aunt Liza and something in her lifelessness made me stubborn in spite of my fear.

"He insulted my father," I said.

The white man smiled.

"See, Sam, your hiding couldn't have been good."

There was a flicker of life in Aunt Liza's eyes. For a brief moment she saw me, looked at me, warmly, lovingly; then her eyes went dead again.

"He's only a child, *baas,*" Uncle Sam murmured.

"You stubborn too, Sam?"

"No, *baas.*"

"Good. Then teach him, Sam. If you and he are to live here, you must teach him. Well—?"

"Yes, *baas.*"

Uncle Sam went into the other room and returned with a thick leather thong. He wound it once round his hand and advanced on me. The man and the boys leaned against the door, watching. I looked at Aunt Liza's face. Though there was no sign of life or feeling on it, I knew suddenly, instinctively, that she wanted me not to cry.

Bitterly, Uncle Sam said: "You must never lift your hand to a white person. No matter what happens, you must never lift your hand to a white person. . . ."

He lifted the strap and brought it down on my back. I clenched my teeth and stared at Aunt Liza. I did not cry with the first three strokes. Then, suddenly, Aunt Liza went limp. Tears showed in her eyes. The thong came down on my back again and again. I screamed and begged for mercy. I grovelled at Uncle Sam's feet, begging him to stop, promising never to lift my hand to any white person. . . .

At last the white man's voice said: "All right, Sam."

Uncle Sam stopped. I lay whimpering on the floor. Aunt Liza sat like one in a trance.

"Is he still stubborn, Sam?"

"Tell the *baas* and *basies* you are sorry."

"I'm sorry," I said.

"Bet his father is one of those who believe in equality."

"His father is dead," Aunt Liza said.

"Good night, Sam."

"Good night, *baas*. Sorry about this."

"All right, Sam." He opened the door. The boys went out first, then he followed. "Good night, Liza."

Aunt Liza did not answer. The door shut behind the white folk, and soon we heard their trap moving away. Uncle Sam flung the thong viciously against the door, slumped down on the bench, folded his arms on the table, and buried his head on his arms. Aunt Liza moved away from him, sat down on the floor beside me, and lifted me into her large lap. She sat rocking my body. Uncle Sam began to sob softly. After some time he raised his head and looked at us.

"Explain to the child, Liza," he said.

"You explain," Aunt Liza said bitterly. "You are the man. You did the beating. You are the head of the family. This is a man's world. You do the explaining."

"Please Liza."

"You should be happy. The whites are satisfied. We can go on now."

With me in her arms, Aunt Liza got up. She carried me into the other room. The food on the table remained half-eaten. She laid me on the bed on my stomach, smeared fat on my back, then covered me with the blankets. She undressed and got into bed beside me. She cuddled me close, warmed me with her own body. With her big hand on my cheek, she rocked me, first to silence, then to sleep.

For the only time during my stay there, I slept on a bed in Elsburg.

When I woke next morning, Uncle Sam had gone. Aunt Liza only once referred to the beating he had given me. It was in the late afternoon, when I returned with the day's cow dung.

"It hurt him," she said. "You'll understand one day."

That night Uncle Sam brought me an orange, a bag of boiled sweets, and a dirty old picture book. He smiled as he gave them to me, rather anxiously. When I smiled back at him, he seemed to relax. He put his hand on my head, started to say something, then changed his mind and took his seat by the fire.

Aunt Liza looked up from the floor, where she dished out the food.

"It's all right, old man," she murmured.

"One day . . ." Uncle Sam said.

"It's all right," Aunt Liza repeated insistently.

10

FROM

Tell Freedom

by Peter Abrahams

(1919–   )

In the long summer afternoons after his work was completed,
Peter Abrahams often played with Joseph, a young black.
From him he learned that black and coloureds are different;
in South Africa whites, Indians, Chinese, mulattoes, and
blacks all have different legal, economic and social status.

Aunt Liza.
Yes?
What am I?
What are you talking about?
I met a boy at the river.
He said he was Zulu.
    She laughed.
You are Colored.
There are three kinds of people:
White people, Colored people,
and Black people.
The White people come first,
then the Colored people,
then the Black people.
Why?
Because it is so.

Next day when I met Joseph,
I smacked my chest and said:
    Me, Colored!
He clapped his hands and laughed.
Joseph and I spent most
of the long summer afternoons together.
He learnt some Afrikaans from me.
I learnt some Zulu from him.
Our days were full.
There was the river to explore.
There were my swimming lessons.
I learnt to fight with sticks;
to weave a green hat
of young willow wands and leaves;
to catch frogs and tadpoles
with my hands;
to set a trap for the *springhaas*;
to make the sounds of the river birds.
There was the hot sun to comfort us.
There was the green grass to dry our bodies.
There was the soft clay with which to build.
There was the fine sand with which to fight.
There were our giant grasshoppers to race.
There were the locust swarms
when the skies turned black
and we caught them by the hundreds.
There was the rare taste of crisp,
brown-baked, salted locusts.
There was the voice of the wind in the willows.
There was the voice of the heavens
In the thunder storms.
There were the voices of two children
in laughter, ours.
There were Joseph's tales of black kings
who lived in days before the white man.
At home, I said:
Aunt Liza.
Yes?

Did we have Colored kings before the white man?
No.
Then where did we come from?
Joseph and his mother come from the
black kings who were before the white man.

Laughing and ruffling my head, she said:
You talk too much. Go'n wash up.

11

FROM

Down Second Avenue

by Ezekiel Mphahlele

(1919–   )

In the following selection Ezekiel Mphahlele, a Black South African, describes the psychological hardships he and his family were forced to bear as residents of Pretoria's black ghetto. He contrasts his first thirteen years in his village with the psychologically debilitating life of the slums. The villagers had to bear physical hardships; the urban blacks had to face not only poverty but the strains of life in a multiracial urban setting.

For high school Mphahlele was sent to St. Peter's School in Johannesburg and went to Adams College, Natal and the University of South Africa, Johannesburg for his undergraduate and graduate education. Even with an M.A. however, Mphahlele discovered that a black has few employment opportunities in South Africa. He was barred from teaching because of his opposition to the government's educational policies, and in 1951 he emigrated to Nigeria. He became a professor at Ibadan University and headed the African Department of the Congress for Cultural Freedom in Paris. At present he is director of Chemchemi, a workshop of the arts in Nairobi. His publications include Down Second Avenue,

The African Image, In Corner B *and* The Living and the
Dead.

LOOKING back to those first thirteen years of my life—as
much of it as I can remember—I cannot help thinking that
it was time wasted. I had nobody to shape them into a
definite pattern. Searching through the confused threads of
that pattern a few things keep imposing themselves on my
whole judgement. My grandmother; the mountain; the
tropical darkness which glow-worms seemed to try in vain to
scatter; long black tropical snakes; the brutal Leshoana river
carrying on its broad back trees, cattle, boulders; world of
torrential rains; the solid shimmering heat beating down on
yearning earth; the romantic picture of a woman with a child
on her back and an earthen pot on her head, silhouetted
against the mirage.

But all in all perhaps I led a life shared by all other
country boys. Boys who are aware of only one purpose of
living; to be. Often the crops failed us. Mother sent us a few
tins of jam and we ate that with corn-meal porridge. Sometimes she sent us sugar which we ate with porridge. Other
times we ate roasted flying ants or hairy tree worms or wild
spinach with porridge. I can never forget how delicious a
dish we had by making porridge out of pumpkin and corn
meal. The only time we tasted tea and bread was when our
mother came to see us at Christmas. On such occasions many
other people in the village came to our home to taste these
rare things. If hunting was bad we didn't have meat. About
the only time we had goat's meat or beef was when livestock
died. A man might have a herd of fifty or more goats, as we
had, and not slaughter one in six months. I can never forget
the stinking carcasses we feasted on. Often we just ate practically dry boiled corn.

Killing other people's livestock out in the veld was common practice among boys. Many times we caught stray pigs.
Then we pushed rags into the mouth to muffle the alarm that
only a pig can give. We had delectable rashers. My brother

had the habit of catching stray chicks, cutting off their heads and legs, putting them in an old rag and coming home to tell us that he had knocked down birds with a catapult. That catapult was nearly the death of him because grandmother would have strangled him with it if Sarah hadn't saved him.

If we milked a goat in the veld or a goat kicked over a pail of milk grandmother found out that the evening's supply was short. Knowing that a beating was sure to follow, I poured out some milk into a second pail, pissed into it so that it soured and thickened. I then invented the story that two or three goats had been too long in milk and that their kids had grown up.

But we were not the only mischief-makers. A number of *hopane*—dry land alligators—could whip their tails round a goat's legs and suck the last drop of milk.

And there was a man in the village who raided kraals in the early hours of the morning to milk cattle and goats. Villagers had tired of taking him to the chief's council. They merely shook their heads and clicked their tongues in leave-him-to-heaven fashion. Matters came to a head when one or two men discovered that he was not only milking the goats but was riding them for his sexual pleasure. The village outlawed him.

'Go away,' Old Modise said to him. 'Go out of this village to a far-off land that side of Mohlaletse river. Maybe when you've shaken off the dust of this village you'll lead a new life. We will not report the matter to the chief. He's not a Christian, but he'll be very angry. You've done a thing that would make a heathen vomit.'

If my grandmother heard any one of us but mention the name of the banished man she flung the nearest object at him.

'You heathen!' she cursed.

My uncle was a big, tall, bony man of about twenty-three at the time. Although he had moments of kindness and pity, he could be just as ruthless as his mother and his elder sister, Bereta. He enjoyed seeing me panic on the back of a bucking donkey as a learner. He laughed heartily when a donkey deliberately entered a mimosa bush in order to unseat me. He loved to send me to drive baboons out of a mealie-land for the fun of seeing them rain mealie cobs on me.

'If you meet a female baboon on the road,' he used to say, 'and you both stand still to look at each other, it'll tell you to get out of its way.'

'And then?' I'd gasp.

'And then, my frightened boy, you'll fall ill as you've never done before, thin down to a ghost and the last thing you'll see, my frightened little boy, will be a female baboon saying, Get out of my way. That'll be when you die if I'm your uncle and you're my nephew.'

It scared the breath out of me. His broad mouth and laughing eyes told me he would never come to my rescue.

Yet another thing that stamped the nightmare of those years in Pietersburg was vermin. Bugs and lice. My grandmother had very clean habits, like the rest of the villagers who boasted that they were Christians. 'Dirty as a heathen' was a popular phrase. But no one ever thought he could do anything about bugs. Big, flat, grey bugs with miniature contour lines on their backs. They fell from the grass thatching at night for their raid. You heard them fall on the mud floor with a thud. You tossed and turned and scratched your naked body and heard the other sleepers on the floor scratch themselves, as if they were scratching pots, and groan and mumble. If you tried to catch the bug it dropped off at a mere touch. We sprinkled water on the mud floor before spreading our grass mats and other bedding, but it didn't help. In summer we slept out in the yard, which was enclosed by mud walls and had a smooth mud floor. But we couldn't do this too often because snakes were many. In winter the bugs disappeared and in summer they came back with a vengeance. It never occurred to anyone that there might be a vermin killer.

We had one set of clothing put aside for Sundays. On week days we put on our rags and other clothing which were all patches. Mother was a very good dressmaker. She often asked us if we were given the clothing she had made and sent for us. She never knew what happened to it. Many years later mother told us that she found out the clothes had been preserved in a box; because grandmother thought she was indulging us and she, grandmother, wanted us to be tough. When mother did discover this, we had already outgrown the clothes. They were given away. I was compelled to put on rags for a stretch of many weeks until they became a nest of lice. I'd sit out in the veld scraping off the eggs and crushing lice between the nails of my fingers. I gave up trying to wash the rags in river water. Yet I don't remember ever falling ill except for occasional stomach upsets caused by eating prickly pears excessively. The only remedy for a constipated stomach after a feast on pears was a sharpened stick pushed in through the anus and turned round and round. Castor oil and other laxatives were practically unknown for loosening the bowels.

When I was about twelve I noticed something that had already begun to take shape in that part of north-eastern Transvaal that fell under the rule of Chief Mphahlele. The young able-bodied men were leaving the villages to seek work in answer to the call of the city. Vaguely I understood that Pretoria was the Mecca. At Christmas-time they came back in dashing clothes: trousers with wide sweeping pipes, shoes with sharp-pointed front; hats with small brims; jackets with fish-tails, trying painfully but in vain to stretch beyond the hips in length; striped ties; belts with iron knobs and spikes worked into the leather; colourful handkerchiefs dangling boldly out of the trouser pocket. They told us about the glamour of the city life, the money (£3 a month) and the electric lights and trams and motor cars we had never seen before and had no hope of ever seeing until we were big enough to go to Pretoria. They brought gramophones which they said they had played all the way in the train. They said the things we saw in Goldstein's general store were for chickens and not eagles compared with those that glittered in Pretoria shop windows. For a long long time they made us believe that there were very small people singing inside the gramophone. They probably believed it themselves. At Christmas-time Jeemee Roe-Jars (Jimmy Rodgers), then in fashion, yodelled plaintively from various parts of the village.

And there was a less glamorous side to all this. Wherever you went—in the fields, at village festivals, at church and every other place where people congregated—you found mostly middle-aged women, old women and old men. The land was not giving out much. The Black man could work only the strip given him by the chief. The chief had no more to give out. The old men at the fire-place complained endlessly that most of their lands had been taken away by the white man. Old Modise pulled mucus through the nostrils and spat out of the mouth as if to clinch the matter: 'Our sons will go out to the city and the chief can't stop them. The cow is too old and it cannot give milk any more. Are we going to beat it for it?' And the old men looked helpless, shaking their heads like that in the glow of the fire.

The non-Christians didn't seem to like change. Their lands turned into patches of sand, but their young men kept on. 'That's the trouble with these Christians,' they said. 'All they can do is go to church and sing and run to the white man to work for him and they've not the brains of a hippo to stay where their ancestors lived and planted them.'

To Christians and non-Christians alike, what the chief couldn't do was impossible. The non-Christians praised him for allowing them to keep to their way of life and the Christians praised him for having built a big school and allowing them to have churches even although he wasn't a Christian.

I never dreamt that I should go back to the city, which I couldn't picture in my mind anyhow. We thrilled at the idea of riding a train, my brother, sister and I, when our mother came in the middle of the year to tell us that she had come to fetch us. Three things stick out in my mind about those few days. The few days when whatever hand it was that drove the train of my life across the trackless wilds suddenly decided to take a capricious turn. First, my grandmother cried. I had only seen her cry at revival services in the Methodist church house. I knew my mother couldn't just come in the middle of the year like that to move a hard-hearted mother-in-law to tears with a kind of domestic joke. Secondly, mother shook off our lousy rags and scrubbed us clean and wrapped us up in brand-new clothes. That couldn't be a joke either. I overheard her say to grandmother: 'I can't change my mind, any more than I can change your son. They're my children and I'm taking them away.' Thirdly, those bright lights we found on Pietersburg station after travelling many miles of dusty road. I heard Jimmy Rodgers yodel. The train arrived. I was too dazed to be happy. Too frightened to ask questions. We found ourselves at Pretoria station the next day. In the midst of a winter's morning we were whisked away by a taxi-cab to Marabastad, a Black location.

That is how a country bumpkin dived into slum life. The springboard was Second Avenue, where my maternal grandmother lived with Aunt Dora and three uncles, all younger than my mother. The eldest uncle was a policeman at Witbank.

After a few days my brother, sister and I went to live with our mother and father at Fifth Avenue. We occupied one room they had hired.

It didn't take long for us to notice that it wasn't all right between our father and mother. They were always quarrelling; especially at week-ends, beginning on Friday evenings. We soon discovered that the main subject of the wrangling was money. Father was not bringing money home. We came to know that was why our mother fetched us from the north. I was thirteen then, my brother three years younger and my sister five years younger.

Mother did dressmaking for an African tailor just outside town. In the evenings she brewed beer out of corn malt to sell. The family's budget was all on her shoulders. She was hard-working and tough. She never complained about hard work. Father walked with a limp as one leg was shorter than the other. It had been broken by a wagon wheel in his teens. But he could cycle fast and he used to bicycle to work. Town was only two and a half miles away. He drank like a sponge, especially home-brewed beer which he had the tendency of commandeering and entertaining his friends with. My mother got very angry but couldn't do anything about it. No pleading could move my father. When he wanted *skokiaan* —brewed with yeast and water—he went to Cape Location, where Coloured people lived, just the other side of the Asiatic Reserve next to us. *Skokiaan* being much stronger than malt beer, my father often said threateningly to my mother: 'I'll go drink skokiaan for you.' But then he was so violent by nature that he didn't really need something to light a fire under him.

We'd never really known Father before. And now living close to him and seeing him at close quarters, I realized that his face was unlikeable. Like his mother, he couldn't laugh heartily. His facial skin clung too close on to the bones. There was something brutal and razor-like about the corners of his mouth; as there was about his limp and the back of his head. He was seldom in a mood to play with us. We kept close to our mother most of the time.

'How long do you want this thing to go on, Moses?'

'What, Eva?'

'Don't pretend you don't know I need money for food. At least you could worry about your children's clothes. Just look at you, drunk as always. What are you standing up for?'

'You don't want to sell me your beer, so?'

'It's there for you if you must drink. But while you're at it, you might think about the bellies of others that want filling.'

My father looked vicious.

'Don't talk to me like that, damn you!' he bellowed. My mother kept quiet. Every gesture of his was menacing, down to the limp. We got used to these quarrels. But we had a sixth companion in the room. Fear.

'I don't want that man here again, hear?' my father said one evening.

'He's your friend and you know he comes to drink.' She told us to go outside as she often did when she saw signs of a storm.

'Don't talk to me like that! Didn't your mother teach you never to answer back to your husband and lord?' we heard him say, through the window.

'You started, Moses.' We looked through the window.

A crashing clap sent my mother down on her knees.

'I'll kill you, I tell you!' He was going to kick her when out of nowhere a hand held him by the scruff of the neck. It was the man from the next room. My father's eyes flickered in the glow of the candle-light. Mother got up and stood in the corner. We went through a restless slumber that night.

'Why does Father do this to you always, Mother?' I ventured to ask one day.

'I don't know, son,' she replied rather curtly.

'I wish Sello's father was my father too.'

'Why?'

'He plays morabaraba with his boys. Father'd never do that.'

'You don't know what you're talking, Eseki. Besides grumbling never takes you anywhere.'

'I'm not grumbling.'

The matter ended. Mother was good at that kind of thing. Probably every trickle of a thought was pain, but grumble she wouldn't.

The tailor for whom she worked went bankrupt. She couldn't get another dressmaking job. Factories were very few and these didn't take in Black labour. So mother started to do white people's washing. She did some sewing at home for people in the location. She made all our clothes—skirts, trousers, jackets, and my sister's frocks and aprons. And I never saw a louse on me again, and she never left my father to go anywhere in dirty clothes.

He, on the other hand, continued to bully, grouse, roar and fume. Mother did a brisk business in selling home-brewed beer. He drank elsewhere and came to her to ask or demand money.

'Don't grumble, Eva!' he'd say when she ventured a comment.

'I'm not going to give you my money if you play the fool with yours, that's what.'

'Let's see if you won't, bitch.'

'You don't need such talk in front of the children.'

'They're mine, anyway.'

'They're mine. What do you do for them?' Her eyes sparkled and I knew from that day that she was going to fight like a tigress to defend her cubs. And from that day I found myself taking sides. I hated my father; his other children no less. Whenever he was in the house we preferred to play outside.

'Eseki, Girlie, Solomon!' We went reluctantly into the room. It was a drunken call. He gathered us in his arms before him.

'I—I—hic—brought you sweets, see? From town—hic.'

My mother was certainly suppressing a laugh.

'See!' He took out a brown packet that smelled of tobacco.

'You give the—hic—others, Eseki, as—hic—the oldest, see!'

This time my mother laughed aloud, as only she could when she was tickled, her big strong arms and shoulders shaking with mirth. She went off into a peal again when my father said, 'Remember, you're my heir, Eseki, and don't let anybody cheat you out of it, see!' His breath smelled of strong beer as he rubbed his rough cheek against mine.

By degrees I drew out of mother the reason why she had fetched us from Maupaneng. He was refusing to maintain us; she had reported him to the Native Commissioner; he advised her to fetch the children—maybe if he lived with us we'd be a constant reminder to him; then she was to report regularly to the Commissioner.

'And those goats and donkeys, I bought them,' my mother said. 'He would hear none of it when his mother wrote to him about donkeys she needed for the plough. But don't think any more about it, my son. You're still young and such things are still heavy for your small shoulders.'

Sunday morning. The day when we lounged in the blankets and silently boycotted the early rising custom. The primus stove was purring softly with a steaming pot on. There was an enticing smell of meat, potatoes and curry.

I was thinking of the years at Maupaneng, Pietersburg. The big dark mountains; the fields; my playmates; Old Modise and Old Segone. I could see through the window that it was cloudy outside; and I hated clouds, as I still do today; had always hated them, because they made my soul gloomier than it was, there at Maupaneng and here in Pretoria. In the country it spelt heavy rains. And goats are impossible creatures to manage when it rains. The goats panicked and dashed about madly as if a huge flea had come among them. The donkeys simply would not move in the rain. How often I cried aloud chasing the goats. If I caught one I belaboured the creature with a stick so that it yelled to the heavens for help. I was sure it must understand why I was angry. Afterwards I'd stroke it and mumble how sorry I was. I learned that there is no domestic animal as proud as a goat, as disdainful; it seems never to have heard about flattering the vanity of the human heart.

Running footsteps. I was startled out of my reverie, and so was my brother. My sister followed close behind her, and she tripped over a strip of wood on the threshold and fell—my mother. When he thundered in we knew he had been chasing after my mother. She kept on her knees, clearly hurt.

'I'll show you who I am!' my father said.

'What is it with you, Moses? What are you standing up to do?'

'Get up!'

'I can't—I can't—my knee!'

'This is the day you're going to do what I tell you!' He limped over to the pot on the stove. In no time it was done. My mother screamed with a voice I have never forgotten till this day. Hot gravy and meat and potatoes had got into her blouse and she was trying to shake them down.

He caught hold of her by the blouse and landed the pot in the middle of her skull with a heavy gong sound. She struggled loose from his grip and fled through the door, crying.

Only then did I have the wits to go and ask for help. I came back with Aunt Dora. An ambulance had already been and carried my mother to hospital. The police came and arrested him. We packed our things and went to live with grandmother in Second Avenue.

A few weeks later my mother came out of hospital, bandaged up thickly, to appear in court against my father. I also went to court.

My mother recounted the events of the Sunday morning and all the other things she had against my father before and after. The magistrate sentenced him to fourteen days' imprisonment with the option of a fine of—I forget how much. I remember that he paid it. That was the last time I ever saw my father, that summer of 1932. The strong smell of burning paraffin gas from a stove often reminds me of that Sunday.

12

"Ibrahimo"

as told by Colin Turnbull

The almost universal problem for a child in colonial Africa was trying to reconcile the long-accepted and personally deep-seated traditions of his rich tribal heritage with the power of Western education and technology. Some Africans tried to ignore their past and grow up as black French and Englishmen, while others totally resisted any innovations from the West. Most African children, however, were forced to live simultaneously in the two worlds and to reconcile them as best they could. Often they were unable to live in either world. As the British anthropologist Colin Turnbull wrote:

There is a void in the life of the African, a spiritual emptiness, divorced as he is from each world, standing in between, torn in both directions. To go forward is to abandon the past in which the roots of his being have their nourishment; to go backward is to cut himself off from the future, for there is no doubt about where the future lies. The African has been taught to abandon his old ways, yet he is not accepted in the new world even when he has mastered its ways. There seems to be no bridge, and this is the source of his terrible loneliness.

"Ibrahimo" is the biography of such an African. He is a Central African boy who grew up in the Democratic Republic of the Congo when it was still under Belgian rule.

I DO NOT think my father was a Christian when he married my mother; I know they married in the way of our own

people anyway. But he became a Christian before I entered
my mother's stomach, and took the name Isaaka. So when
I was born and had shown that I had come to this world to
stay he called me Ibrahimo, because it is our custom to name
our children after their grandfathers. I do not know what my
grandfather's name really was, my father never speaks of him.

By becoming a Christian my father won a good job as a
cook at the Mission. He had to leave because my mother refused to change her ways, and the Mission would not have
her there living with him, because they said they were not
married. So they returned to Ndola and I was born here and
have lived here ever since. There are other Christians at
Ndola, but my father has told me that the Mission does not
want us to have anything to do with them, they do not believe in the same God. Their leader uses his *baraza* [open
porch or veranda] as a church, and has services every Sunday,
but we never go, it would be a sin. My father did not like me
to play with their children, so at Ndola I have no Christian
friends. But I used to have plenty of other friends, and my
mother was always very good to us and gave us plenty of
good things to eat when we were hungry.

As I grew older my father said I should not play even with
my own brothers, and that I should go away to school, to the
Mission on the far side of Matadi. My mother did not like
this, and there was much fighting and beating. In the end,
my mother left my father, and while she was away I was
taken to school.

It was a good place, though all the buildings were made of
brick and were hot, unlike the houses we build. And we were
not allowed to light fires inside at night, to keep us safe and
to keep the mosquitoes away. Even if we could have lit them
it would not have done much good as every wall was broken
open with windows, and the smoke would all have escaped.
But we learned many things, how to read and write and how
to play the strange games of the white man with leather
balls. This hurt my feet terribly at first, for we were not
allowed to wear shoes, although nearly all of us had them.
They said it would spoil the shoes.

I heard that when Bwana Lewis was there the houses were

like ours, made of mud and thatched with leaves, and that there were some trees left to give shade, but as soon as he left Bwana Spence cut down all the trees and built the brick houses. But he also made a big kitchen and fed all the people who worked for him, and all the children at the school. That is why so many come here. Only a few bring their own food because they do not trust food cooked by strangers. They are not real Christians.

But it was difficult to know how to be a Christian, because Bwana Spence[1] did not like to be asked questions. He read to us from the Big Book and often it did not make sense. When I was still new there I would ask questions, and sometimes he would answer them, but usually he said I did not have to understand, I just had to believe what he said. He got very angry if we asked about all the men in the Big Book who had so many wives, when he taught us that when we were older we should have only one. He said that Bwana Yesu said so. But neither Bwana Yesu nor any of his brothers had any wives, so how could they know?

He also did not like us to talk to the girls. We were taught separately, and we lived in separate buildings—those of us who came from far away. Now, it is obviously a bad thing for a boy not to know a girl, and we used to visit each other's houses. Amboko told us it was all right because really they were just like our bachelor houses, it was simply that Bwana Spence had not married until late and did not understand these things. When Bwana Spence had first come to our land he was already a man, but had no wife, and this was not good. He used to look at the women, Amboko said, but never knew them. If they spoke to him he was afraid and ran away. So we understood that there must have been something wrong with Bwana Spence when he was a boy and he did not learn how one should behave. This was one of the things he would never explain to us, merely telling us to do as he said. So we only met the girls at night, when he could not see us and would not be offended.

1 Usually missionaries in a colony were the same nationality as the colonial overlords, but as evidenced in this selection there were exceptions.

But there were some things that could not be just because
Bwana Spence did not understand. In his teachings he told
us to be like brothers to each other, to share everything we
had and to help each other. But while there were many of
us in one house, sleeping in the same room even though we
were from different tribes, he had a house all to himself. He
ate three big meals a day while we had two, and his food was
much better and much more plentiful. He bought all manner of things at Matadi to eat himself, and we never tasted
any of it. He had lots of clothes, and he had many servants
to wait on him and do all his work for him. He never asked
us into his house, although he would come to ours. In the
evenings even if his wife was at the hospital and he was alone
he would not talk to any of us, but just stayed by himself,
eating, and drinking his tea or coffee. He was never without
food, day or night. He must have been very wealthy.

He had a child too, a girl child who had not yet seen the
blood, but he would not let her play with any of us or even
talk to us. There were some other white children at the Mission but they all lived in the white man's houses, and were
taught separately and ate separately and played separately. It
was a pity. They could have had a lot of happiness with us.

Bwana Spence's wife was a proud woman who did not
smile. She gave orders, even to men, and got very angry when
anyone disobeyed her. She taught the white children, and she
worked at the hospital. She always looked as though she was
going to be sick, although when I asked her once if she was
not well she said she was perfectly all right. She lied. She was
not all right. A relative of mine came to the hospital while
I was there because her stomach was full and hurting, but
the child would not come. She had been bound with vines
and had tried everything she knew to make the child come,
but it refused. When Bwana Spence's wife saw her she told
her that the child had not wanted to come because it had
been put into the stomach in sin. It could still be saved, she
said, if my relative would become a Christian and have a
Christian marriage. But my relative was already married,
and said she could not be married again. I think that Bwana
Spence's wife put a curse on her, because the first part of the

child to come out was a hand, and the rest of it was dead.
They say that this was one time when Bwana Spence's wife
smiled.

We were allowed to go home during holidays, but I
liked it at the school because I had many friends there, and
at Ndola the people thought of me as being different, like
my father, and they laughed at me. But the longer I stayed
at the Mission the more I was worried. They were doing very
good things for us, but they did not seem to like us or want
us to be their friends. They were very selfish about their God
too, and although they used to ask Him, when we all talked
to Him together, to look after us and save our souls and
accept us as His children, they never let *us* stand up and ask
for things. They would ask for new motor cars or for money
to make roads so that they could travel farther and meet
more of our people and make them Christians, but they
never let *us* ask for motor cars.

And once when Bwana Spence's girl child was hot with
fever he made us all ask together for her to be made better,
though none of us had even spoken to her. We thought this
funny, because she had been hot with fever before, as we all
were at times, and it was nothing serious. But we asked for
her to be made better, and two days later she was. But that
same week a man was brought in who was very ill indeed,
and Bwana Spence did not even go to see him, and did not
ask God to help him, because, he said, the man was not a
Christian. We all thought this was a terrible thing, and we
wondered and talked among ourselves about what kind of
God this was. We knew we could not ask Bwana Spence, so
we asked Amboko. Amboko was almost as cross with us as
Bwana Spence would have been, for the man was his relation. I think he was cross because he could not explain it
either. I began to wonder if I would be allowed to ask God
to help my mother if she became ill, because she is not a
Christian. Amboko said no, I should have to ask the ancestors, that they would always listen.

I had been at the school perhaps two years when something very bad happened. I was home on vacation and one
day Matungi came up to me and took me into the plantation

to talk with me. This was a great honor, for Matungi is really our chief, and he is a great and good man. I think I knew what he wanted, though, and I was afraid. It had been three years since the last *nkumbi* initiation festival, and it was time for another. At this festival we boys are taken and we are made into men. It is a very difficult and dangerous thing, and I do not know much about it except that our foreskins are taken away from us to make us clean, and we are given the marks on our bodies that make us acceptable to the ancestors. These festivals used to last many months, even a year, but now the Bwana Mkubwa at Matadi does not like it because he says it takes us all away from our work, and the white Christians all say it is evil. They do not know, because they do not understand and are as ignorant about it as little children.

Matungi told me that it was time for me to enter the *nkumbi,* and to learn the ways of my ancestors. He said that he did not mind me learning to read and write, or even being a Christian, but that it was very wrong for me to forget who I was. He said that only by seeing the *nkumbi* could I make myself fit for the ancestors; by becoming like them I could become one of them. This was plainly a good thing, and Matungi further showed me that no matter what the Christians said, nobody could deny that I had a father, and he had a father, and his father before him had a father. Nobody could deny that we did have ancestors, and if we had ancestors how could it be right to neglect and disrespect them when they made life possible for us? I told Matungi that even the Christian teachings said the same thing, and told us that we were to honor our fathers and mothers.

Matungi was very wise, and I told him that although I was frightened, I *did* want to see the *nkumbi.* He was very pleased, and he gave me a cigarette and told me that I would soon be a real man, and that I would be glad. He also told me not to be frightened, that only children were frightened.

I ran straight back through the plantation to the village and told my brothers. They were all very surprised, and they congratulated me and said they were happy, because they had been afraid that I would be separated from them and

not become a man with them. Now we would all do this
dangerous thing together and become men together, and we
would all learn the wonderful secrets about our ancestors,
and learn how to please them and earn a place beside them
in the afterworld. We celebrated by running after some girls
and chasing them into the plantation and playing with them.
It was the first time I had really ever played with my brothers.
I was very happy, and very proud. When we had finished
playing I went to my mother's plantation and told her. I
thought she would be pleased, although I expected her to
wail because women always wail at this time, for they are
losing their children. They would not have it otherwise,
though, because they too are proud and want their boys
to be men. My mother did not wail. She looked frightened and put her arms around me as though I were a
suckling infant still drinking her milk. She held me close
to her breasts so that I could feel their warmth flowing
into me. She told me that my father might not like it,
and that I had better sleep that night with my brothers,
and come to her the next morning. She asked me if I knew
that I was a Christian, and that Christians do not see the
nkumbi. But I told her that my father had seen it, so surely
he would want me to. After all, even white Christians must
have ancestors. She said it was a big matter, and she would
have to talk to my father, and she would get Matungi to talk
to him. She said that she hoped I would never forget my
ancestors, and she pushed me away. When I left, I think she
was crying.

But I was sure my father would want me to do as he had
done, because we had the same grandfather and nearly all
the men of our village were of the same family. I spent the
night with my brothers and told them all about the strange
ways of the white man at the Mission School, how some
things were good and others bad. They laughed when I told
them about the way they tried to keep the boys away from
the girls, and how we tricked them because we knew better.
They said we had done right. . . .

Late that night there was a big noise in the village, and I
was frightened again. But I hid it, and said nothing. I was

sorry, because I had wanted it to be a good night—it was the
first time I had ever slept with my brothers. I dreamed of all
the wonderful times to come, and of all the friends I would
have from now on. Early in the morning I hurried out to
my mother's plantation, but she was not there. I went home,
and she was not there, neither was my father. This was not
strange, as everyone goes about his work in the morning, so
I went back to the plantation to wait for my mother. She did
not come.

At last, when my stomach was crying for food, my father
came, calling my name. I ran up to him and waited for him
to speak, but he hit me on the back with his fist and said
I had done a terrible thing. He had worked hard to send me
to the Mission School, and he had sent me a little money
each month so that I could buy things I needed, and now I
wanted to throw it all away by seeing the *nkumbi*. He took
me back to the house and locked me in, throwing me a little
food that had been left over from the morning. It was cold
and I could not eat it. I called for my mother, but she did
not answer. I didn't know how many days I was kept there; I
only remember thinking that I must truly still be a child
because I cried so much, but I could not help it.

What followed is so bad that I try to forget it, and I do
not like to talk about it. One morning the Bwana Spence's
motor car came and I was put into it and driven away. I still
had not seen my mother, and although I saw Matungi and
called to him from the window he just turned away. If I
had been a man I would have jumped out, but I could not.
I was sick. I was still being sick when we reached the Mission,
and I no longer had the strength to lean out of the window.
I was sick all over the back of the car. When Bwana Spence
saw this he was more angry than I had ever seen him. He had
me taken away to the hospital, to cure my sickness.

He came to see me later, and I told him that I wanted to
see the *nkumbi* just as my father had seen it, that only in
that way could I be a man. I told him all that Matungi had
said, and he replied that Matungi was evil, and when he died
would go to the fires that never go out. I told him about my
brothers, and how they were all glad that I was joining them,

and how it was the first time I had really played with them. Bwana Spence asked me if I did not have enough friends at the Mission, and I said yes, but they were not my brothers— I wanted to be friends with *them,* and to see the *nkumbi* with them and to share their blood, so that we could all live together as men-brothers, and go to the ancestors together. He told me that there was only one ancestor, and that was Bwana Yesu. I said that could not be, because Bwana Yesu was not married and did not have any children. I also told him that I thought Bwana Yesu was a lie invented to make us go to the white man's afterworld and be his servants there. I do not know what made me say this thing, because I *did* believe in Bwana Yesu; but I said it, and Bwana Spence said that I was also evil, but that it was Matungi's fault and not mine. He said he would ask Bwana Yesu to forgive me, and that he would not let me go home again for any more holidays, I could stay at the Mission and help keep the place clean. He stood at the end of my bed and asked Bwana Yesu to forgive me and to make me a good Christian again, then he left. As soon as he left I asked Bwana Yesu to forgive me and to let me see the *nkumbi,* but I knew in my heart that he would listen to Bwana Spence and not me.

The next day I was no longer sick, but they still would not let me out of the hospital. They said I was not there because I had been sick but for another reason, and I did not understand what they meant. They came in and took hold of me and made me walk into a special house they have where they bring people who are dying, and cut them open. I was very frightened and tried to break away, because I knew I was not dying and they had told me I was not even sick. I thought that Bwana Spence was so angry at me for making his car dirty that he was going to kill me. He was there, in the house, and he smiled at me and said not to be frightened, that he had asked Bwana Yesu to stay with me, and that Bwana Yesu had told him how I wanted to be a man like other men, and had made him understand that this was right. At first I thought he meant that I was going to be allowed to return home to the *nkumbi,* but he said no, and told me to lie on the table. Only then did I begin to under-

stand. I fought as hard as I could, but I could not get away.
I remember Bwana Spence leaning on my arms, holding me
down, and smiling. But there was no love in his smile, only
hate. Then someone put something over my face. It smelled
of vomit and I thought I was being sick again. I felt all my
life being taken away from me, and I was sure I was dying.
The last thing I remember is Bwana Spence smiling. And
then I died.

When I woke up I had no feeling. I knew there was a terrible pain in my body, but my mind was empty, and I just
did not care about the pain. All I wanted was to *feel* again,
to feel as though I was alive. But I could not. I saw the wife
of Bwana Spence standing over me, but when she saw I recognized her she turned away. I saw other people, but they
did not mean anything to me. I heard noises, but I just
wanted them to stop because they were empty noises. And
then I knew I was dead. I knew it because the pain got worse,
and as it got worse it no longer came from my whole body,
it came from one place, the place where they had cut me with
their knives. I could not see the cut, I could not see the
blood, because I was covered with a sheet and I had no
strength to move my hands to find what they had done. But
I knew, because the pain came from my penis, where they
had cut off my skin so that I would never be able to see the
nkumbi, and would never be able to be a man. I remember
crying out loud—not because of the pain, but because of
what they had done to me, and I was sick again.

When my body got better I found that Bwana Spence had
gone back to where he had been living for some time with
his wife, near Ndola. This was a good thing, because there
was much hate in my heart for what he had done, and I knew
now that he hated me. Amboko was with him too, so I was
alone, and I was too ashamed to talk of this thing with the
other children. After a while I could not stand it, and I
escaped and walked all the way home. I arrived at night so
that I would not be seen, and went to my father's house.
Nobody was there, so I went in and lay down and went to
sleep.

Later that night I woke up and saw my father sitting on a

chair in the doorway. He knew I was there because when I called to him he was not surprised. I asked him where my mother was, and he said she had left him and gone away. Then I saw that there was someone else in the room, and I knew that my father had taken another wife. I asked him how he could do this when it was against the teachings of Bwana Yesu, the same teachings that had made him stop me from seeing the *nkumbi*. He was silent for a while, then he told me he did not know what he was doing, and he asked me to question him no further. He said there were many things we would have to talk about, and that he was glad I had come home. He knew what had happened to me, and he told me that in his eyes, anyway, I was a man. This made me happy, and I slept well.

Those were difficult days for me, because my brothers made fun of me for not having joined them. They asked me why I walked awkwardly, as if I had been cut, and they laughed. I told them that I had been with a girl and had caught the white man's disease, which had made my penis swell, but they did not believe me. I think they were sorry for me because although they made fun of me, they were kind, but I knew that we could never really be friends now, and never share our blood. One of them told me that after I had been locked up in my father's house my mother had left and gone away to her own village because of the great evil her husband had done, and that shortly afterwards my father had been bewitched by this other woman into taking her as a wife. He had given many goats and much wealth, more than he had given when he married my mother. But although she had bewitched him, I was told, she was a good woman, it had not been her fault. I did not understand them. I was also told that Amboko had had a big fight with Bwana Spence, and that Bwana Spence was going back to Matadi in a great rage. I did not understand that either, because Amboko had been a good friend to the Bwana Spence always, and had suffered much ridicule as a result.

But a few days later my father called me to drink beer with him. I was proud, although we were alone and there were no other men with us, because we sat out in front of

our house, like men, for all the village to see. His wife
brought us the beer and we drank in silence. Then he told
me. He said he had done what he had done because he felt
that our world somehow now belonged to the white man.
He did not know how this had come about, but it was so.
And the only way to be a man in this new world, he thought,
was to be a Christian. There were many good things in the
teachings of Bwana Yesu, and they were not unlike our own
teachings. And we were taught to call him "Father," so perhaps he was an even greater ancestor, further back than .we
had ever thought of, ancestor of black and white alike. This
is how my father once believed, how he still believed when
he sent for Bwana Spence to take me away so that I would
not be forced to enter the *nkumbi*. My father said he did not
know that Bwana Spence was going to circumcise me, but I
think his heart knew it. Anyway it was done.

After the news reached Ndola that I had been cut in the
hospital, and had not even suffered it like a man but had
been asleep, someone put a terrible curse on my father and
caused him to become bewitched so that now he had not only
transgressed against our ancestors, he had also transgressed
against the white man's ancestors. And he knew that they
were different ancestors now, that Bwana Yesu was not really
our "Father," because of a dream he had had. In this dream
Bwana Yesu had appeared to him. It was the first time he
had seen Bwana Yesu, except in photographs, and he looked
very closely. Bwana Yesu was white, and all his children
around him were white. Bwana Yesu pointed to the children
and told my father that unless he changed and became like
that child he could not enter the Kingdom of the Clouds.

I told my father that I had heard Bwana Spence tell the
same story, but he had never explained it except by saying
that we must remain as children. My father said that this
was what worried him so, because what it obviously meant
was that Bwana Yesu was white, and that only uncircumcised
white people could enter the Kingdom of the Clouds. Bwana
Spence had circumcised me so that I would not be able to
enter his kingdom or that of my ancestors. I asked then, in
surprise, if Bwana Spence was not circumcised, and my father

told me about Amboko, and why he had left. Bwana Spence had discovered that his Bwana had never been cut and was unclean.

My father went on to say that Bwana Yesu had added a powerful curse that anyone who harmed one of his children would be drowned in the river. This proved beyond doubt that I was not his child, even though I had been baptized and called Ibrahimo, because otherwise Bwana Spence would not have dared to harm me. I remembered the look on Bwana Spence's face, and at last I understood.

I learned how Bwana Spence had fought with Matungi, and had called him evil, and had cursed him and told him he would never die but would live on forever like a ghost in a terrible world of flames. I learned how he had caused Matungi to be ridiculed and insulted by the administrator at Matadi, and how only the ancestors had saved Matungi from being put away in a box. I saw that my father had no bitterness against Matungi for the curse; for although he was sorry to lose his first wife, my mother, he had been forced by Matungi to give up his mistaken beliefs and come back to the ways of the ancestors. And after a while my mother would come back to him, and he would be blessed with two wives.

I was glad for my father, but for myself I now know that I had truly died when they brought me into that house of the knife. I knew why Bwana Spence had not wanted to explain things, but tried to make us believe that the words of Bwana Yesu were good words and would help us to be good people. I knew now that his Bwana's kingdom really was in the clouds, although he said it was not, and that it was quite different from ours that is in the earth. I knew that in order to go to Bwana Yesu's kingdom I had to be white and uncircumcised, and that I could be neither. I also knew that my ancestors would not want me because I had not seen the *nkumbi*.

I went to see Matungi, and he tried to make me strong. He said that even he did not understand all these matters. He had always thought that Bwana Yesu was a good man, and it was the Bwana Spence who was lying, because he knew of other white men who *were* circumcised. I asked him if he

meant Bwana Banduki, the white man who was circumcised
by the Bafwamiti and who worked growing strange plants
and fruits for the administrator. But Matungi said no, that
even Christian white men circumcise each other.

Then I began to hate Bwana Spence because of all his lies,
and because of all the unhappiness he had brought to my
father and to Matungi and to myself. I felt he was the most
evil thing I had ever met, and I asked Matungi to perform a
special rite to make both my father and myself clean again
in the eyes of our ancestors. But Matungi said he could do
it for my father, but that I had not seen the *nkumbi,* and
he did not know what he could do for me. He said that the
ancestors were able to understand these things, and he would
ask them to look after me, and maybe they would talk to him
in a dream and tell him what to do.

Meanwhile he told me that he thought the best thing was
for me to go back to the Mission School and to continue with
my learning. They would have to take me back after what
they had done, he said. Matungi warned me to have nothing
to do with Bwana Spence, not to trust a single white man
there, not to believe a word they spoke, and never to join
them in their ritual eating and drinking, because this might
offend the ancestors even more. 'But,' he said, 'learn all you
can. See for yourself if what Bwana Yesu says is the same
thing as what the Bwana Spence says. You have been made
one of Bwana Yesu's children by the water ceremony, and
after all your father did not see in his dream whether the
other children were circumcised or not. He thought they
were too young—but maybe the Christians circumcise earlier
than we do—and maybe Bwana Spence has an evil spirit in
his body that makes him do and say these terrible things. If
all that is so, and if you still believe in Bwana Yesu, you may
go to his afterworld. You can not come to ours without seeing
the *nkumbi.*'

All this Matungi told me, and my father said that Matungi
had spoken well. We would have to accept it that in the afterlife we would be separated forever, for my father had decided
to go back to the ways of his ancestors.

I went back to the school, and I am still there. I have

learned a great deal, and I can now read the Big Book my-self. But it does not always make sense, and it speaks of many things of which I still know nothing, and it is all about faraway places and about white men that can have nothing to do with me. I try to talk to Bwana Yesu but he does not talk back to me. I stop my ears when I hear Bwana Spence talking, because I do not want to be tricked by his lies. I look in his face and I know he is lying, and that he hates all of us. Even the young children know this and they laugh at him. I once thought of having a child by his daughter, thinking that in this way I might have access to the white man's afterworld, but Matungi told me this would be a very bad thing.

I do not know what will happen. I am told that the white man is soon going to leave, and then my learning will be useful. But for what? What good is learning if I can not marry a white girl and if none of our own girl-children will have me? If I can not in any way make myself clean and acceptable in this world, how can I be fit for life in the after-world?

I met some BaNgwana the other day, and they told me that they have a god who will accept me and take me into his afterworld if I do certain things. But they are unclean things, and we all know the BaNgwana [an African tribe primarily engaged in trade] to be an unclean people. Perhaps I shall have no afterlife, and in that case I can only do what I can with this life. And in this life I shall never believe a white man again. If I follow his ways it is with my body, not with my heart. In my heart there is only the knowledge that the white man had taken me away from my fathers and brothers for all time, and that he hates me. In that knowledge I can only find strength to hate back.

| | |

AFRICAN CHILDHOOD TODAY:

NATIONALISM AND BEYOND

AFRICANS did resist the colonization of their continent. Some African kingdoms fought the European invaders but were defeated. Other Africans used their Western education to press for greater political and economic rights for their people. After World War II these African nationalists received a broad base of support from other Africans and gained ever larger concessions from the colonial powers. In fact, within fifteen years—because of growing nationalist support, the weakness of Europe, and the Cold War struggle —most of the colonies reached statehood. In 1950 only two black states, Ethiopia and Liberia, were independent. Today thirty-five have achieved nationhood.

The problems that faced nationalist groups and the tactics they employed varied according to their colonial overlord and the number of white settlers present. In West Africa— due to the scarcity of settlers—the road to independence was relatively swift. By constant political pressure—agitation in the press, economic boycotts, petitions, and participation in local politics—African nationalists were able to liberate their

countries peaceably. In Kenya, East Africa, peaceful agitation was unsuccessful, and frustrated Africans turned to the
secret society Mau Mau to further their political ends. In
other areas peaceful methods have proved totally fruitless,
and in South Africa, Portuguese Guinea, Mozambique, Angola, and Rhodesia, African nationalists have turned to guerrilla warfare. Their battle still continues.

Whatever the region of Africa, nationalists not only have
fought for political rights, but have extolled the dignity of
Africa's cultural identity and have questioned the Westernization of Africa. They have pressured colonial powers to
give more political rights and economic assistance to Africa,
and needled their African brothers to take greater pride in
their own race and culture.

A child growing up in resurgent Africa is imbued by the
rising spirit of political and cultural nationalism. His elders'
optimism, positive self-appraisal, and hope for the future cannot help but stimulate the youth.

However, in these exciting days of rising nationalism, an
African child is still caught up in many confusing and dis-
tressing emotions. His past—both tribal and colonial—still
haunts the nationalist and independent African. Eight hundred self-contained tribes are expected to—and at times refuse to—pay allegiance to a new nation. Villages are sup-
planted by cities, and Western-style education continues to
challenge traditional beliefs.

A child growing up in nationalist and independent Africa
has to cope both with the remaining tribal influences of his
forefathers and with lasting Western influences. He must
recognize that in order to prosper, Africa must change but
must also realize the importance of African tradition. Thus,
in many respects an African childhood is still tumultuous.
But as the following accounts will show, with the realization
or promise of independence it is not without hope or joy.

AFRICA TODAY

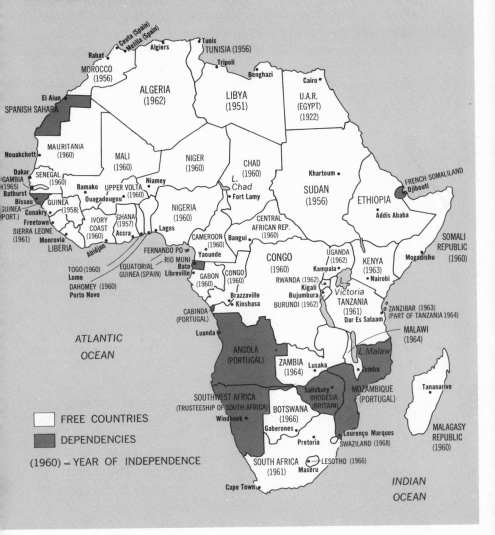

Ceuta (Spain)
Melilla (Spain)
Rabat
Tunis
Algiers
TUNISIA (1956)
MOROCCO
(1956)
Tripoli
Benghazi
El Aiun
Cairo
SPANISH SAHARA
ALGERIA
(1962)
LIBYA
(1951)
U.A.R.
(EGYPT)
(1922)
Nouakchott
MAURITANIA
(1960)
Dakar
MALI
(1960)
NIGER
(1960)
CHAD
(1960)
Khartoum
GAMBIA
(1965)
SENEGAL
(1960)
L.
Chad
FRENCH SOMALILAND
Bathurst
Bamako
UPPER VOLTA
(1960)
Niamey
Djibouti
Bissau
Ouagadougou
Fort Lamy
SUDAN
(1956)
ETHIOPIA
GUINEA
(PORT.)
Conakry
GUINEA
(1958)
NIGERIA
(1960)
Addis Ababa
SIERRA LEONE
(1961)
Monrovia
IVORY
COAST
(1960)
GHANA
(1957)
Accra
Lagos
CENTRAL
AFRICAN REP.
(1960)
SOMALI
REPUBLIC
(1960)
LIBERIA
Abidjan
CAMEROON
(1960)
Bangui
Mogadishu
FERNANDO PO
RIO MUNI
UGANDA
(1962)
KENYA
(1963)
TOGO (1960)
Lome
EQUATORIAL
GUINEA (SPAIN)
Bata
Libreville
CONGO
(1960)
Kampala
DAHOMEY (1960)
Porto Novo
GABON
(1960)
CONGO
(1960)
RWANDA (1962)
Kigali
Nairobi
Brazzaville
Bujumbura
Victoria
Kinshasa
BURUNDI (1962)
TANZANIA
(1961)
ZANZIBAR (1963)
(PART OF TANZANIA 1964)
CABINDA
(PORTUGAL)
Dar Es Salaam
Luanda
MALAWI
(1964)
ATLANTIC
ANGOLA
(PORTUGAL)
ZAMBIA
(1964)
L.Malaw
OCEAN
Lusaka
Zomba
Salisbury
RHODESIA
(BRITAIN)
MOZAMBIQUE
(PORTUGAL)
Tananarive
SOUTHWEST AFRICA
(TRUSTEESHIP OF SOUTH AFRICA)
BOTSWANA
(1966)
FREE COUNTRIES
Windhoek
Gaberones
Lourenço Marques
SWAZILAND (1968)
MALAGASY
REPUBLIC
(1960)
DEPENDENCIES
Pretoria
(1960) = YEAR OF INDEPENDENCE
SOUTH AFRICA
(1961)
LESOTHO (1966)
Maseru
Cape Town
INDIAN
OCEAN

1

FROM

"On the Appeal from the Race of Sheba"

by Leopold Senghor

(1906–   )

*In 1934 Leopold Senghor, a Senegalese student studying in
Paris, joined with Aime Cesaire, a Martiniquais, and Leon
Damas, a Guianese, to form the journal* L'Étudiant Noir. *Its
founding in Paris marked the beginning of the important
literary and cultural movement of Negritude. The basic message of the movement was "black is beautiful," the founders
maintaining that the black race has a special spirituality and
a warmth which the materialistic West can no longer attain.
Senghor urged other Africans to return to the culture of
their forefathers, and while using Western technology, to
reject the Westerners' image of Africa.*

*Senghor's writings are inspired by the poetry of Negritude.
In the following autobiographical poem, he writes on several
different planes. On one level he is a homesick soldier in
Europe who remembers his childhood in a small coastal village of Senegal, West Africa. On another level he is a Westernized African calling to Mother Africa with the "swollen
twisted lip" to help him to return to the spirituality of his
forefathers, to help him maintain his Africanness in the
modern world. He asks Mother Africa to "let me keep the
savour of my blood from the insipidness of the assimilado,
the civilized man," and through his appeal to her he feels*

*fulfilled: "There will spurt up on me and on my sensual lips
the hot salt blood of the bull in the strength of his age, in
the fulness of his flesh."*

Senghor graduated from the Sorbonne, became a professor
of African language and civilization at the École Nationale
de France, a recognized poet, and the foremost African advocate of Negritude. He served in the French army during the
Second World War, was captured by the Germans, and remained in prison camp until 1942. After the war he entered
politics. In 1945 he was elected député for Senegal to the
National Assembly. He formed the political party Bloc
Démocratique Senegalais, which through its appeal to the
peasants became the most powerful party in Senegal. As head
of the Senegal government, he helped found the Federation
of Senegal and Mali in 1959 and became President of Senegal
when the federation failed in 1960. Despite some disaffec-
tion, particularly among students, he still holds the position
of Senegal's political leader. His published works include
Chants d'ombre, Éthiopiques, Hosties noires, Nocturnes,
Nouvelle anthologie de la poésie nègre et malagache, and
Poèmes.

I

Bless you, Mother.
I hear your voice when I am given up to the insidious silence
    of this European night
Prisoner under the white cold sheets tightly drawn, prisoner
    of all the inextricable anxieties that encumber me
When that sudden kite pounces, the sour panic of the yellow
    leaf
Or the panic of black soldiers in the thunderstorm of tanks
And their leader goes down with a great cry, his whole body
    swung around.
Mother, I hear your voice in anger.

Your red angry eyes firing the night and the bush, black as
    once in the time of my escapades
—I could not stay deaf to the innocence of shells, of foun-
    tains, and mirages on the sea flats
And your chin trembled beneath your swollen twisted lips.

II

Bless you, Mother.
I remember the days of my fathers, the evenings of Dyilor
That deep-blue light of the night sky on the land sweet at
    evening.
I am on the steps of the homestead. Deep inside it is dark.
My brothers and sisters like chicks huddle their numerous
    warmth against my heart.
I lay my head on the knees of my nurse Nga, Nga the poetess
My heart pounding with the warrior gallop of the *dyoung-
    dyoungs,* great gallop of my blood my pure blood
My head melodious with the distant songs of Kumba the
    Orphan.
In the middle of the courtyard, the lone fig-tree
The wives of the Man gossip in its lunar shadow, their voices
    solemn and deep as their eyes, as the fountain of Fimla
    by night.
And my father lying on the quiet mat, but tall but strong
    but handsome
Man of the Kingdom of Sine, whilst all around on the *koras,*
    heroic voices, the *griots* set dancing their mettlesome
    fingers
Whilst in the distance arises surging with strong warm
    smells, the classic murmur of a hundred herds.

III

Bless you, Mother.
I am not the East Wind to stir these images like sand on the
    roads
You do not hear me, though I hear you (like an anxious
    mother who forgets to press Button A in the call-box)

But in my head open to the winds and pillage of the North,
I do not raze the footprints of my fathers or my fathers'
fathers.

Mother, in this room full of Romans and Greeks, breathe in
the odour of my heart's vesperal victims.

Guardian geniuses, let me keep the savour of my blood from
the insipidness of the assimilado, the civilized man.

I bring as an offering a hen without blemish; though I have
come late, I stand close to the Elder, so that before the
creamy water and millet beer

There will spurt up on me and on my sensual lips the hot
salt blood of the bull in the strength of his age, in the
fulness of his flesh.

2

FROM

Ghana: the Autobiography
of Kwame Nkrumah

by Kwame Nkrumah

(1909–   )

The foremost African nationalist of the 1940's and 50's was
Ghana's first president, Kwame Nkrumah, who even as a
youth began to recognize the importance of a firm hand in
dealing with Ghana's invaders. In 1949 he formed the mili-
tant Convention People's Party which drew support away
from the moderate and "respectable" United Gold Coast
Convention. The important difference between the goals of
his nationalist movement and those of its predecessor was
that, while the latter had proclaimed a slow but sure road to
independence, Nkrumah's party demanded independence
now. In 1951 his party won the legislative elections, and in
1957 the British government in Ghana was forced to hand
over the reins of power to Nkrumah.

Nkrumah was a strong advocate of Pan-African Unity, and
in 1958 sponsored the first conference of independent Afri-
can states, the All-Africa People's Conference. He remained
president of Ghana until 1966 when he was overthrown by
an army coup. He is now living in Guinea.

AND so, on that particular day in Nkróful [Ghana, West
Africa], my birth was of very little interest to the villagers. I

am told, however, that there was a good deal of commotion going on where I was, for I apparently took so long to show any signs of life that my mother had given up all interest in me as she believed me to be dead. This is not as heartless as it may sound for it is a strong belief among the Akans [tribal group of Ghana, West Africa] that if a mother mourns the death of her child she will become sterile, and this, to an African woman, is the worst thing that can befall her.

But my female relatives, having dragged themselves away from the funeral celebrations, would not give in so easily. They were determined to put life into me and proceeded to make as much noise as they could with cymbals and other instruments, and at the same time jolting me about—and even stuffing a banana into my mouth in an effort to make me cough and so draw breath. They finally succeeded in arousing my interest and, their job completed, handed me back to my anxious mother, a yelling and kicking Saturday's child.

Great importance is attached by the Akans to the day of the week on which a child is born for this determines his Platonic soul. They believe that a man is possessed of three souls: the blood soul (or *moyga*) transmitted by the female and considered synonymous with the clan, the *ntoro* which is transmitted by the male, and the *okra,* or Platonic soul. In order that there should be no mistake about the *okra,* a specific name is given to the child according to the day of the week on which he was born. A male child born on Sunday is called Kwesi; if born on Monday he receives the name Kojo. And so on. For a boy born on Saturday the name is Kwame. There are other superstitions surrounding a child's birth. For instance, the first child is supposed to be less bright, the third child to be precocious and incorrigible, the ninth child to bring good luck and the tenth child to bring misfortune. Sometimes the fear of bad luck at the birth of a tenth child is so strong that the infant may be smothered at birth or during early infancy.

Whilst I can claim to fall into the pattern of things by being born on a Saturday and bearing the name of Kwame, it is surely disheartening that I was the first and only child of my mother and am therefore, according to tradition, less bright than average! . . .

We were a large family, for, although I was the only child of my mother and father, my father had quite a number of children by other wives whom he married by native custom. Polygamy was quite legal and even today it is quite in order for a man to have as many wives as he can afford. In fact, the more wives a man can keep the greater is his social position. However unconventional and unsatisfactory this way of life may appear to those who are confirmed monogamists, and without in any way trying to defend my own sex, it is a frequently accepted fact that a man is naturally polygamous. All the African has done is to recognize this fact and to legalize, or to make socially acceptable, a thing which has been done and will doubtless continue to be done by man as long as he exists. It is interesting to note that divorce in this polygamous community is negligible compared with countries practising monogamy, especially when divorce can be obtained so much more easily than in a monogamous society. For a marriage can be brought to an end for any of the following reasons: adultery, barrenness or impotency, as the case may be, drunkenness, sexual incompatibility, the quarrelsome nature of the woman, unharmonious relationship with a mother-in-law, and discovery of marriage within one's own clan.

All members of a clan are considered to be blood relations and if a marriage takes place between two of the members, it is believed that the whole clan will be visited by the wrath of the gods. In my parents' case, for instance, both were of the same tribe, but my father was of the Asona clan and my mother was from the Anonas. As heredity is governed by the matrilineal line, I belong not to my father's clan, as would be the case in Western marriages, but to my mother's. My father's line descends through the eldest son of his sister, a member of the Asona clan.

Apart from our immediate family, which consisted of about fourteen people in all, there always seemed to be relatives staying with us and our little compound was usually full of people. It is a custom among Africans that any relative, however distant the relationship may be, can at any time arrive at your home and remain under your roof as long as he wants. Nobody questions his arrival, how long he intends staying, or his eventual departure. This hospitality is sometimes very much abused, for if one member of the family does well for himself he usually finds his compound filled to capacity with men and women, all claiming some distant kinship, and all prepared to live at his expense until the money runs out.

My family lived together very peaceably and I can remember very few quarrels. The women of the house used to take turns each week to cook the meals and look after my father and at the same time they either worked in the fields or did some petty trading in order to supplement the family income. It was a wonderful life for us children with nothing to do but play around all day. Our playground was vast and varied, for we had the sea, the lagoon and the thrill of unexplored bush all within easy reach. . . .

I soon learned, however, that life for a growing boy was not all play; at least, not for boys with parents like mine. Although my mother had never had the benefit of formal education herself, she was determined that I should be sent to school at the earliest opportunity. My father, probably due to my mother's persuasive power, was strongly in favor of this also. Even though I could often get around my father, I knew that once my mother's mind had been made up there was nothing I could do about it.

I found my first day at school so disappointing that I ran away determined never to return. But my mother turned a deaf ear to my raging protests and quietly but determinedly dragged me by the arm each morning and deposited me in the schoolroom. Eventually I realized that I had lost the battle and decided that as I was going to be forced to stay there, I might as well get to like it and do what I could to learn something. To my surprise I soon found that I enjoyed my lessons and looked forward to going to school, even though we lived in fear and trembling of the teacher because of his firm and active belief in the adage "Spare the rod and spoil the child." I disliked being forced to do things against my will, for I had not been accustomed to it, and I used to think what a wonderful paradise school would be if we were left in peace to do our studies without the presence of the schoolmaster.

All the various grades were housed in one room and the master used to teach a class at a time. It must have been a hard job for him, and we did nothing to ease his lot. Luckily I was keen on learning, so keen, in fact, that soon my only dread was that my father might one day be unable to afford the school fees, which at that time amounted to threepence a month. Because of this I started rearing a few chickens which I sold for sixpence each. By this means I could not only help to meet the school fees, but I had money to buy books as well. In addition, any fears about my father's poverty were quite unfounded because I can never remember him denying any of us anything we asked and he was particularly generous where I was concerned. . . .

After eight years at the elementary school, I became a pupil-teacher for one year at Half Assini. I suppose I must have been about seventeen at the time; anyhow, I was not very big because I can well remember having to stand on a box in order to write on the blackboard.

In 1926 the Principal of the Government Training College in Accra visited the school where I was teaching and, when he saw the work I was doing, he was sufficiently impressed to recommend that I should go to his college to train as a teacher.

This marks a turning point in my life for in the following year I came to his college, a raw youth bewildered at first by city life and, like most boys who leave home for boarding school, thoroughly homesick. Half Assini, with its roads of sand like tracks in the desert, seemed far preferable to the traffic, the crowded streets and the noise of Accra.

There was also the usual ragging and bullying of freshmen to be gone through. This seemed to last a long time until one day, when I was wondering whether education was really worth the misery of it all, one of my persecutors began to

talk to me as if I was one of them. I had apparently passed
the Test. After that I was dragged in to rag my successors
and realized that my initiation was complete. . . .

About this time the Prince of Wales College at Achimota
was officially opened by the Governor, Sir Gordon Guggis-
berg, before a large and colorful gathering of chiefs and government officials. Among the chiefs was the Kumasihene, the
notorious ruler of Ashanti who had earlier been deported to
the Seychelles by the Governor because of alleged participation in human sacrifices.

But the figure to whom all Africans looked that day was
Dr. Kwegyir Aggrey, assistant vice-principal and the first
African member of the staff. To me he seemed the most
remarkable man that I had ever met and I had the deepest
affection for him. He possessed intense vitality and enthusiasm and a most infectious laugh that seemed to bubble up
from his heart, and he was a very great orator. It was through
him that my nationalism was first aroused. He was extremely
proud of his color but was strongly opposed to racial segregation in any form and, although he could understand Marcus
Garvey's principle of "Africa for the Africans," he never
hesitated to attack this principle. He believed conditions
should be such that the black and white races should work
together. Co-operation between the black and white peoples
was the key note of his message and the essence of his mission, and he used to expound this by saying: "You can play
a tune of sorts on the white keys, and you can play a tune of
sorts on the black keys, but for harmony you must use both
the black and the white."

But I could not, even at that time, accept this idea of
Aggrey's as being practicable, for I maintained that such
harmony can only exist when the black race is treated as
equal with the white race; that only a free and independent
people—a people with a government of their own—can
claim equality, racial or otherwise, with another people.

3

"The Mosquito and the Young Ghanaian"
by Kwesi Assah Nyako

In 1957 Ghana became the first West African colony to achieve statehood. Ghana's first President, Kwame Nkrumah, remarked that his country's greatest national hero was that deterrent to white settlement, the malarial mosquito.

> "Agya-e-e-e! Agyaa-e-e-e-e! poor mosquito!
> Why dost thou bite me
> In this unforgettable midnight?
> When the great church-bells are being tolled,
> To mark this historic sight,
> Vision of the national flag,
> The three colour flag, the black star,
> Hoisted high over the new Parliament of Ghana,
> And the imperial flag lowered?"

> "Young Ghanaian! Young Ghanaian!
> Art thou up in arms against me?
> But I too celebrate this day,
> No blood, no celebration for me?
> "Young Ghanaian! Young Ghanaian!
> Be cheerful, Be cheerful,
> Else thou spoilest the beauty,
> The beauty of this great day."

> "Young Ghanaians! Young, young Ghanaians!
> Let's praise my ancestors, the great mosquitoes,
> Killed thousand invaders of West Africa,

Thereby released us
From settlers, land problem, colour bar."
"Praise be your ancestors, cheerful mosquito,
There is great hope for Africa."

4

FROM

Weep Not, Child

by James Ngugi

(1938–   )

James Ngugi's autobiographical novel takes place in colonial Kenya, East Africa, of the 1950's. The central character, the young boy Njoroge, of the Kikuyu tribe, witnesses his family and country torn apart by racial and nationalist violence.

Historically, Njoroge and his family are caught up in events that led to the Mau Mau uprisings in Kenya. His half-brother Kori is attracted to the nationalist movement of Jomo Kenyatta, Kenya's foremost nationalist and its present-day president. His other half-brother, Boro, eventually a Mau Mau, joins Kenyatta's ill-fated strike for African equality. After the strike fails, repeated police harassment and white repression lead to Mau Mau guerrilla warfare and to Kenya's declaration of emergency in 1952.

Between 1952 and 1963 British administrators met with African leaders to speed reconciliation and form a nonracial constitution. The first African minister, B. A. Ohanga, was appointed to the Colonial Legislative Council in 1954, and by 1960 the majority of ministers were African. On December 12, 1963, when Kenya obtained independence, both its president—Jomo Kenyatta—and its vice-president—Tom Mboya—were Africans.

James Ngugi, a Kenyan, is currently a visiting Associate

Professor at Northwestern University. He has also written the novels The River Between, A Night of Their Own, *and* A Grain of Wheat.

NJOROGE had not reached the courtyard when he saw his brother coming. Kamau had just finished his duties. Njoroge was glad when he saw him for, although Kamau was older, they got on well.

"Let's go, Brother," said Kamau as he pulled Njoroge by the hand. He looked gloomy.

"Today, you're late."

"It is *this* man!"

Njoroge thought that something was wrong. It was not often that his brother was so angry.

"Is he not a good man?"

"Good man! If I didn't know that Father would be annoyed after paying all that money, I would stop coming here. I have now been with him for six months, yet it was only yesterday that he first allowed me to handle a plane. He is always telling me, 'Hold here! Hold there,' and always asking me to watch and note carefully. How can a man learn by watching without practice? Surely not by sweeping the yard and taking away the rubbish and carrying the tools for him. But if I touch something! And you know," and here Kamau spoke in disgust, "his youngest wife actually makes me hold her child just as if she was a European woman and I her *Ayah* [nanny in Swahili]. Oh dear me! It is such a dirty little thing that keeps on howling and—!"

"Why don't you tell Father?"

"You don't know. Father would obviously take Ngaga's side, especially on the question of watching, because this is how people used to learn trades in the olden times. They don't realize that things are changing!"

They kept silent for a while as they made their way home in the gathering gloom, the prelude to darkness. Then Njoroge, as if he had suddenly thought up a great question, asked, "But why does he treat you like that? He is a black man?"

"Blackness is not all that makes a man," Kamau said bitterly. "There are some people, be they black or white, who don't want others to rise above them. They want to be the source of all knowledge and share piecemeal to others less endowed. That is what's wrong with all these carpenters and men who have a certain knowledge. It is the same with rich people. A rich man does not want others to get rich because he wants to be the only man with wealth."

"Probably," Njoroge said, impressed. He had never heard Kamau speak so much at length.

". . . Some Europeans are better than Africans."

Again Njoroge was impressed.

"That's why you at times hear Father say that he would rather work for a white man. A white man is a white man. But a black man trying to be a white man is bad and harsh."

Njoroge could not quite follow Kamau. But he pitied his brother and vowed that he himself would not become a carpenter. The only good thing was education. He tried to change the subject.

"Mother will tell us a story."

"Oh, will she?"

Both loved stories. Storytelling was a common entertainment in their family. Kori, like Ngotho, was a good storyteller and could keep a whole company listening and laughing. Boro, who had been to the war [World War II], did not know many tribal stories. He drank a lot and he was always sad and withdrawn. He never talked much about his war experiences except when he was drunk or when he was in a mood of resentment against the Government and settlers.

"We fought for them; we fought to save them from the hands of their white brothers. . . ."

Then on such occasions, he might talk just a little about the actual fighting. But he very rarely alluded to Mwangi's death. It was common knowledge that they had loved each other very much. Before the war, it had always been said that such love between brothers was unnatural and portended no good.

Boro, Kori, and Kamau were all sons of Njeri, Ngotho's eldest wife. Njoroge's only true brother was Mwangi, who

had died in the war. But they all behaved as if they were of
one mother. Kori worked in an African tea shop called
Green Hotel. Green Hotel was a very dirty place, full of
buzzing flies, while the stench of decay hung in the air like
a heavy cloud. But it was a very popular place because there
was a wireless set. Njoroge looked forward to Kori's home-
coming because he brought with him the town gossip and
what was happening in the country. For instance, when
Jomo [Jomo Kenyatta, present president of Kenya] came
from Britain, it was Kori who brought the news home. Home
was especially a nice place when all the brothers and many
village girls and boys came in the evening and, sitting around
the fireplace in a big circle, they would gossip, laugh and
play. Njoroge always longed for the day he would be a man,
for then he would have the freedom to sit with big circumcised girls and touch them as he saw the young men do. But
sometimes his brothers did not come. Home then was dull.
But the mothers could tell stories. And Ngotho too, when
he was in the mood.

"Our elder mother wanted you," Njoroge said when they
reached home. It was already dark. While Njeri was always
"our" or "my elder mother," Nyokabi, being the younger
wife, was always just "Mother." It was a habit observed and
accepted by all.

"What does she want?"

"I don't know."

Kamau began to move. Njoroge stood and watched in
silence. Then he raised his voice, "Remember to come back
to our hut. You remember the story."

"Yes," Kamau replied. His voice sounded thin in the dark.

Later in the evening Kamau came to Nyokabi's hut.

"Tell us the story."

"Now, now, don't be troublesome," Nyokabi said.

"It is a bad woman this. If I had been my father, I would
not have married her." Kamau liked teasing Nyokabi. Tonight his teasing sounded forced. It did not provoke laughter.

"Oh! But he could not resist me."

"It isn't true," said Ngotho who just then entered the hut.

"You should have seen how happy she was when I proposed to her. Nobody could have taken her. So I pitied her."

"I refused all the young men that wanted me. But your father would have died if I had refused him."

"Don't believe a word she says!"

Ngotho was given food. He began to eat and for a time there was an awkward silence. The children could not joke in their father's presence. Nyokabi broke the silence.

"You children! You never ask your father to tell you stories. Tonight he *will* tell you," she said smilingly toward her husband. She was happy.

"If you all come to my *Thingira* [a man's hut in Kikuyu language], I'll tell you one or two."

Njoroge feared his father. But it always made him feel good to listen to him.

". . . There was wind and rain. And there was also thunder and terrible lightning. The earth and the forest around Kerinyaga [God's mountain] shook. The animals of the forest whom the Creator had recently put there were afraid. There was no sunlight. This went on for many days so that the whole land was in darkness. Because the animals could not move, they just sat and moaned with wind. The plants and trees remained dumb. It was, our elders tell us, all dead except for the thunder, a violence that seemed to strangle life. It was this dark night whose depth you could not measure, not you or I can conceive of its solid blackness, which would not let the sun pierce through it.

"But in this darkness, at the foot of Kerinyaga, a tree rose. At first it was a small tree and grew up, finding a way even through the darkness. It wanted to reach the light, and the sun. This tree had *Life*. It went up, up, sending forth the rich warmth of a blossoming tree—you know a holy tree in the dark night of thunder and moaning. This was Mukuyu, God's tree. Now, you know that at the beginning of things there was only one man (Gikuyu) and one woman (Mumbi). It was under this Mukuyu that He first put them. And immediately the sun rose, and the dark night melted away. The sun shone with a warmth that gave life and activity to all things. The wind and lightning and thunder stopped. The animals stopped wondering and moved. They no longer moaned but gave homage to the Creator and Gikuyu and Mumbi. And the Creator, who is also called Murungu, took Gikuyu and Mumbi from His holy mountain. He took them to the country of ridges [Kikuyu tribe's land] near Siriana and there stood them on a big ridge before He finally took them to Mukuruwe wa Gathanga [mythical place of origin of Kikuyu tribe] about which you have heard so much. But he had shown them all the land—yes, children, God showed Gikuyu and Mumbi all the land and told them,

> 'This land I hand over to you. O Man and woman
> It's yours to rule and till in serenity sacrificing
> Only to me, your God, under my sacred tree. . . .' "

There was something strange in Ngotho's eyes. He looked as if he had forgotten all about those who were present, Kamau, Njoroge, Boro, Kori, and many other young men and women who had come to make the long hours of night shorter by listening to stories. It was as if he was telling a secret for the first time, but to himself. Boro sat in a corner. The expression on his face could not be seen. He did not once move but kept on looking past his father. It was as if Boro and Ngotho were the only two who were there at the beginning when these things came to be. Njoroge too could imagine the scene. He saw the sun rise and shine on a dark night. He saw fear, gloom and terror of the living things of the Creator, melting away, touched by the warmth of the holy tree. It must have been a new world. The man and woman must have been blessed to walk in the new Kingdom with Murungu. He wished he had been there to stand near Him in His holy place and survey all the land. Njoroge could not help exclaiming,

"Where did the land go?"

Everyone looked at him.

". . . I am old now. But I too have asked that question in waking and sleeping. I've said, 'What happened, O Murungu, to the land which You gave to us? Where, O Creator, went our promised land?' At times I've wanted to cry or harm my body to drive away the curse that removed us from the ancestral lands. I ask, 'Have You left Your children naked, O Murungu?'

"I'll tell you. There was a big drought sent to the land by evil ones who must have been jealous of the prosperity of the children of the Great One. But maybe also the children of Mumbi forgot to burn a sacrifice to Murungu. So He did not shed His blessed tears that make crops grow. The sun burned freely. Plague came to the land. Cattle died and people shrank in size. Then came the white man as had long been prophesied by Mugo wa Kibiro, that Gikuyu seer of old. He came from the country of ridges, far away from here. Mugo had told the people of the coming of the white man. He had warned the tribe. So the white man came and took the land. But at first not the whole of it.

"Then came the war. It was the first big war. I was then young, a mere boy, although circumcised. All of us were taken by force. We made roads and cleared the forest to make it possible for the warring white man to move more quickly. The war ended. We were all tired. We came home worn out but very ready for whatever the British might give us as a reward. But, more than this, we wanted to go back to the soil and court it to yield, to create, not to destroy. But Ng'o! The land was gone. My father and many others had been moved from our ancestral lands. He died lonely, a poor man waiting for the white man to go. Mugo had said this would come to be. The white man did not go and he died a *Muhoi* [headman, overseer] on this very land. It then belonged to Chahira before he sold it to Jacobo. I grew up here, but working . . . (here Ngotho looked all around the silent faces and then continued) . . . working on the land that belonged to our ancestors—"

"You mean the land that Howlands farms?" Boro's voice was cracked, but clear.

"Yes. The same land. My father showed it all to me. I have worked there too, waiting for the prophecy to be fulfilled."

"And do you think it will ever be fulfilled?" It was Kori

who asked this to break the silence that followed Ngotho's reply.

"I don't know. Once in the country of the ridges where the hills and ridges lie together like lions, a man rose. People thought that he was the man who had been sent to drive away the white man. But he was killed by wicked people because he said people should stand together [Harry Thuku, the first modern Kenyan nationalist who was deported by the British in 1922]. I've waited for the prophecy. It may not be fulfilled in my lifetime . . . but, O Murungu, I wish it could."

Someone coughed. Then silence. From a corner, a young man tried to make a joke about the coming of the white man and what people thought of his skin. Nobody heeded him. He laughed alone and then stopped. For Njoroge, it was a surprising revelation, this knowledge that the land occupied by Mr. Howlands originally belonged to them.[1]

Boro thought of his father who had fought in the war only to be dispossessed. He too had gone to war, against Hitler. He had gone to Egypt, Jerusalem and Burma. He had seen things. He had often escaped death narrowly. But the thing he could not forget was the death of his stepbrother, Mwangi. For whom or for what had *he* died?

When the war came to an end, Boro had come home, no longer a boy but a man with experience and ideas, only to find that for him there was to be no employment. There was no land on which he could settle, even if he had been able to do so. As he listened to this story, all these things came into his mind with a growing anger. How could these people have let the white man occupy the land without acting? And what was all this superstitious belief in a prophecy?

In a whisper that sounded like a shout, he said, "To hell with the prophecy."

Yes, this was nothing more than a whisper. To his father he said, "How can you continue working for a man who has

[1] Among many African tribes including the Kikuyu land is not owned by individuals but held communally by a clan or tribe.

taken your land? How can you go on serving him?"

He walked out, without waiting for an answer. . . .

Sometimes men came to see his father. Ever since Njoroge was a child, he had seen Ngotho as the center of everything. As long as he lived, nothing could go wrong. And so Njoroge grew up, fearing his father, and yet putting implicit faith in him.

The men who came to see Ngotho usually went to his *Thingira*. But sometimes they went to Nyokabi's or Njeri's hut. This pleased Njoroge for he loved to listen to the mature talk of men. These men were the elders of the village. They talked about affairs of the land. Kori and Boro too brought men at weekends, but these men were different from the young men of the village. The young men of the village usually allowed the elders to lead talks while they listened. But these others who came with Kori and Boro from the big city seemed to know a lot of things. They usually dominated the talks. And because most of them had been to the war, they were able to compare the affairs of the land with the lands to which they had been. They did not joke and laugh as young men usually did, but their faces were grave, as they talked of the foreign lands, the war, their country, the big unemployment and the stolen lands.

Njoroge listened keenly as they talked of Jomo. Already he felt intimate with this man. For Njoroge was sure that he had read about him in the Old Testament. Moses had led the children of Israel from Misri [Egypt] to the Promised Land. And because black people were really the children of Israel, Moses was no other than Jomo himself. It was obvious.

The men also talked of the strike. All men who worked for white men and Serikali (the Government) would come out on strike. The Government and the settlers had to be shown that black people were not cowards and slaves. They too had children to feed and to educate. How could people go on sweating for the children of the white men to be well fed, well clothed and well educated? Kiarie, a short man with a black beard, was a good, compelling speaker. He

usually walked together with Boro. His words stirred Njoroge strangely.

A man asked, "But do you think it will succeed?"

"Yes! Everybody will go on strike. Every black man everywhere. Even those in the police and the army will sit down
too."

"Shall we really get the same pay as Indians and Europeans?"

"Yes!" Kiarie explained with a confident nod of his head.
"All the black people will stop working. All business in the
country will come to a standstill because all the country
depends on our sweat. The Government and the settlers will
call us back. But we shall say, No, no. Give us more money
first. Our sweat and blood are not so cheap. We too are human
beings. We cannot live on fifteen shillings a month. . . ."

The old men and village folk listened with deep interest.
They did not know much about strikes, but if this meant
more money it was a good idea. The solemn voice of Kiarie
had conviction and quiet assurance, which, Njoroge felt,
gave courage and faith to all those around.

"What about those employed by black people?"

"We must concentrate on the Government and the white
people. We black people are brothers."

Ngotho knew of one or two who were certainly not
brothers. But he did not say so.

When Njoroge went to bed, he prayed that the strike be
a success. He hoped it would come soon. If his father had
much money, he could buy a truck like that one of Jacobo.
He slept and dreamed of the happy moment of wealth and
pleasure after the strike.

Mr. Howlands called all his men. This was unusual. But
he had not much to say because he did not want to waste
time. He just warned them that if any man went on strike
he would instantly lose his job. How could he allow a
damned strike to interfere with any part of his farm? Even
the Government could not interfere with this. The blacks
could ask and agitate for anything. Such affairs were clearly

affairs of the Government—affairs that stood outside his shamba [farm]. And yet paradoxically, as the strike approached, he wanted a strong government action—an action that would teach these laborers their rightful places.

Ngotho listened to the warning without apparent emotion. His face did not change and so you could not tell what he was really thinking.

He could not quite make up his mind about the strike. He doubted if the strike would be a success. If it failed, then he would lose a job and that would keep him away from the lands of his ancestors. This was wrong, for the land was his. None could tend it as he could.

Ngotho went home unsure. He went through the African shops. The barber was still at his job. These days he mostly talked about the strike. Ngotho did not go there. He went straight home.

Njoroge had never seen his father quarreling with his wives. Whenever there was a quarrel, the children were never allowed to know about it. So when Njoroge came from school and found Nyokabi crying, he was shocked. He could remember vaguely only one time when his mother cried. It was probably during the famine of cassava or earlier. That was now a dream. But this was not a dream. Njoroge stood stock still, too frightened to enter the house. Ngotho, tall, masculine in spite of age, stood in front of her. Njoroge could not see his face. But he could see the tear-washed face of Nyokabi. Fear gripped him as he witnessed real discord in the home that had hitherto been so secure.

"I must be a man in my own house."

"Yes . . . be a man and lose a job."

"I shall do whatever I like. I have never taken orders from a woman."

"We shall starve. . . ."

"You starve! This strike is important for the black people. We shall get bigger salaries."

"What's black people to us when we starve?"

"Shut that mouth. How long do you think I can endure this drudgery, for the sake of a white man and his children?"

"But he's paying you money. What if the strike fails?"

"Don't woman me!" he shouted hysterically. This possibility was what he feared most. She sensed this note of uncertainty and fear and seized upon it.

"What if the strike fails, tell me that!"

Ngotho could bear it no longer. She was driving him mad. He slapped her on the face and raised his hand again. But Njoroge now found his voice. He ran forward and cried frantically, "Please, Father."

Ngotho stopped. He looked at his son. He ran toward him and grabbed him by the shoulder. Njoroge felt the grip and winced with fear. Ngotho growled something inaudible. Then he suddenly released the boy and turned his eyes away. He walked out.

"Mother!" Njoroge whispered to Nyokabi.

"Why have they bewitched him? My man is changed. . . ."

"Please, Mother!"

But she went on sobbing.

Njoroge felt lonely. Sometimes heavy and cold oppressed him in the stomach. Even the stars that later shone in the night gave him no comfort. He walked across the courtyard, not afraid of the darkness. . . . In the distance, the gleaming lights of the city where the call for the strike had been born beckoned to him. He did not respond. He just wanted to be lost in the darkness, for he could not judge between a father and mother.

In his bed, he knelt down and prayed. "God forgive me for I am wicked. Perhaps it is me who has brought uncleanliness into our home. Forgive me my sins. Help my father and mother. O, God of Abraham, Isaac and Jacobo, help Thy children. Forgive us all. Amen.

"Lord, do you think the strike will be a success?"

He wanted an assurance. He wanted a foretaste of the future before it came. In the Old Testament, God spoke to His people. Surely He could do the same thing now. So Njoroge listened, seriously and quietly. He was still listening when he fell asleep. . . .

Njoroge was a little annoyed when he heard about Jomo's arrest. He had cherished the idea of seeing this man who had become famous all over Kenya. He could still remember a meeting arranged in the marketplace by K.A.U. [Kenya African Union, black socialist movement]. It was many months after the strike that failed. K.A.U. was the society of black people who wanted Wiyathi [freedom] and the return of the stolen lands. The society also wanted bigger salaries for black people and the abolition of color-bar. Njoroge had heard about the color-bar from his brothers in Nairobi [capital of Kenya]. He did not know what it was really. But he knew that the strike had failed because of the color-bar. [A coalition of police, black landowners, and government broke the strike. Leaders were imprisoned or were fired from their jobs.] Black people had no land because of color-bar and they could not eat in hotels because of color-bar. Color-bar was everywhere. Rich Africans could also practice color-bar on the poorer Africans. . . .

Njoroge had gone early to the marketplace. But he had found that many people had already reached the place and blocked his view. All right, he would see him next time.

But now Jomo had been arrested. . . .

Everyone knew that Jomo would win. God would not let His people alone. The children of Israel must win. Many people put all their hopes on this eventual victory. If he lost, then the black people of Kenya had lost. Some of his lawyers had even come from England.

Much rain fell at Kipanga and the country around on the eve of the judgment day. People were happy in all the land. The rain was a good omen. Black folk were on trial. The spirit of black folk from Demi na Mathathi [from the beginning of time] was on trial. Would it be victorious? It was the growing uncertainty of the answer that made people be afraid and assert more and more aggressively that a victory would surely follow.

At school a little argument ensued. It was begun by Karanja, Karanja came from Ndeiya next to the Masai country [northern Kenya]. He said, "Jomo is bound to win. Europeans fear him."

"No. He can't win. My father said so last night."

"Your father is a home guard," another boy retorted. The two boys began to quarrel. Another discussion arose somewhere else.

"The home guards with their white masters. They are as bad as Mau Mau."

"No. Mau Mau is not bad. The Freedom boys are fighting against white settlers. Is it bad to fight for one's land? Tell me that."

"But they cut black men's throats."

"Those killed are the traitors! Black white settlers."

"What's Mau Mau?" Njoroge asked. He had never known what it was and his curiosity overcame his fear of being thought ignorant.

Karanja, who had just joined the group, said, "It is a secret *Kiama* [organization]. You 'drink' oath. You become a member. The *Kiama* [the African Freedom Army] has its own soldiers who are fighting for the land. Kimathi is the leader."

"Not Jomo?" a small boy with one bad eye asked.

"I don't know," Karanja continued. "But Father says that Kimathi is the leader of the Freedom Army and Jomo is the leader of K.A.U. I like K.A.U. and fear Mau Mau."

"But they are all the same? Fighting for the freedom of the black people." This was said by a tall but weak boy. Then with a distant look in his eyes, "I would like to fight in the forest."

All eyes were turned to him. He seemed to have said a very profound thing. Or seemed to have put in words what most of them felt. A solemn air hung over all the group. Then one other boy broke the silence by saying, "I too would like to fight. I would love to carry a big gun like my father used to do in the Big War when he fought for the British. Now I would be fighting for the black folk—"

"Hurrah and victory for the black folk!"

"Hurrah and victory for Jomo!"

"It rained last night."

The bell went, the group dispersed. They rushed back for their evening classes.

That night Njoroge learned that Jomo lost. His spirit fell and he felt something queer in his stomach. He did not know what to think.

"But it was all arranged," Kori explained. They all gathered in Njeri's hut, now together only for comfort. . . .

Again tonight they spoke in whispers. Boro sat in his own corner and seemed more withdrawn than ever.

"It was to be expected," Kori said again.

Nyokabi said, "I knew he would lose. I always said that all white men are the same. His lawyers must have been bribed."

"It is more than that," said Njeri. "And although I am a woman and cannot explain it, it seems all clear as daylight. The white man makes a law or a rule. Through that rule or law or what you may call it, he takes away the land and then imposes many laws on the people concerning that land and many other things, all without people agreeing first as in the old days of the tribe. Now a man rises and opposes that law which made right the taking away of land. Now that man is taken by the same people who made the laws against which that man was fighting. He is tried under those alien rules. Now tell me who is that man who can win even if the angels of God were his lawyers . . . I mean."

Njeri was panting. Njoroge had never heard her speak for such a long time. Yet there seemed to be something in what she had said. Everyone looked at her. Tears were on her face. Boro was now speaking. But it was a lamentation.

". . . All white people stick together. But we black people are very divided. And because they stick together, they've imprisoned Jomo, the only hope we had. Now they'll make us slaves. They took us to their wars and they killed all that was of value to us. . . ." Njoroge convulsively clutched the seat more firmly with his hands. All the wrongs done to the people were concentrated in the plaintive voice of Boro. Njoroge felt ready to do anything to right those wrongs. But inside himself he was afraid.

All of a sudden, Boro stood and almost shouted, "Never! Never! Black people must rise up and fight."

Njoroge's eyes dilated. Nyokabi held her breath while Njeri turned her eyes fearfully toward the door. . . .

It was a hot January morning. Two young men walked along a narrow cattle path, carelessly clutching their Bibles and hymn books. Behind them were a group of men and women, also holding Bibles and hymn books. They were discussing the saving power of Christ. Farther behind still were women gaily dressed in Sunday best. They were joyously singing.

> Nitugu-u-kugoca Je-e-Jesu
> Jesu Ga-a-tuurume Ka Ngai,
> Jesu, Thakame yaku iithera-agia mehia
> Ndakugo-e-ca Mwathani.

> We praise you Jesus
> Jesus the Lamb of God,
> Jesus Thy blood cleans away my sins
> I praise you O Lord.

All of them were going to a Christian gathering a few miles away from the town.

"Are we nearly there?" Njoroge asked the other young man. His name was Mucatha.

"No. We have not yet come to the wood I told you about."

"It is far, then."

"Not very far. I've been there on foot many times." . . .

"There now! This is the wood."

"Oh! It's so thick, it frightens me."

They stood on a rock.

"Do you see over there?"

"Beyond the dark wood?"

"Yes. Beyond, to the left of that hill."

Njoroge could see a small hill in the distance.

"I see."

"That's where the meeting is going to be."

They moved down. Teacher Isaka and the others were nearer. They were still absorbed in their talk of salvation. The cattle path widened and wound through the dense wood. Suddenly, Njoroge heard a voice.

"Stop!"

Both stopped. Fright gripped them. For there, standing in front of them, was a white military officer.

"Mikono juu."

They put up their hands so that their Bibles and hymn books were in the air as if they were displaying the word of God for all to see.

"Kuja hapa."

They went nearer. A pistol was pointed at them. Soon the group of men who had been behind came. They went through the same process and lined up behind Njoroge and Mucatha. The women came, saw the scene, and the singing died with their steps. The women were first interrogated. They were then allowed to continue their journey. It was then that Njoroge looked around and saw that they were surrounded by many soldiers who lay hidden in the bush, with machine guns menacingly pointed to the road. Njoroge clutched the Bible more firmly.

They were all made to squat and produce their documents. Fortunately Njoroge and Mucatha had letters from the former headmaster which indicated that they were schoolboys. The men at the back were not so lucky. One of them was beaten so much that he urinated on his legs. But he did not plead for mercy. The only thing he constantly said was "Jesus."

Isaka squatted and calmly watched the scene. He had no documents. When the white soldier shouted at him, Isaka answered in a calm, almost resigned tone. Where had he left the documents? Satan had made him forget them at home. But the white soldier knew better. Isaka was a Mau Mau. Again Isaka replied that Jesus had saved him and he could not exchange Jesus with Mau Mau. The officer looked at him with reddening eyes. Yet he did not touch him. Njoroge wondered if he was afraid of Isaka. There was something strange in the teacher's calm. When the others were allowed to go, Isaka was made to remain. He did not protest.

"Come this way and we'll see what Jesus will do for you."

He was led into the thick dark wood. Before the others had gone very far, they heard one horrible scream that rang

across the forest. They dared not turn their heads. Njoroge
tried to hold his breath so that his stomach was taut. They
went a few more steps. Suddenly there was one other scream
which was swallowed by a deafening report of machine guns.
Then silence.

"They have killed him," one of the men said some time
after the report. Njoroge suddenly felt sick, sick of everything. It was to him painfully unbelievable that he would
see Isaka, the worldly teacher they used to call Uuu, no more.

"Don't you believe in anything?"
"No. Nothing. Except revenge."
"Return of the lands?"
"The lost land will come back to us maybe. But I've lost
too many of those whom I loved for land to mean much to
me. It would be a cheap victory." Boro was a bit more com-
municative as he sat with his lieutenant on a lookout a few
miles from their new hideout. The old hideout had been in
the wood where Isaka had been summarily executed into
nothing. The patrol had been after the group that was led by
Boro.

Boro had now been in the forest for a considerable time.
His own daredevil action, for he did not care what happened to him personally, had made him a leader of the other
Freedom Fighters. The ripe hour of his youth had been spent
in bloodshed in the Big War. This was the only thing he
could do efficiently.

Boro had always told himself that the real reason for his
flight to the forest was a desire to fight for freedom. But this
fervor had soon worn off. His mission became a mission of
revenge. This was the only thing that could now give him
fire and boldness. If he killed a single white man, he was
exacting a vengeance for a brother killed.

"And freedom?" the lieutenant continued.
"An illusion. What freedom is there for you and me?"
"Why then do we fight?"
"To kill. Unless you kill, you'll be killed. So you go on
killing and destroying. It's a law of nature. The white man
too fights and kills with gas, bombs and everything."

"But don't you think there's something wrong in fighting and killing unless you're doing so for a great cause like ours?"

"What great cause is ours?"

"Why, freedom and the return of our lost heritage."

"Maybe there's something in that. But for me freedom is meaningless unless it can bring back a brother I lost. Because it can't do that, the only thing left to me is to fight, to kill and rejoice at any who falls under my sword. But enough . . ."

5

FROM

"A Conversation with Eduardo Mondlane"

(1920–1968)

Southern Africa is not yet independent, but revolutionary groups have been formed there to achieve black liberation.

In September, 1964, a united front of nationalist organizations called FRELIMO (Frente de Libertação de Moçabbique) launched an armed revolt in Portuguese Mozambique. FRELIMO had not only organized a guerrilla army of some seven thousand men but had established a health, educational, and political structure within liberated zones.

The originator and leader of FRELIMO was Dr. Eduardo Mondlane, an African from Mozambique and assistant professor of sociology at Syracuse University in New York. In an interview with the editor of the periodical Africa Report *in 1967, Mondlane discussed the experiences which brought about his accession to revolutionary leadership.*

In February, 1968, Mondlane was assassinated, presumably by a radical member of his own organization, but the struggle which he began in Mozambique still continues. At this time 100,000 Portuguese troops and 50 percent of Portugal's military budget have been diverted to its African colonies, and Portugal may have to request troops from South Africa.

KITCHEN: Every Africanist knows that you were an assistant professor of sociology at Syracuse University in New

York before you returned to Africa to become leader of FRELIMO in 1962. Can you tell me how this came about?

Mondlane: I was born in 1920 in the Gaza district of southern Mozambique—the last child of my father's third and last wife. My father died when I was very young, and I was raised by my mother and elder brothers. In the beginning, I did not dream of having an education. Even though my father was a chief, no member of my family had ever gone to school. My brothers and mother decided, however, that I would be educated—and she was a very determined and persistent woman. In 1931, when I was 11, I entered the government school at Manjacaze, transferring two years later to a mission school nearer home.

The Calvinist missionaries became interested in me and arranged for me to go to Lourenço Marques [capital of Mozambique] in 1936 to work for my primary school certificate. This was the highest level open to an African in those days, and it seemed that I was already approaching an educational dead end. An opportunity then opened up for technical training, however, and I snatched at that straw. I completed a course in dry-land farming at an agricultural school, and perhaps more important, I learned English. After teaching dry farming for two years in the Manjacaze region, I managed to get a scholarship to attend secondary school in Northern Transvaal [South Africa]. In 1948, I entered Witwatersrand University in Johannesburg [South Africa] on another private scholarship. The bubble burst the next year, however, when my permit as a foreign student was lifted by the South African Government, and I was also arrested and interrogated by the Portuguese in connection with my efforts to organize a Mozambique student association.

The Portuguese authorities concluded that my "embryonic spirit of black nationalism" might be cured by sending me to a university in Portugal. In the end, however, I went to the University of Lisbon on a scholarship provided by the Phelps-Stokes Fund of New York—and was cured of nothing. Although we were under close surveillance and had our rooms searched from time to time, I became friends with

African intellectuals from other Portuguese territories who are today well-known nationalist leaders. . . .

After a year in Lisbon, I asked to have the scholarship transferred to an American university, and subsequently obtained my BA from Oberlin College in Ohio in 1953. My MA and my PhD are from Northwestern University, in sociology, and I spent another year at Harvard doing research in role conflict. From 1957 until 1961, I worked for the United Nations as a research officer on trust territories.

During those five years at the UN, I received many appeals from Mozambicans to take an active leadership role in the nationalist movement. With Tanganyika's independence in 1961 [in 1964 Zanzibar and Tanganyika united to form Tanzania], I decided that the situation had changed completely and that independence for Mozambique might be possible in my lifetime. Now we had a base from which to operate. I resigned from the UN, took a teaching post at Syracuse, and prepared to return to Africa to enter actively into politics. . . .

After months of negotiation, we convened a meeting of the parties in Dar es Salaam [Tanzania, East Africa] in mid-1962 and formally established the Frente de Libertação de Moçambique on June 25 of that year. The three existing parties were dissolved and FRELIMO was established on the basis of complete fusion into a single movement. The new liberation front had a unitary structure—that is, any Mozambican who wished to be associated with the movement had to commit himself as an individual, not as part of a subgroup. We called a first party congress for September 1962 and managed to bring many influential and representative Africans out of Mozambique to help draw up the policy guidelines of the new movement.

Kitchen: What were the major policy lines agreed on at that first congress in Dar es Salaam?

Mondlane: There were three. First, we accepted it as a fact of life that Salazar's Portugal was unable to accept the idea of self-determination and that there was no prospect of negotiating political changes leading toward independence. We had to establish a clandestine political force within Mozambique to prepare the people for the very difficult task of liberating the country. Secondly, we decided to establish a clandestine military program. Thirdly, we agreed to establish an educational program that would emphasize leadership training.

Kitchen: Why were you so certain from the beginning that force would be necessary?

Mondlane: Portugal is controlled by a government which does not even accept the idea of democracy and individual freedom for the people of metropolitan Portugal. Consequently it is inconceivable that it would voluntarily accept the idea that colonial peoples like ourselves should have these rights, much less independence. Portugal cannot be compared with such colonial powers as France or Britain. The Salazar regime does not believe in frank, logical, and peaceful dialogue; it expects obedience. For this reason, we found it necessary to assume from the beginning that liberation would require the use of force.

6

"The Smuggled Account of a Guerrilla Fighter from Africa"

In Rhodesia the revolutionary movement, the Zimbabwe African Peoples Union (ZAPU), has allied itself with the chief resistance organization of South Africa, the African National Congress (ANC). The ANC, unable at this time to oppose South Africa's military might, has been sending freedom fighters to Rhodesia—called Zimbabwe by the nationalists in memory of the great eleventh-century African empire.

The African guerrillas have been fighting South African-reenforced Rhodesian soldiers since August, 1967. Their movement is not as strong as that of FRELIMO in Mozambique or the MPLA in Angola, but it has inflicted serious losses on the Rhodesian army. Together with the struggles in the Portuguese colonies and sporadic guerrilla activity in Southwest Africa, the nationalists of Zimbabwe have created a strong popular front.

The success of the independence movements depends not only on the military strength of the guerrilla forces but on their community backing. Here, the smuggled account of an ANC fighter testifies that Africans both young and old are lending assistance to and feeling part of the movement. The fighter and his specific place of combat have to remain unidentified.

THE fighting alliance made by the African National Congress of South Africa was reflected in our group, which consisted mainly of ZAPU members and a few of us from the ANC. The commander was an able comrade from ZAPU, with remarkable leadership qualities. Both at the political and personal level, our fighting was unique. We all realized that the liberation of Zimbabwe was the job of the Zimbabwe people. But we also knew that the unity of the white regimes and particularly the occupation of Zimbabwe by South African forces made cooperation in the liberation front not only desirable, but indispensable, both for our own victory and for the victory of the Zimbabwe people.

After the last big engagement and the continuous bombing which followed during the daylight hours, our commander split the detachment into a number of smaller groups. Our section made its way to our general area of operations. We were hungry and thirsty, but morale on the whole was good. The previous four months taught us a great deal both about ourselves and the enemy. No one had dared to say during that frustrating, dangerous period of inactivity and waiting that we might not be a match for the enemy; deep in our minds, however, we weren't so certain.

But now at last we'd been through it. We'd seen the enemy run in more than one engagement, leaving his dead and wounded. Doubt was replaced by certainty. It would not be easy, this we knew. A few had already lost their lives, a few had been injured and one, so far, had lost his stomach for the fight and had deserted. But those months had taught us that victory is certain, whether we personally survive the fight or not. The weeks that were to follow strengthened this conviction. We continued to give a good account of ourselves. But more than that, it was our village which taught us. It taught us the reality of this thing called "the people" and how it is possible that an enemy a thousand-fold more powerful than ourselves can be defeated.

I remember that morning clearly. For a week we had had no proper food, and no contact with people. Suddenly the sound of a muffled drum and then a cock crowing and donkeys braying. Imagine our joy! The commander sent two of the men who spoke the local language to investigate. Some hours later the reconnaissance group returned and reported that after making an unsuccessful approach to a man in a house on the outskirts, they had been directed to the main village where, in the first house they entered, they had met Old Man. This was our name for him, even though he was a man in his middle twenties. He had a wife and two young children.

"We are fishermen on the river. We are hungry and we have run out of food. Could you give us something to eat and also . . ." Before they could finish Old Man said: "I am not to be played with. I have heard of the war. You must be honest with me. If you are freedom fighters, say so. If you are not, say so."

After some evasion, they became convinced that his expressions of sympathy for our struggle were genuine, and admitted who they were. His response was warming. He shook their hands and hugged them, and for the first time they saw the beaming, happy smile by which we all came to think of him. He at once gave them 50 pounds of mealie meal, two chickens, salt and milk, while indignantly refusing an offer of money. Before they left he said, "If you really are what you say you are, then I want to see your commander. I want to speak to him about something which is just between him and me." He refused to give any hint of what it was he wanted to discuss.

That night we ate our fill and talked of Old Man. Should the commander go? What if it were a trap? Why in any case should he want only the commander? In the end our commander decided that on balance it was a reasonable chance to take, and with the necessary precautions—he was covered by a few of us—he went to Old Man.

Old Man welcomed him and said almost immediately that he was one of those who had been rounded up during the State of Emergency when he knew no politics. "In the camp," he said, "I started thinking for the first time. Now that the war is on, I want to do something, not only to give food. I sit here idling whilst you fight and die. My life is no more valuable than yours. There are others in this village, young men, who will come forward. I know them. I can get them." Of his sincerity there could no longer be any question.

Thinking back on it, we were much too cautious in our attitude. We wanted to be careful. We had been told to be careful. We had learned from bitter experience that one traitor is worth a hundred supporters. But when can you ever be absolutely certain? In any event, the commander told him that his request to go into the mountains would be considered later. Meanwhile, he should recruit no one and tell no one of our presence without first getting permission. He was to leave food, messages and especially information about the enemy at an arranged spot. Throughout these discussions Old Man's wife sat silent and accepting. He had given an indication that what he did, she would do. Every day thereafter, he did his duty.

During the second week he gave us a message from someone claiming to be a comrade of ours who was being hidden in one of the huts in the village and was trying to meet up with his detachment. From the description we concluded that it might be one of our men who had been sent out some months earlier with an ill-fated reconnaissance unit which had suffered heavy casualties. But we could not be certain. Old Man was instructed to take the man to an arranged spot without giving him an opportunity to talk to anyone.

He was taken there. It *was* our comrade. What a reunion! It was joyous like a township party. We laughed so much, it was getting risky; in the open sound travels dangerously. That night he told us of his reconnaissance unit, of the heroism and death of B, of the battle which their section had put up against superior numbers (they had been ambushed and caught unawares), of how he fought until he was wounded, rolled down a river bank and crawled to safety. From then on he had searched continually, trying to join one of our detachments, helped all the time by ordinary peasants who hid him and gave him food. He told us too that the villagers

who had hidden him were anxious to join our section. Again
we felt that making such contacts was premature—probably
wrongly.

Then, almost casually, he related something which came
to have a most important connection with what was to
happen to us. The people with whom he had been staying
had advised him to carry out the custom which every
stranger for his own good must do whenever he comes to a
village in the area: visit the local Maswikero (fortune
teller). Only *he* would be able to say whether our stay would
be safe.

The first day this was mentioned, it was as a part of the
story of his experiences in the village. We soon noticed,
however, that some members of our group continued to talk
about it. Eventually they raised the matter with the commander. The commander called us all together. He explained that we had received advice from the local people
which some of the men strongly felt should be followed
because we should respect local custom. Many of us spoke
against it: "We can't follow all the traditions in our special
situation. If this is the tradition, then the police must go
there too. Informers must also go there. Is it right for us to
take such a risk?" Someone asked whether this could be done
secretly. The answer given was no.

After two days of discussion, some of the fighters became
impatient. "You despise our customs," one of them said.
"You undermine our traditions. Is it because you are com-
munists? This is Africa, and to achieve our aim we have to
follow our own traditions." In all six months of sharing
hardship and battle (up to now we had already buried six of
our men, four ZAPU and two ANC), there had been a warm,
wonderful comradeship between us. Now for the first time
there was friction, sharpness, even anger. The commander,
who sensed this friction and the way it was beginning to
divide us at a most irrational level—a level at which pure
argument does not always prove to be adequate—decided on
a compromise. If Old Man confirmed this tradition, then he
should take our comrade who had been hidden in the village
to the Maswikero.

Old Man, who confirmed the existence of this tradition, urged us strongly not to send *him,* "because," he said, "I don't want to show my face with one of you." This was obviously right. Instead, he arranged for his uncle to do the job. On Saturday evening they met and set off for the Maswikero. After standing in a long queue their turn came and the uncle, who by then had drunk quite a quantity of the beer sold on the premises, said to the Maswikero, "I have brought a representative of the freedom fighters and they have come to find out whether they will be successful." The answer came: "I see blood in all you are saying. I won't take your money, but everything will be peaceful. I will arrange a mist to cover you on the route to any place you want to go."

On their way out of the hut, the uncle consoled our comrade in loud whispers, saying that he should not worry and not take too seriously the part about the blood. He babbled sympathetically about the freedom struggle, and so on. Not far from the Maswikero they were stopped and questioned by two Security Policemen who had followed them. The uncle explained that his friend had come from Salisbury [the capital of Rhodesia] to see the fortune teller whose fame is widespread. He would be leaving the next morning. For some reason they were allowed to proceed, and our comrade returned safely, after taking extra precautions to make sure that he was not being followed.

The following day brought shattering news. When we went to our supply point, we did not find Old Man, but someone else. He told us that the uncle had been arrested and had collapsed under interrogation. The village was invaded by Security Forces and a search was on for Old Man who had been warned just in time, and was proceeding to a spot in the mountains where it had been previously arranged that we would meet him in just such an emergency. It was now nighttime and the commander decided to wait until first light to keep this rendezvous, since we had not arranged a call sign and he feared that our approach at night might cause Old Man to panic.

At first light, a section was detailed to move toward the

rendezvous point two hours away. We approached in skirmish formation. Suddenly the air was filled with bursts of
gunfire. They came from the direction of the rendezvous
point. We crept closer, and there in front of us, already
moving toward the village, was a large, well-armed enemy
force carrying the limp body of Old Man. We were neither
strong enough nor positioned well enough to invite a battle.

We moved back to base. That day, even the hardest among
us shed tears. The commander gathered us together. We
stood, heads bowed in silence for our brave, smiling Old
Man. We knew then that without people like him, we are
nothing.

A few days later, after taking precautions, we managed to
make contact with the Old Man's wife. There were no tears,
just sadness. She spoke about the struggle for the first time.
She asked why it was that he had to die without a gun in his
hand. "Just running," she said. "Why didn't you carry out
his wish to take him into the mountains with you?" We explained as best we could that Old Man was doing as much
of a soldier's job as if he had carried a gun, that his was the
death of a freedom fighter in battle. "It is often much easier
to be brave with a gun in your hand than to carry on as Old
Man did, risking his life every minute of the day without
defense, and alone." I think she understood for she put an
end to the talk of Old Man by saying, "And how are you
going to eat? And be told things? I will see that it is done."

Old Man's family and friends assembled from many parts
of the country. Among them was a young boy from the Z
area who was appointed to continue the supply work. This
he did with enthusiasm and efficiency. He was in a continuous state of excitement about the reports of fighting in
many parts of the country. He wanted to join us and to
bring some friends along; he also told us of some excellent
terrain in the Z area in which supplies could be stored and
from which operations would be effective, particularly in
view of its proximity to large population groups. We refused
his offer. Again, possibly mistakenly. We were being cautious
almost to a fault.

Some days later we received a message that the house of Old Man's widow was under the strictest surveillance, that it would be dangerous for anyone connected with her to continue doing the supply and contact work, and that another old man, a villager (this time the description fitted the age, for he was also called Old Man), would take over. We were encouraged by this further proof that the reserves of sympathy, loyalty and readiness to sacrifice are large. How it was all discussed and decided in the village was a mystery to us. The new Old Man did his job as the contacts before him had. He refused to be paid for anything which came out of the villagers' own stock. Things like meat and vegetables were given free though we tried to press them to accept some money. It was only for items which had to be purchased at the local store that money was accepted, and then every single penny was accounted for.

The time had come to move. We had built a reasonable stock of food; our physique and weight were back to normal. The commander worked out a plan of march toward the Z area described by the young boy. We were to proceed in two groups, with two hours' distance between us.

I don't know whether it was the result of a leakage of information or whether we had somehow betrayed ourselves by relaxation of vigilance (for example, we cooked at night in an area which was out of bounds to villagers and the fire may have been spotted), but shortly before we were due to move, we suddenly observed a well-camouflaged enemy force of company strength advancing on our base in skirmish formation. It was early in the morning. We knew that once the fight started we would be harassed until nightfall from the air, but we had no option. Our retreat would have been up hilly ground and it was too late to sneak away. Quickly the commander whispered his orders and they were passed on. The group of which I was a member, due to set off toward the Z area, would start moving a short while after the commencement of the battle. The other group, under our commander, would remain to cover our retreat. The order to fire was given, and we punished the enemy badly from our well dug-in positions. The usual pattern was re-

peated. Their ground forces moved away and the aerial
bombardment started. Our group was then ordered to move
as arranged. During the fight we lost two men, one of them
our medical officer.

After moving about half a mile I felt my right leg getting
weaker and weaker. I looked down, and for the first time, a
blood-covered boot told me that I had been wounded. It
must have been shrapnel from a grenade. I could no longer
walk. There was no alternative but to leave me. I was taken
to our new Old Man. He hid me in a dug-out in a field near
the village. I was told that our unit would return for me in
a few days.

Next to the death of Old Man, this separation from my
comrades was for me the saddest time. With them I felt
strong, almost invincible. Alone I felt like nothing. Every
noise and every movement put fear into me. Every night the
new Old Man came to me with food. He nursed my wound
with an impressive skill. He regularly applied hot poultices
of boiled leaves, and used some balm made out of local roots.
After a few days, when the infected area seemed ready, he
applied more and more poultices, and after making a small
incision with a sterilized knife, pressed gently round the
area, and a metal fragment came out. My recovery thereafter
was speedy. But ten days had now gone by. My unit had not
returned for me and there was daily news of increased fighting all over the country, including intensive activity in the
Z area.

After the new Old Man had discussed it with friends in
the village, he suggested that it would be dangerous for me
to remain any longer. The area was now being combed by
Security Forces and my unit was obviously unable to return
for me in time. He suggested that he guide me back to a
place of safety where I could once again join our freedom
forces. This he did at great risk, and with great skill and
devotion.

It struck me later that after the disastrous fortune teller
incident nothing at all was said of it in our detachment. No
recriminations, and no apologies. We were all close once
again. All understood now. It had to be learned, not from

books, but from life. As for the mists, this was not the season for them. But we had all learned that what will really keep us secure and covered in our route are our millions of oppressed countrymen who will throw up thousands of people like Old Man, like his widow, like the youth, like the new Old Man, and like all the other people in *our* village.

7

FROM

"Racialism at the Meeting Point"
by Francis Deng

(1938–   )

European-initiated political entities do not automatically evolve into modern nations. Even after independence, historical, economic, and cultural differences may continue to separate African tribes and peoples, and may continue to impede the development of African national unity and Pan-African solidarity. Three current examples of such antagonisms in East Africa are the hostility between Asians and Africans in Kenya, the hatred among tribes in Uganda, and the distrust between Arabs and blacks in the Sudan.

Francis M. Deng, the son of a Dinka chief, was born in 1938 in the Sudan. The following selection, which takes place in the early 1950's, reveals that during his childhood in the Sudan he encountered not only white racism directed against blacks but also African hatred for other Africans.

Deng studied law at the University of Khartoum and recently received his LL.M. from Kings College, London.

POLITICALLY and socially, the *status quo* has changed rapidly. The ruled have become rulers. This change has meant equality between nations in international organizations; but even more notable, nationals of these newly-independent countries have now the task of asserting their individual equality with others. In doing so, they are obviously questioning old assumptions that 'race' itself is a factor in making some superior to others. This is the origin of the wind of nationalism sweeping Africa today.

Such are the inconsistencies of our accomplishments; becoming more united in one humanity, acknowledging the integrity and competence of others by granting them the right to manage their own affairs, inviting people under our own roof as an expression of good-will and assistance, at the same time we intensify mutual hatred by transforming what was latent prejudice and grudge into active indignation.

I speak of 'we' because in our heterogeneous world today it is difficult to conceive of a country where one will not encounter racialism in one form or another, although certain fields may be more explosive than others. Even as a child in the Sudan, I saw the reactions of one tribe to another, of one ethnic group to others, and of course, the attitude of foreign races towards our own. I am not assuming that I could define 'racialism' or even 'race' precisely, nor do I intend to do so; but in a broad sense I regard all these attitudes as aspects of racial consciousness. Some tribes looked down on others and would not inter-marry. It was normal for some groups to refer to others as 'slaves' because their ancestors had at times raided them in search of slaves. In fact, turning the clock back by twelve years, I recall one of my own experiences. I was walking along a sandy and lonely street one day with several members of my family. It was in a market town of the Baggara Arabs in the Western Sudan. As we walked, we came across a child of about six, playing with muddy sand so that he and his garment matched his surroundings. He got up, and gazing up at us steadily with an innocent smile on his face, he said, '*abiid*.' Taking it for '*tayibiin*' which is a greeting in that part of the world, we responded accordingly; but to our surprise, one of the party who had heard him rightly went up and slapped his face. We had little sympathy for the child when we knew that he had said 'slaves,' though we could not help being amused.

He was surely too young to know what he was saying, but he was clearly expressing the spirit of the community in which he was growing up.

I can quote, too, another case which illustrates the sense of racialism in the same setting. A prominent chief of a friendly neighbouring tribe wanted to marry into our family for diplomatic reasons. When the matter was put to the girl concerned, she objected to the suggestion. The Arab chief, in order to add weight to his proposal, sought the support of the British Administrator at that time, who tried to discuss the matter with our family and the girl. Writing about the incident, this Administrator reports: 'When I asked her about it, she laughed. "The man is all right," she said, "but he is an Arab. I'm a Dinka. We don't marry outside our people." '

Unfortunately, most Africans do not pay much attention to such cases, even though they may deplore them. Racialism to most people is a struggle between the Blacks and the Whites, usually taking the form of a colour-bar, or being given more definite form as a policy of subjection and segregation of the Blacks by the Whites. But history teaches that racialism is not necessarily 'colourism' and that it can be practised by Whites against other Whites. I have shown that race prejudice can be practised by Blacks against Blacks, though unacknowledged.

8

FROM

"The Price of Nigerian Victory"

by Charles Keil

Recently the worst tribal conflict in Africa has been the Nigerian Civil War in West Africa. In the 1960's economic jealousies and historical and cultural rivalries paralyzed Nigerian politics. In 1967 the Ibo tribe of eastern Nigeria seceded from the Nigerian republic to form Biafra. For three years Biafrans and Nigerians engaged in combat until the final Biafran surrender in February, 1970.

Whatever the politics of the conflict, the toll in human lives—particularly due to starvation—is staggering. According to the American Africanist Charles Keil, an estimated 500,000 Biafran children died.

THE central problem of genocide seems to be simple comprehension—how to grasp the fact of mass murder emotionally and intellectually. A newspaper headline will help us to empathize with the mother of a kidnaped baby, but when hundreds of children die each day, week after week, month after month in a distant land there are no newspaper headlines and the weeping mothers are too many. The vulgar search for immediate images: How many pages will be needed to give small obituaries for 500,000 Biafran children?

Jerone, 8, a fast learner, wanted to teach one day.

Rose, 10, hoped to be a nurse.

Kusuwe, 4, dreamed only of food, more rice, and died dreaming.

Amede, 3 months, faced a dry breast and never lived at all. One hundred abbreviated lives in progress on each page and still 5,000 pages. Emotionally, the death of half a million Biafran children is completely incomprehensible.

9

FROM

A Nigerian Villager in Two Worlds

by Dilim Okafor Omali

(1927–   )

Africans experience not only intertribal antagonisms but also tensions between modern and traditional Africa. As Dilim Okafor Omàli's account illustrates, a child growing up in urban Africa in the 1940's had a markedly different childhood from that of the village children. A visit back home was a strange and even frightening event.

Okafor Omali was born in 1927 at Port Harcourt, a commercial city of eastern Nigeria, West Africa, and has been attending a technical college in London. His first book, A Nigerian Villager in Two Worlds, *is a biography of his father's life and indirectly an autobiography of his own youth.*

MOST of Nweke's people who went abroad in the early 1920s were Christians, and their children were the first to be brought up under a largely Christian system of education. These children were sent to school when they were five, and later took jobs where their parents were living. Hence, some never visited their home village till they were grown up and had adopted Western ways of life.

The tragedy of it was that these carefully educated children, who had been given more attention than their counterparts in the home village, could not, when they returned, fit into the traditional social structure. They had been given personal names which had no connection with the system of names used in the village. Moreover, as they had lived most of their early life abroad, they had learnt to talk, not their mother tongue, but the white man's language, or the foreign language spoken where their parents lived. Even when they attempted to acquire their mother tongue, they were often unable to speak with the correct accent. It is very sad to meet a grown-up person who is fluent in the white man's language, but who can hardly say a word in his mother tongue without apologizing for mistakes.

At the beginning, parents did not understand what harm this ignorance would do in the cultural education of their children and in home affairs. But later they realized the mistake—when the appalling situation arose in which a young man did not fully understand his own language, was ignorant of his rights in the village, did not know his father's property, his own inheritance, and had no knowledge of the people and affairs of the village.

Strenuous efforts were made by parents and by the community to counteract these evils. Those who lived abroad sent their children back to the village to attend school, and to learn something about village matters. Young men who were working abroad regarded it as a duty to travel home whenever they had leave. And the town union made it binding on every citizen to return home with all the members of his family at a specified time. . . .

Among the early Christian parents were my father and mother. I was the first son, and was born in the township of Port Harcourt, the seaport of the Eastern Region of Nigeria. My father gave me the long name Sigismund, meaning 'Conquering Protection.' It was his intention to express a particular circumstance by this name. If he had not been a Christian he could have done the same, more easily, with a native name. He found this name only after much research, and he thought it came closest to what he wished to express. None of his fellow tribesmen ever took the name, Sigismund, and many found it difficult to pronounce. They criticized him for overlooking the common Christian names and wondered where he found this one.

My father, shortly after my birth, worked in a non-Ibo speaking community where the lingua franca was the white man's language. As a result, I learnt to talk the white man's language. Until I was five years old, I could not speak a word of my mother tongue.

I was five years old when I was taken by my father to Enugwu-Ukwu [eastern Nigeria] for the second time, the first time being when I was a little over a year old. The mere sight of the villagers and the strangeness of the environment alarmed me. My conduct was very amusing. When my maternal grandmother approached to pick me up I screamed wildly and ran away. I ran to my mother and cried, "Mamma, look that dirty woman, who bi that? Ee dey touch me." As I said this, I was shivering violently and would not look up. Poor me! it was the grandmother whom I later became very fond of, but I did not know her then. I next ran to my father and complained, "Papa, which place bi this? Make we go now!" I was very uncomfortable during my stay in the village—although it was my own village! Poor me, I did not understand! I screamed whenever any villager came near me and did not allow most of them to touch me. No amount of persuasion from my parents could make me mix with the people. My conduct was the subject of much talk among the villagers. Their common remark was, "Well, there is a Christian child, and that is how they behave!"

One incident during this visit is always fresh in my mind. It was my first experience of horror. For the first time, I saw adult men and women crying and wailing, and women throwing themselves on the ground. It happened one bright sunny morning. Somebody, I learnt later, had died in the adjoining village. He was a middle-aged man, one of the very few people I would talk to, who had also returned on leave, bringing with him his wife and two children. In the morning of the day previous to his death he was well, but in the afternoon he suddenly fell ill, and died the following morning. He had been very sociable and was loved by one and all. His sudden death was a great shock to all the villagers— hence the frantic expressions of grief, and the stampede to his house.

Within minutes, all the adults in our compound had rushed out to the compound of the deceased. I saw my grandmother running with her hands clutching her head. We children, the very little ones, were left behind.

The children, mostly about my own age, moved from one part of the compound to another, playing and enjoying themselves. There was no Papa, no Mamma, I could hang on to. I was scared to remain alone, so I trailed after the other children. They soon started leaving the compound. Where they were going I did not know. At the front gate, I hesitated and looked back. The compound was deserted. I had no alternative but to stay with them. I did not understand their language, and they did not understand mine. They made their way along a sandy path. Once, my foot sank into the sand. I thought I was falling into the ground, and was about to scream. Just in time, one of the children took me by the hand and pulled me out and along. Soon we left the sandy path, and started going through winding passages in the bush. The bright light was gone. It was a world of shades. I was horrified by the strangeness of this new world. I looked around, to see matted branches overhanging everywhere. I wanted to go back, but the view behind was equally terrifying. I was drawn on by the exuberance and cheerfulness of the other children. I was already ten yards behind, but two of them came back; one took my right hand, the other my left. I followed, my eyes half shut in horror.

Next came a sharp turning to the left and I lost sight of the other children. They had raced down the adjoining slope, which led to the village stream. "What sort of place is this?" I thought. I looked at the face of the boy on my right, then at the one on my left. They spoke to me but I did not understand them. They urged me on with encouraging gestures and stepped down the first part of the very steep slope. Their step was firm—mine slipped. Then both feet slipped. Though they managed to hold me back, terror struck my heart. I was a victim of a dreadful misadventure, I thought. Papa and Mamma were not there to help me. Again I looked at the two boys, again I looked down the precipice.

At that unfortunate moment, I caught sight of the creature I most hated to see. It was a snake crossing the path. My declining courage was shattered. I screamed, and pulled my hands away from the two boys. I screamed at the top of my voice for Papa and Mamma to hear me and come to my rescue. The children down by the stream looked up, amused. When I looked for help and sympathy, they laughed at me. For quite a long time my screams mingled with the cries of the birds. I felt an intense hatred for anything connected with the adventure. I lost faith in the children because they laughed at me. When they could do nothing for me, they called their elders. The elders, as they approached me, started laughing too. "They are just the same," I thought. I had no confidence in them. All their efforts to pick me up failed. I was screaming all the time. But my saviours soon arrived. A real saviour, I thought; one of the only two who do not live with snakes in this horrible wilderness; who give me sympathy when I want it and do not show their teeth in laughter. It was my father. Peace had come to me again. He picked me up and asked, "What ting dey do you?" "This people, them take me for bush. I see snake. Bush people. Papa make we go." Looking scornfully at those around, I crept into the circle of his protecting arms.

I told my story to my mother. For the rest of the day I did not step out of our house. I refused to play with the other children, and whenever I saw those connected with my unhappy adventure, I would beckon to my mother, and say, "Mamma, mamma, look them!"

After a brief stay my parents left the village for a new station, Enugu, an Ibo-speaking town. I now had an opportunity to pick up my mother tongue. I mixed with my fellow children in play and at school, and gradually learnt to express myself in Ibo. Though circumstances did not permit my father to send me home to the village to attend school, and I continued to live abroad, I nevertheless visited home occasionally. I had little opportunity to associate closely with

the villagers, but I made a special effort to become ac-
quainted with local affairs, and later in life I championed
the cause of the village in which, when I was five years old,
I had refused to live.

10

FROM

Ambiguous Adventure

by Cheikh Hamidou Kane

(1928–   )

Ambiguous Adventure, *written by Cheikh Hamidou Kane, is an autobiographical novel. More specifically Kane, a Senegalese, has written a philosophical treatise which deals with the problem of Africa's Westernization. The central figure, the young boy Samba Diallo, is raised by pious Islamic West Africans. His parents reluctantly send him to a French school to learn the power of the West, but there Samba Diallo gradually discovers that he cannot live in both worlds. He cannot resolve the incompatibility of Islamic Africa's mysticism with the West's pragmatism. Although he prefers his own culture to that of the West, he is torn from the strength of his own traditions—by attending a French school, by accepting the material comforts of the West, and by studying Western philosophy—and eventually he can live in neither world.*

Kane does not resolve the problem of the attraction of the West, either for Samba Diallo, for himself, or for his countrymen. He merely states that he does believe that Africans must compromise with the West and must accept some Western technological advances. But at the same time he pleads with his countrymen not to become too attracted by the West so as to forget their own traditions.

In the following excerpt from Ambiguous Adventure, *Samba Diallo, as a young boy, is just being introduced to Western institutions and ideas. He, like his father, still receives comfort from his own culture, but he is already becoming influenced and confused by Western ideas and culture.*

Kane, born in 1928, has been director of the cabinet within the Senegalese Ministry of Development and Planning and governor of the region of Thies. Ambiguous Adventure *won the 1962 Grand Prix for French-speaking Black Africa.*

THE country of the Diallobé [tribal group of Senegal, West Africa] was not the only one which had been awakened by a great clamor early one day. The entire black continent had had its moment of clamor.

Strange dawn! The morning of the Occident in black Africa was spangled over with smiles, with cannon shots, with shining glass beads. Those who had no history were encountering those who carried the world on their shoulders. It was a morning of accouchement: the known world was enriching itself by a birth that took place in mire and blood.

From shock, the one side made no resistance. They were a people without a past, therefore without memory. The men who were landing on their shores were white, and mad. Nothing like them had ever been known. The deed was accomplished before the people were even conscious of what had happened.

Some among the Africans, such as the Diallobé, brandished their shields, pointed their lances, and aimed their guns. They were allowed to come close, then the cannon were fired. The vanquished did not understand. . . .

Others wanted to parley. They were given a choice: friendship or war. Very sensibly, they chose friendship. They had no experience at all.

The result was the same, nevertheless, everywhere.

Those who had shown fight and those who had surrendered, those who had come to terms and those who had been obstinate—they all found themselves, when the day came, checked by census, divided up, classified, labeled, conscripted, administrated.

For the newcomers did not know only how to fight. They were strange people. If they knew how to kill with effectiveness, they also knew how to cure, with the same art. Where they had brought disorder, they established a new order. They destroyed and they constructed. On the black continent it began to be understood that their true power lay not in the cannons of the first morning, but rather in what followed the cannons.

Thus, behind the gunboats, the clear gaze of the Most Royal Lady of the Diallobé [the sister of Samba Diallo's father] had seen the new school.

The new school shares at the same time the characteristics of cannon and of magnet. From the cannon it draws its efficacy as an arm of combat. Better than the cannon, it makes conquest permanent. The cannon compels the body, the school bewitches the soul. Where the cannon has made a pit of ashes and of death, in the sticky mold of which men would not have rebounded from the ruins, the new school establishes peace. The morning of rebirth will be a morning of benediction through the appeasing virtue of the new school.

From the magnet, the school takes its radiating force. It is bound up with a new order, as a magnetic stone is bound up with a field. The upheaval of the life of man within this new order is similar to the overturn of certain physical laws in a magnetic field. Men are seen to be composing themselves, conquered, along the lines of invisible and imperious forces. Disorder is organized, rebellion is appeased, the mornings of resentment resound with songs of a universal thanksgiving.

Only such an upheaval in the natural order can explain how, without either of them wanting it, the new man and the new school come together just the same. For neither of them wants the other. The man does not want the school because in order that he may live—that is, be free, feed and clothe himself—it imposes upon him the necessity of sitting

henceforth, for the required period, upon its benches. No
more does the school want the man because in order to survive—that is, extend itself and take roots where its necessity
has landed it—it is obliged to take account of him. . . .

A letter had announced to the knight [Samba Diallo's
father] that the older members of the Diallobé family, the
Most Royal Lady as well as the chief, had decided to send
Samba Diallo back to him so that he might be enrolled in
the new school.

What the knight felt when he received the letter was like
a blow in his heart. So, the victory of the foreigners was complete! Here were the Diallobé, here was his own family, on
their knees before a burst of fireworks. A solar burst, it is
true, the midday burst of an exasperated civilization. The
knight was suffering deeply in the face of this irreparable
thing which was being accomplished here, before his eyes,
upon his own flesh. Those who, even down to his own family,
were racing headlong into the future, if they could only
understand that their course was a suicide, their sun a
mirage! If only he himself were of the stature to rise up
before them on their road, and put an end to that blind
contest!

"In truth, it is not acceleration which the world needs,"
the knight reflected. "What we must have is a bed, a bed
upon which, stretched out, the soul will determine a respite,
in the name of its salvation. Is civilization outside the balance of man and his disposability? The civilized man, is he
not the expendable man—expendable for the love of his fel-
lows, expendable above all for the love of God? But, a voice
within him will object, man is surrounded by problems
which prevent this quietude. He is born to a forest of questions. The substance of matter in which he participates
through his body—which the soul hates—harasses him with
a cacophony of demands to which he must respond. 'I am
hungry. Give me something to eat,' his stomach orders. 'Are
we going to rest at last? Let us rest,' his limbs keep murmur-
ing. To his stomach and his limbs, a man gives the answers
that are called for; and this man is happy. Then a voice im-
plores him: 'I am alone. I am afraid to be alone. I am not

sufficient in loneliness. Find me someone to love.' And this voice, particularly plaintive, lamenting day and night: 'I am afraid. I am afraid. What is my native country? Who brought me here? Where are they taking me?' The man rises and goes in search of man. Then he isolates himself and prays. This man is at peace. Man must respond to all the questions. You, you wish to ignore some of them. . . . No," the knight objected for his own part, "no, I only wish for harmony. The most strident voices try to drown out the others. Is that good? Civilization is an architecture of responses. Its perfection, like that of any dwelling house, is measured by the comfort man feels in it, by the added portion of liberty it procures for him. But, precisely, the Diallobé are not free—and you would like to maintain this condition? No, that is not what I want. But man's slavery amid a forest of solutions—is that worth anything more?"

The knight was turning these thoughts over and over in his mind, in a thousand ways.

"Happiness is not a function of the mass of responses, but of their distribution. There must be balance. But the West is possessed by its own compulsion, and the world is becoming westernized. Far from men's resisting the madness of the West at the time when they ought to do so, in order to pick and choose, assimilate or reject, we see them, on the contrary, in all latitudes, a-quiver with covetousness, then metamorphosing themselves in the space of one generation, under the action of this new egotism which the West is scattering abroad."

At this point in his reflections the knight had something like an hallucination. A spot on our globe was burning with a blinding brilliance, as if a fire had been lighted on an immense hearth. At the heart of this fierce light and heat a swarm of human beings seemed to be giving themselves over to an incomprehensible and fantastic mimicry of worship. Emerging from all sides, from deep valleys of shadow, floods of human creatures of all colors were pouring in; and in the measure of their approach to the hearth, these beings took up, insensibly, the rhythm which encompassed them, while under the effect of the light they lost their original colors, which gave way to the wan tint that filled the air round-about.

The knight closed his eyes to banish the vision. To live in the shadow, to live humbly and peaceably at the obscure heart of the world, to live from his own substance and his own wisdom. . . .

So when he had received the letter from the chief of the Diallobé the knight had remained seated for a long time. Then he had got up, gone to a corner of the courtyard, turned his face toward the east, and prayed long and earnestly to his Lord. Samba Diallo would go to the school, if such was the will of God.

He had refrained from any sort of outburst at the time of the boy's return. But through his calm and his affectionate solicitude Samba Diallo had perceived profound grief. In the face of this disapproval which was not expressed, this sadness by which the knight was not crushed, in the face of this silence of his father's, Samba Diallo had melted into tears, and a thousand times regretted his departure from the Glowing Hearth.

On that first night, it would seem that Nature had wished to associate itself with a delicate thought of the boy's, for the luminous twilight had scarcely died away when a thousand stars had sprung forth in the sky. The moon was born at the heart of their scintillating festival, and a mystic exaltation seemed suddenly to fill the night.

The house was silent. The knight, stretched out on a chaise longue on the veranda, was absorbed in meditation. The women, grouped around the mother of the family, were talking in very low tones.

Samba Diallo quietly left his room on the court, walked up and down and across, and then, slowly, recited the prelude to the Night of the Koran,* which he offered to the knight. His voice, scarcely audible at first, gradually rose and grew stronger. Progressively, he felt that an emotion was

---

* It was the custom that the child who had completed his studies in the Koran and returned to his parents should, in their honor, recite the Holy Book from memory throughout all of one night.

sweeping through him in an experience he had never had before. Every word had ceased, throughout the house. The knight, at first lying down indifferent to what was going on about him, had stood up when he heard the voice of Samba Diallo, and it seemed now that in listening to the Word he sustained the same levitation as that which increased the teacher's stature. Samba Diallo's mother had detached herself from the group of women and come close to her son. From feeling himself listened to, so, by the two beings whom he loved the most, from knowing that on this enchanted night he, Samba Diallo, was repeating for his father what the knight himself had repeated for his own father, what from generation to generation through centuries the sons of the Diallobé had repeated for their fathers, from knowing that he had not failed in this respect and that he was about to prove to all who were listening that the Diallobé would not die in him—from all this, there was a moment when Samba Diallo was on the point of fainting. But he considered that it was important for him, more than for any of those who had preceded him, to acquit himself to the full on his Night. For it seemed to him that this Night marked an end. This scintillation of the heavens above his head, was it not the star-studded bolt being drawn upon an epoch that had run its course? Behind that bolt a world of stellar light was gently glowing, a world which it was important to glorify one last time. His voice, which had progressively risen as if linked to the thrust of the stars, was raised now to a pathetic fullness. From the depths of the ages he felt, springing up in him and breathed out by his voice, a long love which today was threatened. In the humming sound of this voice there was being dissolved, bit by bit, a being who a few moments ago had still been Samba Diallo. Insensibly, rising from profundities which he did not suspect, phantoms were assailing him through and through and were substituting themselves for him. It seemed to him that in his voice had become muffled innumerable voices, like the voice of the river on certain nights.

But the voice of the river was less vehement, and also less close to tears. The voice of the river did not carry along with it this refusal which was now being cried out in the voice of Samba Diallo; nor did it have the accompaniment of this nostalgic chant.

For a long time, in the night, his voice was that of the voiceless phantoms of his ancestors, whom he had raised up. With them, he wept their death; but also, in long cadence, they sang his birth. . . .

The knight took off his eyeglasses, closed his Koran, and for some time remained motionless, with his face to the east. His countenance was at once grave and serene. Samba Diallo, lying on a rug near him, slipped the pencil from his right hand between the pages of the book he was reading, and looked at his father.

"The Word must continue to echo within him," the boy said to himself. "He is one of those who do not cease to pray when they have closed their prayer book. To him, God is a constant Presence—constant and indispensable. It is this Presence, I believe, which stretches the skin tight across the bones of his forehead, the deep-cut orbits of his eyes. His mouth holds no smile, nor does it hold any bitterness. All the profane exuberance of life must certainly be burned out of this man by his profound prayers. My father does not live, he prays . . .

"But wait a minute! Why did I think that?" he caught himself up. "Why did I think of prayer and life in terms of opposition? He prays, he does not live. . . . Certainly no one else in this house would have thought that way. I am the only one who could have this bizarre idea of a life which could be lived, in some fashion, outside the presence of God. . . . Curious. Bizarre idea. Then where could I have got it? This idea is foreign to me. The astonishment into which it plunges me is proof of that. It is, in any case, an idea that has evolved. I mean to say, an idea that marks a progress in precision over my previous state of mind: it distinguishes; it specifies. There is God and there is life, two things not necessarily intermingled. There is prayer and there is combat. Is this idea right? If I listened to that man sleeping more and more profoundly within me, I should reply, No, this idea is even mad; life is only of a secondary order: it is from time to time. God alone is, continually, uninterruptedly. Life is only in the measure and of the fashioning of the being of God.

"So this man within me would say; would he be right? Evil is of life; is evil of God? There is something even more simple and prosaic; let us take work. I cannot struggle, work, to live and support my family, and at the same time be fully with God. My teacher at the Glowing Hearth prays all the time, except when he is busy cultivating the soil—and even then, to be sure, he is still chanting litanies. But he does not pray in the same way as when he is before the hearth, on his prayer rug. So it is with my father. With him, the case is even more clear. While he is in his office, he is less close to God than the teacher is in the field. My father's work absorbs his thought. Carried to its limit, a work in which a man was completely absorbed would keep him all the time outside God. There is no work, it is true, which completely absorbs the man who is engaged in it. But there are countries where great masses of men have long been alienated from God. Perhaps . . . Perhaps it is work which makes the West more and more atheistic. . . . A curious idea . . ."

"What are you reading?"

Still seated on his rug, the knight was smiling at his son, in a pause in his prayer.

Samba Diallo held out the book he was still holding in his hand.

"*Les Pensées* . . . Hmm . . . Pascal. Of the men of the West, he is certainly the most reassuring. But be distrustful even of him. He had doubted. Exile had known him too. It is true that he came back afterward, running. He wept, sobbing, over having gone astray, and he called upon the 'God of Abraham, Isaac, and Jacob' against that of 'the philosophers and scholars.' The road of his return began like a miracle and ended like an act of grace. The men of the West know less and less of the miracle and the act of grace. . . ."

"But just then I was thinking that perhaps it is because the West works—"

"What do you mean to say? I don't know if I understand your objection."

Samba Diallo did not dare to reveal to his father the whole tenor of his thought, and in particular the formidable break which he had believed he discovered. In considering how much he himself had been surprised, he was afraid of worrying him. He tempered his words, therefore:

"You have spoken of Pascal's exile, thinking no doubt of his life which preceded the *Mémorial*. . . . Now this period of dereliction was also a period of intense scientific toil. . . ."

"Yes, I understand you. But your idea is bizarre."

The knight regarded his son in silence for several seconds. Then, instead of answering his implied question, he asked,

"Why, in your opinion, does one work?"

"In order to live."

"Your answer pleases me. But in your place I should have been less categorical. My reply would have been enumerative, in the following form, for example: 'One can work to live, one can work to outlive, so to speak, in the hope of multiplying the life one has, if not in its duration—one cannot do that as yet—at least in its intensity. The aim of work is then accumulation. One can work—in order to work; that happens.' My enumeration is not restrictive. Do you admit that I am more in the way of truth than you are, and that my enumeration is just?"

"Yes."

The knight clasped his beautiful hands over his knees. His gaze was lost in the distance before him. "Even while he thinks, he has the air of one praying," Samba Diallo said to himself. "Perhaps he is really praying? God has indeed entered into his entire being."

"Therefore," the knight went on, "one may work from necessity, for the cessation of the great pain of need which wells up from the body and from the earth—to impose silence on all those voices which harass us with their demands. Then, too, one works to maintain oneself, to preserve the species. But one can also work from greed. In this case, one is not trying to block off the pit of need; that has been wholly filled already. One is not even seeking to defer the next date when that need's claims will come due. One accumulates frantically, believing that in multiplying riches one multi-

plies life. Finally, one can work from a mania for working
—I do not say to distract oneself, it is more frenzied than
that; one works like a stereotype. It is with work as with the
sexual act: both are aimed at the perpetuation of the species;
but both may have their perversion when they do not justify
themselves by this aim."

His gaze, which had been far off, seemed now to come
closer. He changed his position and leaned toward Samba
Diallo. "Oh, how handsome he is!" he was thinking. "And
how I love him for being so impassioned over his idea!" He
asked,

"Would you like us now to enlarge upon and examine
these ideas in relation to God?"

"Yes. Let us take the case where work is aimed at the
preservation of life. Let us reason about that, since it is the
case of necessity. Even in this case work diminishes the place
of God in the attention of man. There is a reason why this
idea offends me: it seems to me contradictory. The conserva-
tion of life—thus the labor which makes it possible—ought
to be a work of piety. The contemplation of God is the
work of piety *par excellence*. Whence comes the clash of these
two aims, which are nevertheless in other ways the same?"

All the time he was talking, Samba Diallo had kept his
eyes lowered, partly to follow out his idea better and partly
to escape the knight's gaze. When he had finished speaking
he raised his eyes again. The knight, still in the same posture
of prayer, was now smiling, with an air at once delighted and
mocking. His eyes were gleaming. "He is sparkling, the
monk is sparkling," Samba Diallo thought.

"Why do you so stubbornly keep your eyes on the floor?
Let us rather discuss together, apprentice philosopher," his
father said. He lost his sparkling expression as he continued,
after a short pause: "I prefer the ideas that are tried out in
the full light of day to those that are allowed to grow rancid
within oneself. It is these last that poison, and sometimes
kill."

He recovered his serenity on the instant and began to
smile again.

"To come back to the idea that is worrying you—it seems

to me, my young philosopher, that we ought to get a better hold on it, to get it pure and simple, so to speak. Now the idea of work for the preservation of life does not appear to me as sufficiently simple. It has anterior stages."

"Certainly: for example, the very idea of life, insofar as it has value."

"Bravo! Let us consider work in the case where it is linked to life by a relation of justification. I say that everything which justifies life and gives it its meaning, in the same way and *a posteriori,* gives work its meaning, too.

"I see your conclusion," Samba Diallo said. "When a life justifies itself before God, everything that tends to preserve it—hence, work—is also justified in His eyes. . . ."

They were silent again for some time. Then the knight spoke once more:

"The West is in process of overturning these simple ideas, of which we are part and parcel. They began, timidly, by relegating God to a place 'between inverted commas.' Then two centuries later, having acquired more assurance, they decreed, 'God is dead.' From that day dates the era of frenzied toil. Nietzsche is the contemporary of the industrial revolution. God was no longer there to measure and justify man's activity. Was it not industry that did that? Industry was blind, although, finally, it was still possible to domicile all the good it produced. . . . But already this phase is past. . . . After the death of God, what they are now announcing is the death of man."

"I do not understand," Samba Diallo said.

"Life and work are no longer commensurable. In former times there existed a sort of iron law which decreed, in action, that the labor of one single life was able to provide for only one single life. Man's art has destroyed this law. The work of a single being supplies nourishment for several others, for more and more persons. But now see: the West is on the point of being able to do without man in the production of work. There will no longer be need of more than a very little life to furnish an immense amount of labor."

"But it seems to me," the boy objected, "that we ought to rejoice in this prospect instead of regretting it."

"No," his father replied. "At the same time that work gets along without human life, at that same time it ceases to make human life its final aim; it ceases to value man. Man has never been so unhappy as at this moment when he is accumulating so much. Nowhere is he thought so little of as in the places where this accumulation is going on. That is why the history of the West seems to me to reveal the insufficiency of the guarantee that man offers to man. For man's welfare and happiness we must have the presence and the guarantee of God."

He paused, then added, thoughtfully:

"Perhaps Pascal had caught a glimpse of this. Perhaps his piercing gaze had seen from afar what the methodological myopia of the scholars had not seen."

Suddenly the knight raised his eyes toward the sky, and said:

"But now it is the hour of twilight. Let us pray."

11

"Pardon Me"
by Ismael Hurreh

(1940–   )

Urbanization, Western-style education, and increased inter-tribal communication have radically changed black Africa. In "Pardon Me" Ismael Hurreh reluctantly recognizes the inevitability of this transformation.

Ismael Hurreh was born in the northern region of So-malia, East Africa. He graduated in 1965 from the University of New Mexico and is teaching secondary school near Moga-discio, Somalia.

pardon me father if I am a disappointment to what you
expected of me

                                            pardon me father

if I cannot slaughter other tribesmen
if I do not say my prayers in the morning
if I turn my back on some of your advice

                                            because father

although your blood runs in my veins
although I too have been a nomad
although I've slept under roofless huts

                                            eyeing the moon

and raising my hands to God
and envying His might
time has unfolded many strange sheets
and spread them between us

time has uprooted me
time has transplanted me to grounds
where prayer is of no use,

and mother pardon me for digging your bones out
(your bones that were buried here)

                                        pardon me

if I had forgotten that you were buried here.

12

"The Vultures"

by David Diop

(1927–1960)

Despite economic problems, tribal strife, and the strains of modernization, the youth of independent Africa is still hopeful; for whatever the problems of independent Africa, solutions no longer depend on the vagaries of imperialist powers but rather on the Africans themselves.

In those days
When civilization kicked us in the face
When holy water slapped our tamed foreheads
The vultures built in the shadow of their talons
The bloodstained monument of tutelage
In those days
There was painful laughter on the metallic hell of the roads
And the monotonous rhythm of the paternoster
Drowned the howling on the plantation.
O the bitter memories of extorted kisses
Of promises broken at the point of a gun
Of foreigners who did not seem human,
Who knew all the books but did not know love.
But we whose hands fertilize the womb of the earth
In spite of your songs of pride
In spite of the desolate villages of torn Africa
Hope was preserved in us, as in a fortress,
And from the mines of Swaziland to the factories of Europe
Spring will be reborn under our bright steps.

Some Highlights of Black African History*

*This chronology, due to its brevity, has to ignore massive numbers of historical events in Africa, but its aim is merely to give readers an idea of the very broad scope of African history.

West Africa

A.D. *1000–1600: Period of the Trans-Saharan Trade and the Great Sudanic Empires*

ca. 700—Rise of the Sudanic empire of Ghana (east of the Niger River

ca. 800—Founding of first Kanuri empire of Kanem-Bornu (near Lake Chad)

1076—Capitulation of Ghanaians to Almoravid raiders and subsequent decline of Ghana

1230–1255—Rise of Sudanic empire of Mali (same area as Ghana)

Early 1400's—Decline of Mali, rise of Old Oyo (western Nigeria) and rise of Benin (central Nigeria)

1470—Defeat of first dynasty and founding of second empire of Kanem Bornu

ca. 1470–1492—Rise of Songhay (east of the empire of Mali)

Late 1400's—Portuguese explorations of West African coast

Early 1500's—Rise of Hausa states (northern Nigeria)

1591—Invasion by Moroccans and decline of Songhay

A.D. *1500–1850: Era of the Slave Trade and the Rise of the Coastal States*

1500's—Period of Portuguese contact with West Africa

1600's—Period of Dutch trade in Africa

1700's—Rise of Britain as a naval and shipping power, height of the slave trade, rise of Ashanti empire (Ghana), rise of Fante States (Ghana)

1700–1880—Decline of Old Oyo and Yoruba wars of the nineteenth century (Nigeria)

1790–1830—Development of the Sierra Leone colony

1801—Fulani Jihad (holy war) in Northern Nigeria

1807—Official British ban of the slave trade

A.D. *1850–1970: Colonial Contact and the Rise of Nationalism*

1850's—Decline of the slave trade and rise of legitimate trade

1850's—Missionary and explorer's interest in West Africa, conquest of Senegal

1863—Bombardment of Lagos and declaration of the protectorate (Nigeria)

1826–1901—British-Ashanti wars (Ghana)

1874—Gold Coast declared a British colony (Ghana)

1884–1885—Berlin Conference and division of Africa into spheres of influence

1884–1900—Period of the scramble for Africa

1900–1914—Imposition of colonial hierarchy

1918—Britain's and France's takeover of German Togoland and the Cameroons

1940–1955—Rise of nationalist movements in West Africa

1957—Independence of Ghana

1958—Independence of Guinea

1960—Independence of French West Africa and formation of Senegal, Mali, Mauritania, Upper Volta, Ivory Coast

1962—Independence of Nigeria

1967–1970—Nigerian Civil War

East and South Africa

A.D. *900–1800: Ascendancy of the East African Coastal States*

900's—Height of gold and ivory trade with Oman, China, and India

1000's—Construction of great Zimbabwe (Rhodesia)

1200's—Height of trading city-state of Mogadishu (Somali) and rise of Kilwa (Tanzania)

Late 1400's—Decline of Kilwa and rise of Mombassa (Kenya) and Pate (Kenya)—all coastal trading city-states

1400's—Lwoo migrations (Uganda)

1490–1733—Formation of Bunyoro and Ankole and Buganda states (Uganda)

1498—Vasco da Gama anchors at Kilwa (Mozambique)

1500–1850—Growth of long-distance trade between coastal and upcountry Africans

1600–1700—Portuguese ascendancy on East African coast

1652—Arrival of Dutch in South Africa

1700's—Dutch trek into South Africa

1779—First Kaffir wars (South Africa)

1700–1850—Expulsion of Portuguese from East Africa by local Swahili and Omani allies

A.D. *1800–1970: Colonial Contact and the Rise of Nationalism*

1800–1880—Caravan trade from the coast to the interior for slaves and ivory

ca. 1810—Decline of Mombassa (Kenya)

1830's—Rise of Zanzibar and the sultanate of Sayyid Said

1818–1828—Rise and rule of Shaka (South Africa)

1830's—Rise of Moshesh and creation of the Basuto nation (Botswana)

1839–1859—Rise of Mirambo and unification of the Nyamweze (Tanzania)

1884–1885—Berlin Conference

1884–1900—Period of tribal resistance

1902–1970—Development of the policy of apartheid (South Africa)

1952—Mau Mau revolt (Kenya, East Africa)

1960—Declaration of Congo independence and civil war

1961—Angolan rebellion

1961—Independence of Tanzania

1962—Independence of Uganda

1963—Kenya's independence

1964—Formation of FRELIMO (Mozambique)

1964—Revolution in Zanzibar

1965—Unilateral Rhodesian declaration of independence

Starter Bibliography of Black Africa

General Works

Anene, J. C., and G. N. Brown, *Africa in the Nineteenth and Twentieth Centuries*. Ibadan, Nigeria, Ibadan University Press, 1968.

Beier, Ulli, *Introduction to African Literature*. Evanston, Ill., Northwestern University Press, 1967.

Carter, Gwendolyn, ed., *African One-Party States*. Ithaca, N.Y., Cornell University Press, 1964.

Collins, R., *Problems in African History*. Englewood Cliffs, N.J., Prentice Hall, 1968.

Emerson, Rupert, and Martin Kilson, *The Political Awakening of Africa*. Englewood Cliffs, N.J., Prentice Hall, 1965.

Fage, F. D., *An Atlas of African History*. London, Edward Arnold Ltd., 1966.

Fortes, M., and E. E. Evans-Pritchard, *African Political Systems*. London, Oxford University Press, 1969.

Hodgkin, Thomas, *Nationalism in Colonial Africa*. New York, New York University Press, 1967.

July, Robert, *A History of the African People*. New York, Charles Scribner's, 1970.

Legum, Colin, *Pan-Africanism*. New York, Frederick Praeger Inc., 1962.

McKay, Vernon, *Africa in World Politics*. New York, Harper and Row, 1963.

Mphahlele, Ezekiel, *The African Image*. London, Faber and Faber, 1962.

Oliver, Roland, and F. D. Fage, *A Short History of Africa*. Baltimore, Penguin Books Inc., 1964.

Parrinder, Geoffrey, *African Mythology*. London, Paul Hamlyn, 1967.

———, *African Traditional Religion*. London, S.P.C.K., 1962.

Wallerstein, Emanuel, *The Politics of Independence*. New York, Random House, 1961.

West Africa

Achebe, Chinua, *Things Fall Apart* (a novel). London, Heineman, 1964.

————, *A Man of the People* (a novel). London, Heineman, 1966.

Ajayi, J. F. Ade, and Ian Espie, *A Thousand Years of West African History*. Ibadan, Nigeria, Ibadan University Press, 1967.

Boahen, Adu, *Topics in West African History*. London, Longmans, Green & Co., 1968.

Bovill, E. W., *The Golden Trade of the Moors*. London, Oxford University Press, 1968.

Crowder, Michael, *West Africa under Colonial Rule*. Evanston, Ill., Northwestern University Press, 1968.

Curtin, Philip, *Africa Remembered*. Madison, Wis., University of Wisconsin Press, 1967.

Kimble, David, *A Political History of Ghana: The Rise of Gold Coast Nationalism 1850–1928*. London, Oxford University Press, 1965.

Little, Kenneth, *West African Urbanization: A Study of Voluntary Associations in Social Change*. London, Cambridge University Press, 1966.

Porter, Arthur T., *Creoledom*. London, Oxford University Press, 1966.

Post, Kenneth, *The New States of West Africa*. Baltimore, Penguin, 1964.

South Africa

Ballinger, Margaret, *From Union to Apartheid*. New York, Frederick Praeger Inc., 1969.

Carter, Gwendolyn, *The Politics of Inequality*. London, Thames and Hudson, 1958.

Duffy, J. E., *Portugal in Africa*. Baltimore, Penguin, 1963.

Gray, Richard, *The Two Nations*. London, Oxford University Press, 1960.

Keatley, Patrick, *The Politics of Partnership: The Federation of Rhodesia and Nyasaland*. Baltimore, Penguin, 1963.

Kuanda, Kenneth, *Zambia Shall Be Free*. New York, Frederick Praeger Inc., 1963.

La Guma, Alex, *And a Threefold Cord* (a novel). East Berlin, Germany, Seven Seas, 1964.

Omer-Cooper, John D., *The Zulu Aftermath*. Evanston, Ill., Northwestern University Press, 1966.

Paton, Alan, *Cry, the Beloved Country* (a novel). New York, Charles Scribner's Sons, 1948.

Rotberg, R. J., *The Rise of Nationalism in Central Africa*. Cambridge, Mass., Harvard University Press, 1965.

Roux, Edward, *Time Longer Than Rope*. Madison, Wis., University of Wisconsin Press, 1964.

East and Central Africa

Beattie, John, *Bunyoro*. New York, Holt, 1960.

Bennet, George, *Kenya, A Political History*. London, Oxford University Press, 1963.

Bennet, Morman, ed., *Leadership in Eastern Africa: Six Political Biographies*. Boston, Boston University Press, 1968.

Cliffe, L., ed., *One Party Democracy*. Nairobi, Kenya, East African Publishing House, 1967.

Kenyatta, Jomo, *Facing Mount Kenya*. New York, Vintage Books, 1963.

Mboya, T. J., *Freedom and After*. Boston, Little, Brown and Co., 1963.

Ngugi, James, *Weep Not, Child* (a novel). London, Heinemann, 1967.

Nye, J. S., Jr., *Pan-Africanism and East African Integration*. London, Oxford University Press, 1966.

Ogot, B. A., and J. A. Kieran, *Zamani: A Survey of East African History*. Nairobi, Kenya, East African Publishing House, 1968.

Rosberg, C. G., Jr., and J. Nottingham, *The Myth of Mau Mau: Nationalism in Kenya*. Nairobi, Kenya, East African Publishing House, 1967.

Thompson, Virginia, and Richard Adloff, *The Emerging States of French Equatorial Africa*. Stanford, Calif., Stanford University Press, 1960.

Young, Crawford, *Politics in the Congo: Decolonization and Independence*. Princeton, N.J., Princeton University Press, 1965.

About the editors:

Jay David is the editor of the critically acclaimed book *Growing Up Black,* as well as many other volumes.

Helise Harrington graduated from Stanford University and received a master's degree in African history from Columbia University.

AFRICA IN 1914

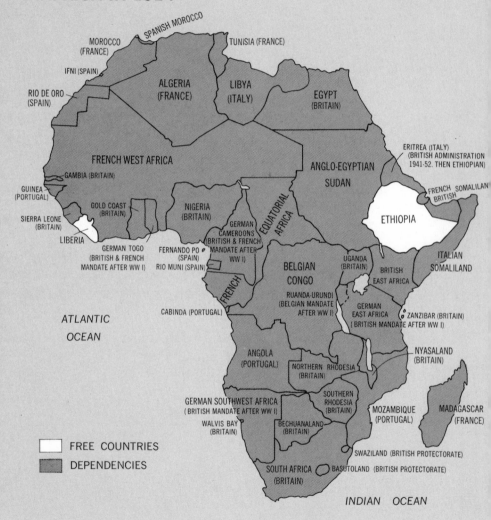

SPANISH MOROCCO

MOROCCO
(FRANCE)

TUNISIA (FRANCE)

IFNI (SPAIN)

RIO DE ORO
(SPAIN)

ALGERIA
(FRANCE)

LIBYA
(ITALY)

EGYPT
(BRITAIN)

ERITREA (ITALY)
(BRITISH ADMINISTRATION
1941-52. THEN ETHIOPIAN)

FRENCH WEST AFRICA

ANGLO-EGYPTIAN
SUDAN

FRENCH SOMALILAND
BRITISH

GAMBIA (BRITAIN)

GUINEA
(PORTUGAL)

GOLD COAST
(BRITAIN)

NIGERIA
(BRITAIN)

ETHIOPIA

SIERRA LEONE
(BRITAIN)

GERMAN
CAMEROONS
(BRITISH & FRENCH)
MANDATE AFTER
WW I)

EQUATORIAL
AFRICA

LIBERIA

GERMAN TOGO
(BRITISH & FRENCH
MANDATE AFTER WW I)

FERNANDO PO
(SPAIN)

RIO MUNI (SPAIN)

UGANDA
(BRITAIN)

ITALIAN
SOMALILAND

FRENCH

BELGIAN
CONGO

BRITISH
EAST AFRICA

CABINDA (PORTUGAL)

RUANDA-URUNDI
(BELGIAN MANDATE
AFTER WW I)

GERMAN
EAST AFRICA
(BRITISH MANDATE AFTER WW I)

ZANZIBAR (BRITAIN)

ATLANTIC

OCEAN

NYASALAND
(BRITAIN)

ANGOLA
(PORTUGAL)

NORTHERN RHODESIA
(BRITAIN)

SOUTHERN
RHODESIA
(BRITAIN)

GERMAN SOUTHWEST AFRICA
(BRITISH MANDATE AFTER WW I)

MOZAMBIQUE
(PORTUGAL)

MADAGASCAR
(FRANCE)

WALVIS BAY
(BRITAIN)

BECHUANALAND
(BRITAIN)

SWAZILAND (BRITISH PROTECTORATE)

FREE COUNTRIES

DEPENDENCIES

SOUTH AFRICA
(BRITAIN)

BASUTOLAND (BRITISH PROTECTORATE)

INDIAN OCEAN